SMUGGLER'S

Shouts—a scream—the chokes of the astonished broke out in a chorus with the unearthly shrieks of the creatures themselves. Then Ned saw, very clearly, three alien heads and three snouts, hunched shoulders and brandished sets of claws, all turned toward him and the other cadets. The creatures let out screams through their bared teeth, one scream on top of the next.

And there were more teeth inside. Snapping extra jaws.

The dogs of hell, not of Earth, not of Heaven, not of the Veil. Jack o'lanterns!

The breath left Ned's body as if he'd been punched. He felt the air pump from his mouth and not come back in. Like prey before a cobra, he and his clan were held still in shock as death rolled before them. He wanted to grab out for Pearl, to drag her back, but the seconds shot by while he was bound by fright. Without willing it or thinking about it, he held his ground before a squall line of demons.

Shrouded in gassy stink, the creatures twisted, never still, pitiless in their posture, and they hissed and screamed, rising before poor Pearl, tiny thing that she was. Her shoulder blades came toward one another as she looked up at them.

The creatures hissed again, and one of them retracted its center jaws, then all three pivoted their pod-like heads around toward the smugglers.

Handlebar Moustache, huge man that he was, stared for a moment of detachment at the drooling creatures before him. Whether possessed by dementia or blunt reality, he fixed his eyes on the nearest creature, digested what he was seeing, reviewed in his mind all the rumors and legends and fact, then raised his sawed-off rifle and blew a hole in his own head.

ALIENS™

CAULDRON

DIANE CAREY

*Based on the motion picture
from Twentieth Century Fox*

DARK HORSE BOOKS®
Milwaukie

ALIENS™: CAULDRON

© 2007 Twentieth Century Fox Film Corporation. All Rights Reserved. TM indicates a trademark of Twentieth Century Fox Film Corporation.

Book design by Debra Bailey
Cover painting by Stephen Youll

Published by Dark Horse Books
A division of Dark Horse Comics
10956 SE Main Street
Milwaukie, OR 97222

darkhorse.com

First Dark Horse Books Edition: June 2007
ISBN-10: 1-59582-113-9
ISBN-13: 978-1-59582-113-3

Printed in U.S.A.
10 9 8 7 6 5 4 3 2 1

Special thanks and devotion to Captain Alley and my shipmates
aboard the Pilot Schooner *Virginia*,
for drawing a wayward seafarer back to Chesapeake Bay.

And there we were . . .

CHAPTER ONE

Pan-Galactic Cruiser Virginia
Chesapeake Class, Near-Space Registry Tango Lima Fox 33
Dual Classification 200-Pack
Captain Nicholas Alley, Special Override Authority

Heat doesn't rise. Cold sinks. Everybody knows that. Nobody admits it.

A punch in the ship's side would confirm the whole theory and wreck a pretty good day.

"Jonsy, adjust the pitch! Correct the amplitude right now, right now!"

The captain's call skittered under the whine of the ship's engines in the grip of oscillation. Jonsy Coyne perspired over the helm console that spoke to him in that sonorous female robot voice: "*Transverse oscillation on longitudinal axis thirty-two degrees. Correct now, correct now, correct now.*"

"We're not supposed to have a center of gravity yet!" Jonsy spat, that little wedge of spittle formed in the right side of his mouth, the same as when he was a teenager trying to apply for a job.

"It's that moon," Captain Alley called over the howling mechanical struggle. "We're too close. The ship thinks we're trying to land on it. Track the imbalance. Find our gimbal. Give the ship a new protocol. Hurry up!"

Droplets of sweat fell from the end of Jonsy's hooked nose and slapped onto the console, just as a second band started flashing and the warning vixen droned, "*Transverse axis pitch through center of gravity forty-four degrees. Correct now, correct now, correct now.*"

Oily palms twisted the gimbal joysticks. Jonsy shouted "There goes the pitch amplitude!"

The captain's voice cut through to Jonsy's rattling brain. "Breathe through your nose and ignore it or we're going to be dead in about thirty seconds."

"I'm not ready for dead!"

"You're halfway there, skeleton boy." Nicholas Alley squeezed his compact form past Jonsy to the helm support station, his hands flashing across the switches and keys like they did on the strings of his old guitar. "Keep an eye on our apparent altitude. Tell me if there's a change. Stay calm, stay calm, lean into it . . . close that circle of declination. Not too fast—"

Jonsy blinked at the captain's talent for dispensing humor and horror at the same time. His pale eyelashes picked up beads of sweat from his cheeks and flipped them up into his eyes as he burned with hatred for Alley's contagious stability. He managed to slow down and push the right buttons in the right sequence. He didn't want to be the only one who panicked! Plain embarrassment was the final force that held Jonsy down to a job when all his senses said, "Scream and run, idiot!"

But Nick Alley was a longtime tug skipper and tight maneuvers were a way of life for him. The crew of the *Virginia* had heard all about those days. Suddenly, those days were today.

He spouted orders one after the other, deliberately speaking clearly and even slowly, so he wouldn't have to waste time repeating. "Colleen, lose the draggers. We need speed. Gunny, compensate with thrust. Dave, give us more aft thrusters, favor starboard. Power astern, one quarter . . . bow thrusters, one half—everybody work together, quick! Jonsy, keep that helm equalized! Rockie, make sure all the coms are in sync. No blackouts, now. Make sure everybody can hear me. Compensate for engine noise!"

From the aft quarter where she was supposed to be working the intra- and inter-ship communication grid, Jonsy's wife Rockie blurted, "Why can't we just land?!"

"Only if you want to retire here," Alley responded, his eyes scanning back and forth, back and forth, flitting from one display unit to the next and back. "You, me, and the Board of Interplanetary Trade."

"Once we're down we can't launch again!" Jonsy cranked the gimbals, gaining some ground before the enormous transport ship slipped sideways to starboard. He wanted to stop fighting the ship and hand over the problem to somebody else, but how would that look? Rockie would never respect him. Rockie's respect came dear.

Even in the midst of action, impending destruction, he stole a glance at her, to appreciate her slick black hair, cut in a bowl around her dark exotic face, two carefully trimmed strands curving just under almost perfectly round cheekbones. In a world of homogenous genetics, where people looked more and more ordinary and races blended to a medium-tan, Roxanne Coyne was an exotic star. *How did I get her? How did I deserve her?*

"If we go down another fifteen degrees, we'll have to land," the chief mate warned from the stabilization cube. Nobody knew Clyde very well yet, but he was a friend of the captain's and that got him a command job aboard. He seemed to know his stuff and wasn't pushy, a good quality in a career sailor who had just stepped aboard a matter of days ago. "Nick, you want me to calculate an approach?"

"No, I want to fight it!"

"Fight'n it, aye." He tapped the communications grid on the arm of his chair. "All hands, no approach, no approach. Push for rafting maneuvers, everybody!"

Jonsy tried to feel part of the amalgamous body of effort, the whole crew working in sync at stations all over the massive cruiser. The cooperation to save their ship and each others' lives, their passengers and cargo, was cut now by Rockie's glare as she cast her resentful eyes at Clyde. Jonsy saw it. Suddenly he was suspicious, too.

Rockie stumbled forward and gripped the back of Jonsy's chair with her long brown fingers, as if she could control the situation if she controlled Jonsy. But the chair pivoted and almost threw her off her feet. Jonsy wasn't putting enough weight into the chair to stabilize it, but was instead working the controls at a crouch. His knotted thighs pressed back against the edge of the seat, and for a moment it was as if Rockie were the ventriloquist and Jonsy the puppet.

Captain Alley saw something on a monitor and reacted. "Shift four degrees lateral port, Jonsy. Clyde, give him thruster support aft. Move, move, hut, hut. Let's save our behinds!"

How did he do that?

Clyde, almost reclining now in his chair—a bizarre vision for a moment of action—pressed his knees forward into the cushioned bar below the thruster panel, gritted his teeth as if he were physically moving the ship with his body, and pressed into his task. Spikes of perspiration made his short-cropped hair gleam like a helmet. Straight blond brows were drawn over a pair of unblinking keen eyes. To Jonsy, Clyde looked like one of those kids' action-figure toys, with a small wiry body and two strong arms protruding from wide shoulders, always held in a ready-to-strike pose.

Why can't I have arms like that? And hair that glistens at the right moments? Why can't I be shorter and quicker? Is Rockie looking at him? Jonsy's whole body made a single tremendous shudder, a sympathetic vibration that buzzed through the whole ship from the cargo holds to the flank bays, and up to the pilot house. For a moment he couldn't believe what he saw and felt—the *Virginia* heaved like a big horse finding that last bit of energy to levitate itself from a ditch.

Was it true? Did he see what he thought he was seeing? Yes!

"Gimbals are stabilizing," Jonsy rasped.

"How are we doing with the moon?" Alley asked.

"Losing its grip," Clyde reported, victory lacing his choked voice.

Jonsy almost whooped, but his joy was swallowed by a huge black shadow that crossed two of his screens. "Collision! Captain—!"

Nick Alley was suddenly at his side. Together they scanned the twelve high-resolution screens showing different parts of the *Virginia*'s black exterior, bare processed metal gleaming with day-glow markings. No longer in the grip of the moon's gravity, the elephantine ship swung freely toward the twenty-deck *Mequon*.

"Brace yourselves!"

Almost immediately on Alley's words came the collision, a grinding crunch as the thousand-foot *Virginia* knocked hips with the *Mequon*. Both ships were enormous bulk carriers, but hanging in space, without the grip of the moon, there was no resistance except for the mass of the ships themselves. The triple-hulled *Virginia* swung over and jammed into *Mequon*'s port quarter. Kinetic energy transferred in a thrumming *bongongong* down the sides of both ships and they began to swing through space together, like a giant bell and its clapper.

"Use it!" Alley commanded. "Aft grapples, take in! Ease line four, take both spring lines!"

Clyde stood up and reached for the sensitive dials. "Easing four . . . taking two and . . . three."

"Hold three . . . take one! Jonsy, help him!"

Jonsy stumbled out of his seat and dived for the line dials. He caught a glimpse of Rockie's eyes watching his every move.

This went on for four minutes, easing umbilicals and taking orders. Each minute was a stepdown in the level of tension as the two ships shimmied against each other, bow to bow, stern to stern, flank bays touching, all buffered by auto-compensating gas-filled fenders and self-adjusting grapples that would keep compensating whenever they sensed drift. The ship groaned and endured hollow booms inside her massive boxy frame, her length almost proportional to her height, yet she had a series of sculpted curves that ran the length of her hull and gave her a streamlined, attractive appearance that worked well in ads because the human eye found them pleasing. Inside, the holds and bays were so big that echoes were unavoidable, despite considerable devotion to special sound-inhibiting structures, resins, and compounds. *Virginia* was a high-class VIP cruiser, posh and polished on her passenger decks, but she was also a state-of-the-art bulk carrier, and cargo was her real bread and butter.

"Rafting complete," Clyde reported. "All umbilicals taken in. Hardpoints established, fenders engaged. And . . . we . . . are . . . rafted."

"That is what we in the industry call 'a narrow escape'!" the captain exuded, and clapped his hands together once in sharp punctuation. "Sheesh, what a morning! Can't believe we didn't die." He put his nose to the monitor showing the panoramic gray side of the other ship and the giant painted letters M E Q and part of a U. "What the hell is going on over there? I want to talk to Butch Burton right now! What was the point of that?! They almost took us both down!"

The pilot house fell into a busy silence for a few moments as Rockie did her only job—inter- and intra-ship communications, recordings, and network interface. She had been in training to do other things, but was too comfortable in her one duty to bother studying very hard for anything else. Besides, she had other plans.

With a moment finally to spare, Jonsy cannily gazed at his wife, and noticed that she was watching Clyde.

"I can't get an answer to our hail," Clyde reported, clearly annoyed. "Oh—there it is, here it is . . . They want to do a fully automated transfer. Right now it's just the ship talking to us."

"Burton just doesn't want us to see his face after that mess of a rafting," Captain Alley deduced. "Fine! I'm not in the mood for a name-calling session. If they want to hide, let 'em. Jonsy, do your thing." He handed Jonsy a flat plastic sealed case the size of a man's palm. "Let's board this zoo and get going for our rendezvous with the *Umiak* before I rip off a binding strake and beat that guy to a pulp with it."

Jonsy accepted a grimy little rag from Rockie and mopped his face as he steadied himself before the intership coordination console. He gave his wife a glance of both relief and amazement that they weren't now cleaning up from a major disaster. Falling back into routine felt good, but weird at the same time. He wished there were a cooling-down period. His voice betrayed his unsteadiness as he made the formal required announcement into the computerized loading system. "This is John C. Coyne, Chief Bosun, PCG *Virginia*, authorization

Zebra Roxanne nine-four-five. Confirm identification and tie-in with PCG *Mequon*."

While the computer system happily processed his voiceprint and passcode, he cracked the plastic case by bending it slightly until it made a noise, which then released a compound inside. Once mixed, the compound began to glow bright green in narrow rows that spelled out a numerical and key-word code. Jonsy continued speaking into the system, the way a person talks to a machine. "Begin transfer clearance procedure of test cargo containers Alpha, Beta, Charlie, limited clearance code as follows: One. Yellow. Eight. Emerald. Three. Eight. Niner. Five. Everglade. Go for auto-check."

"That's what I like!" Alley slapped Jonsy on the back, making Rockie jump half out of her jacket. "This is the fun part! Rockie, put me on shipwide. Thanks, kid." The captain flexed his shoulders to shake off the morning's stress and leaned over the communications relay. "Attention all personnel, passengers, guests, mascots, and stowaways, this is your intrepid captain speaking to you from the bridge of a sweetheart of a ship that just saved its own ass and yours too. Now you can tell your grandchildren that you once participated in a near-miss collision with a transfer vessel the size of a city block and almost got to write your name on a moon. So shake it off and go to your nearest viewing screen, open a can of your favorite lubricant, and kick back for the sideshow of all time, which will begin in roughly—"

He looked at Jonsy.

"Sixty-five minutes," Jonsy supplied.

"Approximately one hour, after we clear the first three as test containers. This is the best part, watching two gigantic spaceships co-mingle by doing *all* the work themselves. Ladies and gentlemen and other life-forms, I give you the brilliant human enterprise of fully automated supercontainer transfer!

Autographs will be signed later in the VIP lounge where all bribes, tips, and kisses will be accepted with a somewhat craggy smile. We will be giving out a prize to the person who can answer the following question: What was the capital of Assyria? Yee-ha!"

He grinned at the bridge crew and pulled out a cigarette.

"I can see why everybody hates you so much," Clyde commented. "You're such a hard-ass."

"A hard-ass, *sir*," Alley required, lighting up.

"Oh—*sir*. Pardon."

"Let's do some visual scans and see if there's damage that requires immediate attention, or what can be done robotically or what needs hands-on, and all that. Let's keep the EV activities to a minimum until we're on our way. Don't want to take a chance of squishing anybody while we're rafted up."

Jonsy evaluated whether or not to speak. "Are . . . you gonna lodge a shipmaster malconduct complaint?"

"I should. But, hey, everybody's entitled to a screw-up now and then. Burton's probably kicking himself a lot harder than I want to kick him. He can't afford to lose his license. Still got children living at home. He's got a forty-three-year-old daughter who's still 'finding herself.'"

"You're too forgiving."

"Gotta be forgiving in space. It's cold and lonely. Forgiveness is the only warmth."

"Plus you get to avoid the hassle," Clyde commented.

"What? Avoid two weeks of bureaucratic protocol and forms and depositions and hair-pulling? Yeah, someday I'll be the slob who needs to be cut some slack."

Nick Alley scanned the bank of screens that displayed the ship's exterior from many angles—forward and abaft of the beams, on both the quarters, the bows, the flank bays, the tumblehome, the hull, and the cap-structure. When she moved through space, the *Virginia* created a velvet-black spot in space, delineated only by the beautiful emblems, logos, call letters, and her gigantic name in hyper-bright gold paint, and, most impressive, a bigger-than-life mural of the strange United States ironclad *Monitor* once again plying the waters of Norfolk Harbor, blocking the bigger Confederate ironclad *Merrimack* from achieving her goal of dominating those waters. In one of history's greatest coincidental equinoxes, the rafty *Monitor*, with its hatbox turret, and the *Merrimack*, a metal roof with a hull underneath, moved in space seemingly without artificial support. Nobody spent money on painting the naturally black hulls of modern cargo haulers, but everybody spent it on proudly displaying identities and loyalties with complex dazzlepainting, scrollwork, mosaics, murals, and chromataphoric enameled renderings that changed in the constant self-illuminants embedded into the outer structure like theatrical fresnels. In the tradition of the European exploration ships the 1600s, a ship's brightly patterned hull was a badge of the financial success of their owners and captains. Giant dazzlepainted movers plowed the charted spacelanes in an eruption of commerce. Artists made big fortunes with clever illumination using lights and paint. The perfect amalgamation of frugality and décor was always in demand. How cleverly could a giant black billboard be decorated so that the display was provocative while profits could still be made?

Besides, Captain Alley thought, it made a good story for the kid passengers. And then came the punch line . . . the ironclad *Merrimack* had been made from the plated-over hull of a ship called the CSS *Virginia*. Oooooh. Aaaaah.

On *Virginia*'s massive black side, the signature encounter of her namesake's history sailed now through open space, forever engaged. No longer locked in 1862, the Battle of Hampton

Roads had moved to outer space and would live in elegant immortality.

Flushed with the relief of having corrected the dangerous approach, the captain smiled. The art of bringing two ships together was as dicey in space as it had ever been on water, just a fact of life. For millennia, ships had been the workhorses in the most hostile environs mankind had traversed. Into the tropics, the arctic, the Horse Latitudes, the Great Lakes, Hudson Bay, enduring storms and doldrums, the typhoons and ice and biting flies, ships had been the mothers of progress. When mankind moved into space, he moved in ships. Finally, after decades of ferrying only the hardiest sacrificial pioneers and soldiers into space, Earth had taken the next step. Space was now a pathway for more than just mining, salvage, military, and bare-bones settlements clinging by fingernails to the scruffy cusp of new ground. Ships were safer now, spacelanes charted, guides experienced, and regulations relaxed. Now, an embryonic market appeared for tourism, entertainment, capitalism, and even plain old education for its own sake. Today there were chances to go to space just to look around. A whole new breed of ships was being constructed for these purposes, the newest of which was the *Virginia*. She was a tour and museum vessel, taking people out into space while conducting seminars and presentations of the history and future of human expansion.

Those were the passenger decks, anyway. In the multiple holds, the *Virginia*, like all other ships in space, shuttled cargo. Every last inch of room aboard was packed with necessities for outlying settlements and the bright new cities springing up where once there had been only outposts.

And then there were the people who were still pioneering spirits. They rode the ship on one-way tickets to new lives. This ship might be the last civilized habitat they would experience for a long time.

Captain Alley believed in all those missions, and he nodded in agreement with his thoughts.

He really believed.

"If this gets out, we're dead."

On a ship in space, night and day were said to blur into one continuous night, but that wasn't true. Jonsy Coyne had always felt the difference. Now, preparing for a loading maneuver, it was all-hands-on-deck, but Jonsy felt the tug of lightheadedness, as if it were the depth of the night. Ordinarily he would have been asleep right about now. But he couldn't think about that. He only had minutes to commit subterfuge.

Sweat sheeted his face and chest, leeching through his crew shirt, a new layer of sweat, worse than the sweat from the rafting maneuver just forty minutes ago. This was a full-body paste, as if he'd lathered himself with oil. He could barely keep a grip on the bosun's box, a hand-held computer unit specially made to store and manage the ship's complex cargo manifests, locking codes, transfer orders, loading plan, and myriad other necessities of a job with endless details. Jonsy buttoned through scan after scan, manipulating the codes to accept the complex deceptions he had forced the machine to digest. To do what needed to be done today, he had severed the link between his personal box and the ship's mainframe. He still didn't believe it had worked, or that it would keep working. The ship's computer was probably looking for the bosun's box link right now, sending out signal after signal, trying to get a response, calling and calling like a desperate mother bird. Any minute now it would set off alarms, send out warnings, make announcements in that wily lady's voice, and the cover would be blown right off the pot.

He and Rockie huddled in a blade of shadow in the ship's cavernous and dim starboard hold. Lights were at a minimum, to save energy, creating a cave-like environment of narrow, dark passages and high, sheer walls. Shadows made sharp black knife-shapes that speared the cavern. They hid next to one of the three test-loaded containers he had just boarded from the *Mequon*, close enough that Jonsy's bosun's box could connect directly with the locking panel on this specific container. The test-load, part of the procedure for every transfer, had gone flawlessly, in record time—only nine minutes—and that somehow made him nervous. At his order, the two ships had seamlessly shifted six containers, three each, to make sure the cranes, airlocks, winches, grav-shifters, and other mechanisms in the jungle-like loading canopy were working properly. Regulations were satisfied. In a few minutes, the remaining five thousand house-sized containers aboard *Virginia* would be switched with over eight thousand containers waiting aboard the *Mequon*. The ships were linked up, entertaining the final transfusions before intership autoload. Once it started, there would be no stopping it without giving away their plan. Rockie's plan.

Frantically manipulating the bosun's box, Jonsy looked up, up, up at the huge Brittany-blue container. The other two test containers, he didn't care about. This one . . . this was the one. This battered old container with scratches that showed its many layers of paint, with dents that decried its dependability. It had seen many transfers, but none like this. He'd jiggered every protocol to make sure this old blue jug was one of the first three. Its coded locking system, only inches from his face, placidly displayed its authorizations, all faked. He kept thumbing the controls as if he were playing a computer game, countermanding every successive protest from the system. He chased each code protest as it popped up, leading to the next one. The box didn't like what he was doing, and he coddled it one protest at a time. He prayed it would soon run out of failsafes and relax, and allow this container to remain aboard.

"Rockie, are we completely, I mean *completely* sure about this?"

"Honey, we're sure!"

He leered at the container as if seeing through its walls to the cryogenic tubes inside, to the contents held there in stasis. Fourteen very important, very rare, and monumentally dangerous tubes. The bosun's box kept flashing red anger at him, and he kept tapping away the flush. Red, green, red, green, red, yellow, green . . . red . . .

"Illegal to own, illegal to transport, illegal to experiment on—what if these things are infected or viral? What if they're toxic? I don't want to fiddle with a bomb like that."

"It's nothing like that," she insisted.

"It's *something* like that! Why else would anybody pay us so much?"

"So *much*, honey." Rockie put her teeth together and parted her lips, sucking in the fragrance of ambition. She clasped his lanky torso in a full-body hug, hunching to make him feel taller. "Enough to start a whole new life. Enough to buy our own transport ship! You'll be a captain, like you deserve. This is a dream come true, our dream, coming true! This isn't the time to lose your nerve. The job is done. All we have to do is ride it out."

She spoke with dangerous intensity, as if their secret were the secret of the century, the one great secret a couple could share, the secret that would only bear the weight of two people. To tell anyone else would snap it like sugar threads.

Squirming in her embrace, Jonsy nearly choked on his own bile. "Maybe we should drop it right now, fess up, y'know, give in . . . Do we know what, y'know, what we're doing? The laws are ironclad on this. No transportation of these—these animals—these creatures, whatever they are, in any stage . . .

"You can't even transport *any* dangerous substance without a whole bible of paperwork, never mind *these* monsters. No weaponized cells or bacteria, no cloneable tissue—What we're doing carries a mandatory death sentence, Rockie—*death*. Y'know, *death*? I looked up the history of these things . . . it's not pretty, I'm telling you."

He stole a quick glance up at the massive blue container with the yellow chevrons. All around them, here in the starboard hold, thousands of containers waited to be moved. Each container was stamped with giant bright markings that identified it, like the rectangular bodies of dressed knights' horses in repose on a tournament ground, each declaring the colors of its house.

And in the cavern of transport containers, this one box, this blue one with the yellow chevrons . . . this battered old gravity-puffer seemed to know it was completely alone today.

Rockie pursed her lips and tipped her chin up to bring her mouth close to his. "They're dead, baby, they already had their death sentence. They died in the—what'd they call that stage? You know the right words."

"It's the . . . the proto-xenomorphic stage, between the infant stage and the adult stage."

"See how in control you are?" She flickered her eyes at him and smiled in admiration. "You know they're just dead tissue, just frozen cells for somebody to play with or mount or—who cares? Remember what you told me? There's that clause permitting transportation of non-living scientific research specimens."

"Not this kind. There's no loophole *these* things can squeeze through."

"They're frozen, baby. Dead, dead, dead, tissue, tissue, tissue. Like clipped fingernails. Like hair on the barber's floor. They can't hurt anybody. Unless maybe you eat 'em." Her shoulders rolled back and forth in a series of shrugs as she cast off his worries.

"I guess . . ." His gaunt face hurt. Tense muscles twitched, his lips, cheeks, eyes. Code after code flashed between his fingers, faster and faster as the system fought the new protocol pattern he was forcing down its throat. "What would anybody want these things for?"

"What do we care?" Rockie dismissed, waving her long fingers. "Medical experimentation, science research . . . maybe a museum wants to put them on display. Remember once you moved that frozen mammoth so it could be thawed and stuffed?"

He nodded, managing a smile. "Taxidermists must be a little sick in the head, y'know?"

The bosun's box flickered with warnings. It was being scanned by the mainframe. Where are you? Why aren't you answering? Do I have to shut you down?

Banishing thoughts of being fired, or arrested, charged, imprisoned, maybe even executed, he let Rockie lead the way by feeding his ambitions. While he poked the box's feeder panel, calming it down, his wife caressed the corner of the big illegal container.

"I found this deal," Rockie said. "You know my sources are good. It's a shortcut to success. Just this once, baby."

"You're too much with shortcuts," Jonsy murmured. "You need to get that prison colony out of your head."

"It made me tough." Her eyes turned to hard obsidian disks. "Tough, so I would be ready for today. My whole childhood in that pot of criminals, it carved me for today. Guards for foster parents. They taught me the only things they knew—angles. Guards know all the angles. This is fate playing out."

In the murmur of impending activity, the *Virginia* hummed with hot systems. Everybody, every circuit was happy to be alive and blessed with duties. Roxanne's eyes narrowed to the Polynesian wedges that Jonsy had first found so irresistible. He imagined her on some tropical island, raising her hands to the gods of fire, with flowers around her wrists and vines around her head like a crown.

"That place," she uttered. "Nobody there was worthy of respect. Everything was a scam or a deal or a dodge. You don't get respect and you don't give any." She turned to him and surveyed him from head to foot in a way that made him feel bigger than he was. "Now I'm married. A respectable woman with a husband who works a respectable job."

"Maybe we shouldn't shake the tree," he attempted again.

"Why settle for peanuts? You should be more! Have more! You shouldn't be taking orders from somebody else. You have all it takes to be a captain."

"I don't have a commercial captain's license—"

"But if you own your own ship, you don't need one. That's ancient maritime law. You taught me that. You have all the contacts to get your own cargos. Why should you wait around on some long list, hoping for some bureaucrat to give you permission to make your own fortune? Forget it! Success is in your hand, right there!" She tapped the bosun's box. "It's just this once. You've never cheated a freight manifest before. You're entitled one little cheat. One little step to get you all the way up the ladder."

"Just let me finish before they find me . . ."

The container's locking panel began to flash numbers at him in coded sequence, matching the new codes he had forced into the bosun's box against all its failsafes. He had to let them come up, kill them, replace them, then do it again with slightly altered codes. The box was now communicating with the container, giving new loading and locking codes that would disguise the fact that it was completely contraband. If his thumb slipped, if one numeral was wrong, the container's own security system would start blaring. The *Virginia* would hear it, and all the alarms would wake the dead.

The shadows slicing down around him seemed blacker by the moment. Eyes of night predators leered at him from the depths—or were those just the pairs of red safety lights? In his left ear, Rockie's voice murmured on, as smooth as a buzz from fine wine.

"And we can strike gold today, baby, you and me . . . Tomorrow you won't be just a bosun on somebody else's ship. Tomorrow you'll be on the market for your own ship! You know everybody in every spaceport. Shouldn't all this be yours? Just because you didn't come up through the military, you don't have some big backer, just because other people got lucky, shouldn't you be lucky just once? You need connections to move up. Today, we've got the connections. If we just do this one time. Just once!"

Eyes . . . those were only lights, just faint red lights to help him in his escape.

Jonsy nodded, pumped up by her enthusiasm, like the last time and the time before as she kept his ego from slipping into despair. He knew he was good enough. All he needed was the down payment on a ship.

He'd never cheated before. Never once betrayed a captain or an owner or an employer. He knew Rockie would go further than he would himself, push acquaintances and use connections if she could find them, and somehow she had found them. What kind of people was she dealing with? After all this, would they come through? Or would he and his wife be hung out to dry?

"I didn't go through all the training for being a captain," he sputtered. "I don't have a master's ticket—"

"I can get you whatever you need to show anybody." Rockie saw the doubt in his face. She could always see through him. So she kept talking. Talking, so that his thoughts would be crowded out. "It doesn't matter how deep into debt we go.

You'll be able to get cargo. No approval from anybody else. No standing around with your hat in your hand. Own the ship . . . own the ship . . . Keep that in front of your mind. Own the ship . . . own the ship."

Her enthusiasm and confidence infected him. The creatures inside, the contraband tissues inside, they were all dead. Some rich nose-picker probably fancied to hang them on his wall and pretend he hunted them. So what? Who would it hurt?

And he knew . . . the manipulation he'd done on the codes and locks and overrides, the hiding of combinations inside other combinations, the blurring of identities between these containers . . . what he had done, nobody would ever know. In a gross violation of every regulation ever invented, two of the containers had the same identification protocol. At first, the idea had just been a challenge. Rockie had dared him to do it. She pretended she didn't believe he could, and he hadn't been able to sleep until he did it. He had to prove to Rockie that he was worthy of this marriage. How else could a man like him hold a woman like her?

The container panel and the bosun's box abruptly began to flash a bright chartreuse clearance code—identical numerals, identical letter codes. Done! It worked!

He dropped sideways against the container, pressing his shoulder to its cool side, the locking panel flashing softly on his face. You did it, did it, did it . . .

His fingers clenched on the bosun's box, now vibrating softly as it reconnected with the ship's mainframe, pretending it had nothing to report. In the glow of Rockie's gaze, he swallowed a couple of times, and found his voice.

"It is just once."

CHAPTER TWO

With its dark passages, looming escarpments of stacked containers, and dim pathways lit only by energy-efficient blood-red lamps, the belly of a transport ship was an unsettling place, almost nightmarish. The pathways were nothing more than metal bridges, hooded by the bridges overhead, each one completely movable, so there was access to the containers, no matter how high they were stacked. Preparing for an autoload, this cave-world was as bright as it would ever get—generally the containers reposed in near-darkness, because so much was automatic and machines didn't need eyes.

Despite the difficulty in seeing very deep into the hold, Nicholas Alley enjoyed watching the gantry cranes, rotating winches, and grav-floaters move house-sized containers along the centerline bulkhead of the self-trimming holds, using drums and mooring cleats, chafe gear, self-adjusting winches, drum ratchets, lock-downs, and tricks of gravity efficient only in space. Because of the gravity tricks used in heavy-load transfer, and the constant pressurization and depressurization of the hold as the automatic shifting went on, the crew was able to take most of this time off. No humans were allowed into the hold during auto-transfer, so the system was free to change pressure, increase it to crushing strength, or drop to the vacuum of space as needed to move and stack the giant containers as if they were children's building blocks. Only Jonsy and a couple of bosun's mates were at work in their various cockpits, overseeing the transfer. The two ships would automatically coordinate with each other, making sure that the bulk cargo was exchanged in a way that maintained balance so the ship could hold her course without straining against her own mass. Imbalance caused thruster stress and wasted energy. When balance was no longer possible, when more cargo needed to be moved off one ship than was compensated for on the other, the ships would begin a process of artificial compensation with computerized tricks of imaginary ballast.

"Everybody ready?" Alley flopped into the comfortable chair that had been saved for him. Around him, his crewmen were chipper and pleased with themselves, having survived their close shave this morning. Usually, those things happened only in safety drills, and today had been the payoff for drilling.

The crew on a ship like this was a total of twenty, but ten of those attended to the forty passengers on the upper decks of the ship. Even in space, people liked the idea of "upper" and "lower," though those concepts didn't really apply, and some of the "upper" decks were technically lower than the "lower" decks. Still, the VIPs were given the idea they weren't riding in steerage, even though space was at a premium and the cabins were small. Elegant, but small. The stewards and other attendants ran that part of the ship like a hotel, and seldom did the two crews mesh.

The crew that tended the ship, those Alley felt were the real crew, those who didn't rotate off every season, had grown into a family typical of the ancient bond between shipmates. They were more than just people who worked together, more than just people who traveled together. They were people who had to work in close quarters, under situations of dullness and duress. Even if they hated each other, they had to work as if they didn't, and they had to trust each other with their lives. After all, you had to sleep some time, and that meant somebody else was driving.

The normal ebbs and tides that happen between people, especially those living in tight quarters, were suspended today for the sake of enjoying the autoload and having a sort of in-house picnic. This was official time off, not just off-watch, and tensions of all sorts were eased for now. There were only a handful of them, counting Alley and Clyde as the two commanding officers. The others each had his own specific duty and skills. There was some crossover, of course, but spaces were limited and each person was of particular value for the sake of his or her own job. Three of the crew were bosun's mates, all stationed in critical positions in cockpits to oversee the load. They all reported to Jonsy, who was in his cockpit right now, and probably Roxanne was with him. Those two were a little weird. Clingy.

The ship's cook, Keith Kavanaugh, was doing his chef imitation, wearing a big white piece of paper rolled into a tube as a hat, handing out trays of bread glazed with a red-and-white substance.

"What's this?" Alley asked.

"Sourdough rolls drizzled with peppermint," the big bearded man said. In another life, with more white than gray hair, he could've been Santa Claus.

"Ah . . . more cuisine from the dark side," Colleen said. She was their coxun, a small-engine specialist who ran and maintained the pumps, motors, drivers, and a hundred winches, windlasses, gantry motors, and all the motive power that pushed things other than the ship itself. It was a big job on a ship that moved heavy loads internally. In preparation for this autoload transfer, she had been on the job twenty hours a day for the past three days. This was her reward—to sit and watch.

Keith gave her a double helping of the drizzled rolls. "I consider this a signature dish."

Dave LaMay, a platinum-blond surfer-type, the ship's second mate and extra-vehicular specialist, intercepted the second roll Keith was handing to Colleen. "I thought the salad with chocolate chips was your signature dish. You lied to me, didn't you?"

"That was last week."

"Okay, kiddies," Alley continued, touring the happy faces around him, "today we're moving the equivalent of forty-seven working farms, ranches, and zoos, as well as fundamentals for sixteen wildlife sanctuaries, campgrounds, and controlled natural habitats. Entire food chains from algae on up. Clyde, let's hear that manifest."

"Starting with the ones closest to us, the red containers with the gold 'XG' have ten thousand Merino sheep and a couple thousand Highland cattle and Texas longhorns, right along with sixty border collies."

Two by two, enormous boxes, beautiful in their way, floated by on gantry cranes and rotating cranes, up ramps and down the centerline travel system as Clyde gave the crew the tour and their imaginations did the rest of the work.

"There goes a pack of macaque monkeys, some specially bred alligator/crocodile hybrids, ninety or so various pit vipers, tree snakes, mambas, and the mice and moles to feed them, some cobras to eat the other snakes . . . And that one with the orange markings, it's carrying three million micropods."

"Three million?" Dave "Gunny" Gunn, sitting between Voola and Clyde, was the ship's engineer, responsible for the smooth running of the main engines and all the thrusters that maneuvered the *Virginia*, both in space and in close quarters. He had a boyish face under a cap of auburn hair, and a welcoming personality that they all appreciated. He had sweated through the bumpy rafting maneuver this morning and had been only nominally relieved to find out that none of it had been because of a mechanical fall-off. "Three million of what?" he persisted.

"These would be . . . silkworms."

"Silkworms! They're serious out on Zone Emerald, aren't they?"

"Oh, they're serious," Alley assured. "They're planning to manage all this wildlife on separate ranches, and gradually build an ecosystem. They've been transplanting bugs, plants, and birds for about five years now, and they're moving on to larger animals."

"How can they do that?" asked Voola Vendini, a comedic name for a no-nonsense woman. As the ship's nurse, she was responsible for the crew's general health, but was, even more crucially, the ship's interior maintenance chief, the one responsible for making sure the ship's transport decks were clean, orderly, well-appointed, and even, in some places, sterile. To her, cleanliness was both science and religion. Her large-boned body and the barrel of extra pounds she carried belied the fact that she could clean the whole ship in half a day and was untiring in her fastidiousness. Every ship in the merchant fleet wanted her, and *Virginia* was lucky to have her. She was everyone's mother—or at least their silver-haired auntie from the old country. Almost never completely at rest, she sat here now mending a fabric-sheathed bone splint with a micro-stapler.

"Whole-planet ecosystem is too complik-kated," she insisted, "to put on some Noah's Ark. It won't not work."

"That's right," Colleen confirmed. "Two at a time, and all . . . two butterflies, two mealybugs, two congressmen . . ."

Dave LaMay leaned toward her, tucked his chin, and gave her a look of intense inquiry. "Voola . . . you're Dutch."

"I am not Dutch," Voola declared without looking at him. "I am an American."

"She's Eastern-European," LaMay injected. "It's got to be Romania."

"Turkey," Clyde contributed.

"Or," Captain Alley invited, "maybe it's none of anybody's business. Just ignore them, Voola. You have the captain's permission to spit on them if necessary."

"I will no spit. I am an American. Dat's all dere is toot."

"She's got a point about the animals," Colleen caught up the previous conversation. "They'll fiddle till they get some kind of hybrid that'll destroy everything. Like the hooved imports in Australia that finally had to be hunted out before they wrecked everything."

"Those weren't hybrids," Clyde said. "Those were imports."

"Still. L'Dave, hand me some more of those yum-yums."

"Yum-yums on approach . . . Incoming!"

"Zone Emerald's a haven of scientists and geniuses," Alley explained. "The best brains Earth could produce. They've got naturalists, animal husbandry guys, whatever they need. It's a long-term plan. Ranching and farming and hunting, controlled natural preserves . . . and they're ready to see what evolution does on its own once they turn it loose. They'll end up with whole new species in a hundred years, like the Galápagos Islands or Australia."

"Sounds like playing God to me," Dave said.

Gunny snorted, "So what?"

At the same time, Clyde elaborated, "Mankind's been playing God since we learned to control fire."

"Somebody always says that!" Alley protested. "Every time technology makes a leap forward, somebody says, 'Oh, no, we're playing God! Eeee!' They keep oh-noing until they need their particular disease cured, then it's a 'modern miracle.' People always say that. It's a 'modern miracle' if it comes out good, but it's 'playing God' when they don't know how it's going to turn out."

Dave put his chin up vauntingly and shook his blond hair from his eyes. "Captain, are you calling me a hypocrite?"

"Are you being hypocritical?"

"I don't know, but I'll certainly check my files and report back to you."

"We can spit you out an exhaust lock and not notice."

"I'm an EV specialist. I can live in space. I have a snorkel."

"Hey, here come the elephants," Clyde interrupted. He pointed at four white containers moving on collapsible boom davits, swinging elegantly together, emblazoned with giant green pine trees and the name of their parent shipping company, "FOREST CARTAGE." "Twenty-nine African elephants. Probably a whole family."

"Right behind them are the four hundred thoroughbred horses, some Arabians, Fresians, and . . . Clydesdales. Wow, Clydesdales . . . they're big, aren't they?"

Alley nodded and swallowed a sip of punch. "There's a Scottish nobleman who's moved his entire estate there from the Borders, rock by rock, house and all, and he's establishing his own mini-Scotland."

"No kidding."

"I've met him a couple of times. He's one of the main sponsors of the cultural and strategic operations on the ship we're going to meet up with."

"The *Umiak*."

"Such beautiful name for ship," Voola said, wistfully pausing in her work. "*Umiak*."

Alley smiled. "He made the connection with the travel agency on Earth that's supporting a whole scholarship program for teenagers to gain spacefaring skills."

"Is he a former spacefarer?" Colleen asked.

"Nope. Just a former dreamer. Now he makes other people's dreams come true. I love rich people."

Keith made a face. "You love rich people?"

"Sure! Only a wealthy and productive society can explore and expand. I love expansion! Besides, when's the last time you were employed by a poor man?"

The cook paused and stood to his full height. "That's true . . . I never thought about that! Now we know why you're the captain."

"Be proud. *Virginia* is going to be known as the ship that helped supply a new Atlantis, a dream colony. Well, not a colony for long—they're working on a new constitution, with the goal of becoming an independent republic. Limited government, maximum freedom, property rights, individual rights, and the only things in herds will be the animals. They're doing it on January seventh, the colony's seventy-sixth year. Zero one, zero seven, year seventy-six. It honors the year 1776 on Earth."

"How do they get seventy-six years?" Gunny asked. "That colony's been there for almost two centuries."

"The first century was eaten up just with terraforming. This coming year marks the seventy-sixth year of their colonial charter."

"That's nice. I like that."

"Imagine this," Clyde went on. "We, fellow shipmates, are carrying no less than five woolly mammoths. Real woolly mammoths from the Ice Age. Check that!"

"I guess they're partially cloned and partially bred, using African elephants," Alley said.

"What are they going to do with mammoths and all these other big animals?"

"Beats me. Maybe use them for big game hunting or who knows what."

"Oh, brilliant," LaMay commented. "Bring back prehistoric animals so they can be hunted to extinction again?"

Everybody laughed.

"Either way, they're dead," Colleen said.

Alley sat forward. "Hey! Are these in the same container as our elephants?"

"No," Clyde said, "but the same shipper."

"I'll bet we've got mammoths and their mommies! Sure, that makes sense! How about us—sitting here on the cusp of scientific advancement, bringing the Ice Age to the Galactic Age!"

As the crew applauded merrily, Colleen asked, "So what's the capital of Assyria? Because we're all dying to know."

"Chicago," La May said.

"Nineveh," Volla offered.

"The correct answer," Alley told them, "is 'I don't know,' followed by a scream."

Laughter rolled through the observation deck as the crew kicked back in their lounges and appreciated themselves and the infectious humor of their captain. But even humor and contentment didn't cloud his alertness. He sat up, peering at one of the monitors. "What's that?"

Clyde tilted sideways. "Got a blip?"

"One of the test containers. Why's the loading code amber instead of green?"

"Might be a system infection. I've seen that before."

"It's not an alert about clearance?"

Dave leaned forward to look. "That would show up in red or orange."

"Maybe you'd better have a look," Alley said to Clyde. "Do it quick, so we can get cracking."

"Having a look, aye."

Clyde got up, briskly stepped through the tangle of his shipmates' legs, and disappeared into the companionway.

"This is so dangerous . . . I should ring the bell on myself right now before I jump out the airlock and put myself out of my misery. The captain could lose his license . . . if this gets out, we're just dead—just dead—"

No longer in the main starboard hold, Jonsy and his wife were now up in the safety of the bosun's cockpit, a protected bubble where the loading master could oversee operations. Now they looked down at the rows upon rows of stacked spaceworthy containers, each of which would soon be dancing on cranes, one after the other. Only the three test containers, down there to the left, would be left in repose, having already been transferred. Jonsy kept glancing at that one container, the hot potato in his pocket, as if he expected it to suddenly come to life.

Rockie closed her hand on his arm and pinched off his tirade. "What do you care about the captain? He's nothing to us."

"Everybody likes him," Jonsy sputtered. "Everybody wants him for a friend. That dope Colleen and Gunny and Dave, even my stevedores. They want to listen to him more than to me. That's not the chain of command. They're supposed to listen to me first. How does a captain do that? All my other captains, they were bastards. We didn't want to be around them so much. How does he act so friendly and stay a captain? How does he keep discipline?"

"You're as good as he is." Quietly overruling his doubts, she moved closer, the scent of her hyacinth shampoo making his head swim. "This is it! When you're a captain, you can do anything you want. Anything. You can be a tyrant or a god, or whatever you want. Any style you want. Make up your own style . . . be your own legend.

"Listen, baby, listen. I listen when the captain talks. I overhear when the officers talk. I know what's happening. All these years in space, hardscrabble people, hardscrabble lives . . . you don't have to like the captain to listen to what he says about that, how he talks about mankind's dreams, how we're going out into space now for riches and development . . . we conquered all the frontiers, we put clothes on the natives, and now it's happening . . . Look at Zone Emerald! Not a prison colony! Not a shake-and-bake! A palace for rich people, a shining new city, all the time expanding . . . and what do they want? Stuff! They want all the things that anybody wants that can be shipped—everything from shoes to poodles—"

"From forks to fountains," Jonsy assisted.

"And when the wealthy start moving . . .

"There's more wealth to be earned," he recited. "Investors coming in with capital. There are fortunes to be made—"

"Fortunes," she hissed, twisting her body as if in a dance, but without taking a step, and her eyes gleamed. "To be made. This is the time to go! The boom time that doesn't last very long. This is the Gold Rush of space!"

Jonsy let her spin intoxicants as he worked the bosun's cockpit dashboard in preparation for the main autoload. He wasn't doing anything illegal now, but his hands still felt dirty. His only job now was his regular one, to facilitate the clearances for the ship to take over its unloading and loading, in coordination with the *Mequon's* automatic system.

"It's done now," Rockie murmured, sensing that he needed encouragement. "The hard part is over. The little ugly whatevers are aboard in their peapods, sleeping away eternity while they make us rich."

"Don't even talk about them. I don't want to chance some ship system picking up our conversation and recording it."

"There's nothing like that here—"

"I don't want to take chances!"

"Okay, baby, okay . . . you're the man."

Jonsy elbowed her away enough to free his arm when he noticed what was happening with the electronics. "Damn! The airlocks aren't engaging. It's supposed to be completely secure in the hold . . . I'm supposed to be able to open the space doors! Why aren't they working?"

"Did you do a bio-scan?" Rockie suggested. "Maybe there's a mouse or something in there being picked up by the infrareds. The space doors won't open unless there are no life-forms—"

"The container!" Jonsy's whole body went cold, his hands numb, as he peered through the big observation window down into the hold. "Crap! Somebody's down there!"

Rockie crushed her hands to her mouth. "Clyde! What could he want? Why is he there?"

"Let me handle it!" His panicked whisper broke into a squawk. "Stay here!"

She seized his arm. "Make it sound good! Tell him, just say, 'Clyde, this is my job, go do your own job, I've got my own system going and I don't have time to teach you'—"

"Don't tell me what to say! Stay here!"

The cavernous starboard cargo bay was chilly. The air was dry. Dry enough that Jonsy was forced to clear his throat as he approached the blue container with the yellow chevrons. He might otherwise have wanted to sneak up on Clyde, to put forth a kind of proprietorial stealth that would prove he was more proficient at slipping through the canyons between containers. He was the bosun, this was his territory. He was the expert at the safari of the ship's hold.

But his cover was blown. When he came around the corner to the broad side of the container, Clyde was unflapped at his sudden appearance.

"Hey, what are you doing?" Jonsy asked. "I'm trying to close the hold off so I can open the space doors and start the autoload."

"I know, but I'm checking something," Clyde said. He didn't honor Jonsy with a glance, but poked relentlessly at the container's black-and-silver locking panel.

Jonsy tried to sound authoritative. "But, y'know, as long as you're down here, you're gumming up the works. We can't get started."

"It can wait a minute or two. There's a blip on this container's clearance code."

"Oh—oh, yeah, it had a little flurry, but I combed it through. It's just an older-style lock. Uh, hey, Clyde, don't forget you're supposed to lock down EV activity until after we're, y'know, all loaded up."

"I won't forget. What's in this container?"

"Uh, it's chickens." Jonsy held up the bosun's box showing the codes and lock-down authorizations. "Eight thousand chickens in individual cryopods. A whole poultry farm ready to be . . . farmed. Plucked. Egged. Whatever they do on a poultry farm."

"Cryopods? Isn't this one of the old gravity-puff containers that holds cargo in zero-G and keeps it in the middle with puffs of air?"

"Uh . . . it's been converted to cryo."

"Why would anybody do that?" Clyde's straight brows made a single serious line across his forehead. "I thought the black ones with the red stripes over there had the chickens."

"Uh, well, yeah . . . they all do."

"Are they from the same source as this one?"

"Yeah, it's a shipping company out of Cargo City. Those orange ones are theirs too, loaded with ducks and quail, pheasants, game birds . . . There are fifty-two containers filled with just pigs and hogs and wild boar—"

"But if this one and those all have the chickens in stasis, why don't they look the same as each other if they're from the same shipping source?"

"Uh . . . I'll check. But that happens all the time. Even old and banged up, these jugs are valuable."

"Not that valuable." While Jonsy made a show of playing on his bosun's box, Clyde pecked persistently at the coded locking system, but the signals kept flashing orange—access denied.

"How come every time I try to unlock it, it goes 'tilt' like it doesn't want me to look inside?"

"Maybe because you're not authorized to look," Jonsy contrived, letting his exasperation show. "I'm the bosun, not you. I'm supposed to be the one minding the locking systems."

Clyde glanced at him. "What's your problem?"

Jonsy sweated every peck, every touch of Clyde's finger on the panel. Tap. Tap. Tap-tap. Tap. And the mechanical resistance from the locking computer. Epp. Epp. Beep. Bawk. Epp. "Uh, well, y'know you're new here and we have our tricks that maybe you don't know about yet. We already have multiple boarding clearances satisfied—see, they're all right here—and if we add your personal clearance into the code, it's just a big complicated mess for, y'know, no really good reason to add steps, an' all. If we add you to every one of eighty-two hundred containers, we'll never get any of them boarded and we'll miss our rendezvous point. If you want to explain to the captain, I guess I can go through the protocols and dismantle the whole grid and reprogram the—"

"Okay, okay, you made your point." Clyde quit poking at the locking panel. "Can you get inside?"

"Uh, I could, but I've got six hundred crates to confirm before this one, and if I don't do it in order, that'll take twice as long. I'll have to go back to the cockpit and rifle through the cross-checks. But if you stay here and wait, the hold won't move forward on its loading procedure. If you leave, it can at least do some ballast shifting till I get back."

"Yeah . . ." Clyde looked up in exasperation at the silent blue container and the giant yellow chevron that came down to end at his feet. "Okay, I didn't mean to foul up your order. Just check the contents by sight before we break raft, will you? We're not opening any cracks for smuggling."

"Yeah, I'll check it."

"Okay, but I want a report confirming."

As Clyde walked away, Jonsy watched him go, measuring the stride and wondering if he could replicate it. "Sure, you do," he muttered.

Back on the crew observation deck, Keith the cook had buttered the cheerful mood with rum-laced chocolates that he called "tots," and some kind of punch with lemon drops floating in it. Though the chocolates didn't really have rum and the drops weren't really lemon, he claimed to be an expert at extract and the crew was expected to comply with proper imagination. Not much in a spaceship's pantry was real. Instead, cooks made do with concentrates, freeze-dries, extracts, illusions, and palate-fooling textures. In space, cuisine was the art of sensory deception.

Captain Alley pretended the tots were yummy, gave Keith a nod of approval, and began singing to the tune of "Old Smoky." "On the good ship *Virginiaaaaa* . . . in space we do dwell . . . we eat Keith's spaghetti . . . and tell him it's swelllllll—"

"Uh-oh," Colleen uttered. "He's singing."

"It's a space chantey," Gunny said.

"And we'll transfer our carrrrr-go," Alley sang on, louder, "while eating our tots . . . and hope that the mustard . . . doesn't give us the trots!"

"Ew!" LaMay snarled. "That's not very 'yar'!"

"There's not mustard in these, is there?" Colleen eyed the tray of chocolates Keith held before her. "Tell me there's not mustard!"

Keith ignored the question. "I'm either being insulted or immortalized."

Alley grinned merrily and sang on. "On top of spaghettiiiii . . . the crew gets their wish . . . we get strawberry sprinkles . . . on garlic and fish!"

"Carry me back to Old Virginny," LaMay said, "soon!"

While they laughed, Clyde returned from checking that one old blue container, saving them from further serenades.

"All clear?" Alley asked.

"I'll know in a few minutes," Clyde reported.

Gunny spoke with food in his mouth "What's the plan for break-off after the transfer? Are we striking right out for our rendezvous?"

Alley rocked back and grinned. "Translation—Captain, do we get a few hours of sleep before we have to get up and work again?"

"Oh, fine, thanks. Like you and I haven't been side by side on enough dirty, smelly, greasy jobs, that you have to treat me like this? That's it. I quit."

"You quit last week, Gunny."

"This time I mean it."

"Oh, look! The holds are reconfiguring themselves!"

Everyone paused to watch the transverse bulkheads begin to slide and climb, reshaping the hold to specifications only the computer fully understood. Reconfiguration would use the space most efficiently for bulk freight, even if some spaces were completely empty, and would re-trim the ship's cubic capacity to fit her most spaceworthy balance. A dozen swivel-derricks on telescoping masts adjusted themselves to work with the quadrant davits, now in new places, preparing to work with different bitts and bollards embedded into the ship's structure to give them purchase. The dance of constant movement was beautiful in its industrial way.

"Our mission for the next ten hours," Alley interrupted, "while the ship stabilizes the new cargo, is maintenance surveying. We will check for crazing, pinhole corrosion, and those little structural devils that make first mates nuts."

"Thank you for your concern," Clyde acknowledged. "Speaking of which, where are the zinc disks kept?"

"Ask Jonsy. He's the bosun."

"He'll tell you they're right next to the rivet guns."

"That's what he always says for everything when he doesn't know where they are. 'Right next to the rivet guns.' The end of the rainbow is next to the rivet guns."

"What's 'crazing'?" Keith asked.

"Little random surface hairline breaks in the laminate. They're caused by normal hull stresses. They have to be repaired quickly or they could penetrate all the way through. We fill them with loomed fiberglass and an epoxy resin compound."

"Filling them isn't the hard part," Colleen said. "Finding them is the hard part."

"Sounds gooey."

"It's the way of things to come. Computers do the fancy work on ships, and gradually humans are only needed for the menial labor that requires fingers."

"There's a pleasant prediction."

"So what you're saying—"

"Oh, now don't hold me down!"

"What you're saying—tell me if this is what you're saying—is that crewmen will eventually be needed more than captains."

"Nah, they'll always need captains," Alley trumpeted. "We provide style!"

Their laughter was a welcome decoration, interrupted only by the ship's com system. "Clyde, this is Jonsy."

Clyde jumped for the console. "Wow, that was fast . . . What've you got for me, Jonsy? Hey—shhh, the rest of you!"

"The permits and records are all clear on that blue jug. It's one of the cartage company's older boxes. They're phasing out gradually and changing to the new red-striped ones with better capacity and more dependable monitoring systems. That's . . . y'know, that's why it looks different. And why the lock didn't work right."

"Did you check the contents yourself?"

"Uh, yeah, it's loaded with individual stacked cryopods of poultry. Rhode Island reds, black striders, prize Leghorns, speckled Cornish hybrids, giant Golden Orpingtons—"

"You saw these chickens in cryosleep with your own eyes?"

"Uh, sure did."

Clyde paused, rolled his tongue inside his left cheek as if feeling for a bit of unchewed food, and for a moment seemed to balk at accepting the explanation. "Okay, good. Thanks for checking."

"Get us—we got Orpingtons."

"Sounds like the trots."

As Clyde dropped back into his lounge chair, Alley asked. "Something bothering you?"

Clyde offered a shrugging nod. "Why do half Jonsy's sentences start with 'uh'? Makes him sound uncertain."

"Same reason half my sentences start with 'aw, heck.'"

"Does the policy say anything about different sizes and styles of containers from the same source?"

"Hell, read page eleven million two thousand whatever, it's right there."

Clyde shook his head. "Somebody ought to comb through that system and simplify it."

"We do," Dave said. "We simplify the code by ignoring most of it."

"The Bureau of Shipping keeps adding regulations, as if that helps," Alley explained. "Makes it harder to check when something seems fishy."

"Is something fishy?" Keith asked.

Clyde shrugged. "Yeah, but it cleared with multiple failsafes, double-checks, coordinated security locks, and confirmation by sight."

Dave nodded, eyes bright with anticipation. "Can't do better than that."

"So we're 'go'?" Alley asked.

"Captain, I do believe we are 'go.'"

"Great!" The captain clicked on the main communications system with an announcement to all posts. "All scanners on. All systems, all stations, we are go for autoload!" He clicked off and dropped back into his chair, then put his foot up on the padded bar in front of him. "I love this part. I love watching the ship follow its last order, transferring cargo entirely by automated means . . . I love watching the cargo shift itself around like big bears coming out of hibernation. I love the winches and the gantries and the magnetics and tilt-locks, and that big chunking sound when a ten-thousand-ton jug clicks into place. Chhhhunnk! That deep vibration! It's like making love! Yeah!"

"You're just a moving man by nature," Colleen commented.

"You bet I am! What's any gathering of human beings without their supply train? Tugs and trains and freighters . . . I love 'em all."

"I hope you love livestock, 'cuz that's 90 percent of what we're loading today."

Alley accepted a refill on his pseudo–fruit punch and watched a pretend lemon drop make the circuit around the rim of his glass. "As long as they don't wizz in my cargo holds, what trouble can they possibly be?"

CHAPTER THREE

"Trust me. They'll never notice."

This was great. This would be monumental. What a coup. Keith the Dark Chef and Gunny, his unwitting sidekick in evil, crept through the ship on a stealth mission into the underworld—the tomblike starboard hold. Their timing was perfect, just after the autoload, when the computers had secured everything and the crew was concentrating on the port side autoload. Keith calculated a window of several minutes during which nobody would miss them and nobody would look in here.

"This is stupendous," Keith editorialized. "Legendary. We're going to be big names in space lore."

Gunny's mind was on something else. "There are a dozen containers with birds in them. How do you know which ones have chickens?"

"Sixty thousand chickens in various containers. I've got it all figured out."

"Did you ever cook a real chicken? What if we steal a bunch of chickens and then you end up burning 'em?"

"If you're sure you can break into the lock, then I'm sure I can cook chickens."

"I can break into *any* lock."

"I can cook *any* chicken. At the last port, I secured a hundred ninety pounds of real potatoes. Not flakes, not powder. Real potatoes. Yukon golds. Such pretty little nuggets—I been peelin' 'em all day . . . there it is! It's right over there.

The blue old one with the dents. It's the only one without the modern approach alarms. We can walk right up and do our business."

Gunny followed Keith down a T-section in the walkway, trying not to look down through the walkway slats which allowed for ventilation, but didn't do much for acrophobia. "Sounds like you want to use it for a toilet. You sure we won't get in trouble for this? Stealing cargo?"

"Stealing twenty chickens out of sixty thousand," Keith told him. "It's twenty chickens, not twenty elephants. *Chickens.* Ten times that'll die of natural causes. If I can find any dead ones, I'll take them too, if that makes you feel better. I've got it all figured out."

"I'm not eating no chicken that died in cryo. You sure the blue one has chickens inside? Looks like somebody rolled it down a hill. Looks like a big dumpster."

"Chickens. Eight thousand Rhode Island reds, speckled Cornwalls, black Herpingons, leghorn longhorns . . . just think about it. Tomorrow is Thanksgiving! I can serve real roasted chicken breasts stuffed with pesto croutons. On Friday we'll have grilled drumsticks and thighs. On Saturday, chicken stew a la Dark Chef. On Sunday, chicken tenderloin salad with celery salt, and on Monday I'll render the bones into broth and pour it over noodles. I can smell it, I can just smell it now. Real chickens. Not chopped . . . not minced . . . not freeze dried . . . not condensed. . . not air-puffed . . . not jerked . . . real . . . fresh . . . living . . . clucking . . . roasted chickens . . ."

"You're slipping into a fantasy world." Gunny's snarl of doubt showed in wedge-like shadows on his craggy face. His squinted eyes reflected the red track lights, making him look like a crouching demon waiting for orders. "You better be right. I want a real chicken dinner."

Keith shook off the image. "Everybody does. Don't you think a non-synthetic Thanksgiving dinner would be nice for everybody? Don't you think they deserve it? Centuries of culinary science and storage, and there's still nothing like the taste of fresh, real meat. Nature's had billions of years. We've had a couple thousand. Fresh is bound to be better."

"You're just a thief, is all—"

A loud chunking noise drove them both almost to their knees, sounding as if the whole deck structure were about to come down on their heads. Gunny looked up and made a foul noise. "Aw, it's just the swivel hooks going back to their stations. Damn, they're loud!"

Keith turned, and held up one warning finger. "I'm not a thief. I'm Robin Hood. I'm not doing this for myself. "

"Are you gonna eat some?"

"Only after the crew eats. You have a small mind, don't you?"

"If you're Robin Hood, what does that make me?"

"An enabler. I hope you're the wizard you think you are."

The container sat in repose on the third level, stacked on top of the other two test containers that had been boarded first. The mobile walkways provided easy access and would be in place until the next autoload. The starboard hold was a very quiet place right now, because all the activity was in the port hold, where the second phase of loading was just finishing up. The two holds sandwiched the habitable decks of the ship, the storage and utility decks, and Keith's home base, the galley.

"This is really tangled up," Gunny said. "It's been manipulated out of sequence. Maybe it malfunctioned. Sure is old . . ."

"Bring it back to life for five minutes," Keith encouraged. "Then it can die a peaceful death in some industrial boneyard."

Gunny stopped talking as he focused on the locking box. He never talked while he worked, as if his brain could only manage one protocol at a time. Keith dutifully went silent, knowing that Gunny did better work when nobody was talking to him. Chicken recipes bowled through Keith's mind, pesto chicken, orange and pineapple chicken, country captain, chicken with pine nut stuffing . . . wouldn't the crew be surprised when there was no rock candy drizzled on the meat? No seaweed twists?

In the depths of the hold, a throaty mechanical sound thrummed, then ended with a clank.

"What's that?!" Gunny drew his hands under his chin like a big squirrel. "Somebody's coming!"

"Just keep working," Keith said. "I'll have a look."

He picked along the edge of the walkway, shivering slightly in the cold air of the hold. By not heating the enormous holds, the ship could afford the power to make the living quarters comfortable, but trips to the hold were chillers, and he and Gunny were already on their nerves' edges. Around him the sheet sides of stacked containers loomed like cliff faces, giant letters and markings clawing high up and sinking down until he couldn't see where the colors ended. Dim red lighting, designed to ease the eye, blurred into black shadows like blood draining into pumice.

When the click-snap came behind him, he almost jumped off the walkway. He spun around. "Did you get it? Is it unlocked?"

Gunny didn't answer, but looked up at the huge container hatch. The hatch, a garage door in the blunt end, suddenly cracked with a chunky mechanical shift. Air rushed in as the gasket suction abruptly released. That should've been it, but instead of just opening, the hatch sucked air and resisted releasing its tongue-in-groove seal. The whole container began to hum from inside with a long breathy *mmmmmmsssssk*.

Gunny jumped back. "Why's it pressurizing? This jug isn't supposed to be depressurized!"

"Try not to talk so much," Keith suggested.

But Gunny's weatherworn face turned ghastly. "Cryocontainers aren't supposed to be depressurized! We're opening the wrong container, Mr. I've-got-it-figured-out!"

A chittering sound made Keith's shoulders hunch—not the sound of mechanics or air or a computer, but an animal sound, a sound of living creatures, and with it the squirming feeling of not being alone anymore. The gush of air from the gaskets fizzled out and the hatch opened automatically, its folding parts retracting in sections. A short gray ramp came out like a tongue and shoved Gunny back until he fell on his buttocks, engulfed in spraying fog from deep inside the maw.

There was a moment of sudden silence. Enough for Keith to take one step forward, to lean inward—to be knocked back by a streaking mass, as if he'd been smacked in the neck by a wet towel. Then another—and another!

He spun and landed on one knee, guarding his face with a crooked arm as two more wraiths shot past together, then another, then two more.

Teeth gritted and eyes crimped, he peeked over his bent arm. Into the depths of the hold went the thin chittering noises, until they faded completely away as if disappearing into a canyon. Almost like sea birds crying in the clouds.

Gunny jumped up, slammed the flat of his hand to the control panel and the locking mechanism. The hatch groaned, thunked, retracted its ramp, and unfolded its segments until it once again made the shape of a single door, then drew itself back inward and began the humming and hissing process of repressurizing.

Gunny stumbled back, twisted around, and looked out into the hold.

"What—were those! Were those chickens?"

Keith hunched his shoulders. "Why were they awake? Did we wake 'em by opening it?"

"This is bad—this is real bad—"

"Forget it . . . They'll just go off and starve someplace. It's not like there's chicken feed on the deck."

"This is bad . . ."

"They're chickens!" Keith insisted, forcing himself to believe the only good answer. "Forget about it."

"Forget the whole thing!" Gunny snapped. "I'm not *this* hungry."

"What's going on?" a third voice cut through the gloom.

Gunny let out a *yowp* of shock and spun around just as Jonsy Coyne materialized out of an angular shadow and demanded, "What are you clowns doing up here?"

"Nothing," Keith attempted unconvincingly. "Nothing at all."

But Gunny folded without interrogation. "There was these little ugly things . . . we thought they was chickens!"

"Little things?" Jonsy's face abruptly dropped its color, and with it all the personality he possessed. "Where?! Where?!"

"This blue jug—"

Jonsy seized Gunny by the collar and drove him back into the container's hatch. "You didn't *open* it!"

"Of course not," Keith said. "He's making up stories."

"They run off!" Gunny howled. "We just wanted chickens for dinner! Roast chickens! Chicken salad! Thighs! Wings! Drumsticks!"

Jonsy suddenly breathed in choppy gasps. "Oh, God! Where?! Which compartment?! Oh, God save us!" He broke into a full run, pounding down the middle of Container Canyon, the walkway ringing under his boots. "Rockie! Rockie!"

"What's the problem?" Keith called after him. "They're chickens!"

Jonsy's voice got higher, fainter, and more frantic as he ran down the thousand-foot hold. "Oh, God, God, God, oh, God! We've got to get off the ship! We've got to get off the ship!"

Like the chittering things, Jonsy's cries faded off into the hold, deeper and deeper, increasing in panic as they decreased in volume.

Keith stood there, looking across the walkway at Gundersion, as the hatch made its final slurping noise and locked itself again.

"Because of chickens?" he asked.

CHAPTER FOUR

"Okay, happy campers! It's time to give the ship the Big Hug!"

She had a lilting voice, like music on a stringed instrument. Not like a sailor or a worker or anything so earthbound, but the voice of a cheery sprite, rallying the morning dewdrops. Yet Dana, pacing the deck in the imitation of a drill sergeant, didn't smile nor show any facial expression of the sound she made in her voice.

"You'll be divided into a 'soles and bowls' crew, and a wash-down crew for the holds and the outer hull. The outer-hull wash includes remote operation of cleansing equipment, so it's more complicated than it sounds. Inside, 'soles and bowls' means cleaning the interior soles and ceilings—that means the thing you're walking on and the side bulkheads—and, of course, complete sanitation of those wonderful sanctuaries of repose and reflection . . . the ships heads."

She was the first officer of this muscular ship. Ned Menzie was impressed as Dana spoke to the collection of teenagers of which Ned was part. Like Dana, Ned had dark hair, but his was not so fluffy nor appealing, nor did it have those little umber highlights under the utility lights. Her skin was deeply tanned, or perhaps just naturally golden, while his was pale and unremarkable. And she had nut-brown eyes, while he had only his dad's simple greens.

But it was easy to be impressed here, for a farm boy. He'd always known he and his family lived in the past, and this adventure had thrust him whole-hog into the modern age of outer-space science.

Whole-hog. Hee. Pun intended.

Ned pressed a smirk out of his lips. Usually in the company of the sheep, goats, deer, and his herding dog, Kite, Ned could let fly any facial expression he pleased, and since he liked to talk to himself and the animals always laughed, his expressions were many and varied.

Here, among these other teens and the adult crew of the space cruiser *Umiak*, he restrained himself from being the star of the braeside show. This was a whole new thing for him and his sister Robin—he glanced at her, a few kids down—and though they were out of place and had never before this been across so much as an ocean, they knew this whole expedition was set up to handle them. There were adults here whose job it was to take care of the teens, and no matter how strange and mystifying this environment, this far-flung reach into the stars, he knew they would be taken care of. Therefore, a sense of humor and a light heart were the order of his day. Things would happen in their own time, and he would ride them out. This was a one in a million chance, to take part in this special program for young spacefarers, an exclusive program which would be the tale of his lifetime.

Then he would go home and tell the sheep and Kite what happened.

Just as First Mate Dana parted her lips to continue speaking about the duties of the day, one of the teenagers popped up with a question.

"We have to clean bathrooms?"

Not the best of informational trawling.

Dana raised one brow. She could've been a model in an advertising campaign for perfume or—

No, wrong. Ladies' outerwear. The autumn line. Jackets, cloaks, ruanas, and wraps.

Who do you think does the cleaning on a ship?" she asked, while Ned envisioned her in a corduroy camp jacket with plaid lining and leather riding boots. And a scarf. Lamb's wool. He knew just the one, of course, being a farm boy from a wool farm. It was his stock in trade.

"The slaves, apparently," commented a bold young man two down from Ned. By his aristocratic demeanor, superior clothing, and polished appearance, the boy with the sweeping golden hair was unimpressed by Dana or any of the other crew members. Ned guessed the tall boy was here against his will. Or at least against his inclinations. He had the air of someone who thought his time was being wasted.

"Going to space is a big thing," Dana went on, brushing smoothly past the unfriendly comment. "Appreciate it. This cadet program is a new adventure in human history and you guys are right at the cusp of it. You're cutting new ground for human beings. Live up to it. Clean the heads with gusto."

"I'll clean the heads," Ned volunteered. He hadn't intended to speak up so soon, or at all, but he knew where his talents lay. If trouble could be averted, wouldn't that be better?

"As will I," his sister spoke up immediately from two kids down.

"That's the spirit!" Dana applauded. She was a tall woman just out of the Coast Guard on Earth, with previous experience in the Colonial Marines, but Ned couldn't imagine her as a soldier. She looked like an actress, with a perfect frame, long limbs, and dark chocolate hair and the facial features of a painting. Artists never painted soldier girls. Men, but not girls.

Yet, there was something about her that held distant. She used that artificial tone of voice, the way an adult talks to children at camp, but none of the enthusiasm transferred to her expression. She spoke in this encouraging, rousting way, but none of it was in her eyes. It was a job to her. She was going through the steps.

But if she treated them decently, what else was needed? Ned decided not to judge. She seemed comfortable, competent, and experienced, and he would follow her directions.

"You're going to start where all sailors have started for centuries," Dana went on, gesturing to the other crewman standing near her, a fellow no older than twenty. "You are now in the clutches of Dustbin Dustin. Dustin is in charge of all the small engines, pumps, motors, and other intra-ship power systems. When he's not doing that, he's our head janitor. The rest of us, we're the assistant janitors, and you cadets are the apprentice janitors—oh . . . Captain."

She fell quiet as a statuesque man entered the salon. The man was still on the young side of middle-age, and Ned had never seen him before, despite having been in space now for nineteen days. Nineteen days of travel at breakneck speeds, soaring deeper and deeper into the night sky, until all they knew was far, far behind. They looked out portals and through telescopes at special bodies and nebulae and trunk formations, and went on tours, experienced the ship's mess, and the food of their funny round cook. The first two weeks had been only the end of their school year, a series of tightly organized classes geared to each of their age requirements, from fourteen to seventeen, so they could tag along with another outgoing convoy for the first six days to get safely into space, but not miss getting full credit for the year. Ned and Robin had been out of place on this aspect, not having attended Earth's finest primary education schools, not having achieved the world's highest scholastic merits, and not having parents with influence. Ned had no illusions about competing on brain power. Still, the ride would be something to talk about.

Ned's attention was now held by the magnetic man whose presence drove all to silence. Until this minute he had remained isolated from the teenagers, as if the ship were two cities and he lived in the other one.

"Well, Captain, we have a fine show of cadets here, anxious to serve the good ship *Umiak*," Dana told him. "I respectfully submit that Mr. Nielsen read the manifest to you."

"Granted." The captain folded his arms and gave her a nod. The long sleeves of his silver shirt displayed naturally muscular arms. The shirt seemed to gleam as bright as a midsummer moon beneath the salon lights.

Ned took all this as a nice show, for the benefit of the teenagers, and supposed the others took it in the same way. Then again, as he looked down the line, the variance of expressions told different tales.

Mr. Nielsen, the ship's education officer, a specialist himself in the art and science of teaching arts and sciences, stood up from where he'd been perched at the end of the bench. He was a friendly and open fellow of a fatherly age, with a family back home, and he seemed to genuinely like the kids and enjoy teaching. Ned got the feeling that Mr. Nielsen would teach even if he weren't paid to do it.

"Thank you, Captain. Thank you, Dana," he began. "On the port side we have Daniel, Adam, Christopher, Leigh, and Pearl. On the starboard, we have Stewart, Mary, Dylan, Ned, and Robin."

Ned suddenly found it amazing that the two groupings of teens hadn't really interacted at all, but had been kept separate by the watch schedule. Only now did he realize that he didn't even know the names of the other group. They'd been on completely different schedules, awake while the others were asleep, and even had separate classes, run by the education officer. He knew Mary and Dylan well enough for lunchtime talk as classroom acquaintances went, but the others—they were yet strangers to him. Nineteen days in space, and he still hadn't met so many of these important people . . . he made a secret vow to be a little more forthcoming.

"Thank you, Mr. Nielsen." The captain surveyed the teenagers, lighting briefly on every face, then scanning on before anyone became self-conscious. He was not a tall man, but broad of shoulder and perfectly proportioned under those shoulders. He gave the image of being bigger than life, with a topper of rich brown hair, neatly cut, but enough to wave in an imagined breeze. He seemed to move and stand as if he were constantly being filmed . . . move . . . stand . . . stride . . . fold arms . . . turn . . . lay a hand on some part of the salon, the table, a monitor hood, a display case. In fact, there were lots of places here in the main salon to be theatrical, for it was a place as solemn and polished as an English library. Ned had seen such a place once, on a trip to London for a medical treatment. This place was paneled in wood burnished to a depth like wine, with brass-lined display cases carrying a collection of artifacts or mementoes—Ned couldn't yet tell which, but they looked old and cherished. Was this the captain's personal shrine? Was the captain doing this step-pause-step on purpose, or was he in fact just poetic by nature? The movements were elegant, calculated, and he cocked his hip just slightly with every pause. Ned watched, wishing he could do that.

Between the captain and Dana, the impression was that all persons who ventured out into space were the dashing characters of myth and lore, blessed with heroic looks and the self-confidence of prize racehorses. Only the presence of the rest of the crew muted that impression, for the others—the engineer and the cook, the boatswain and the cockswain, the second mate and the education officer—were scruffy and work-worn, and one engineer even had a missing tooth right in the top front. Only Mr. Nielsen was clean-clothed in his khaki shirt and trousers, for his job didn't involve mucking out the ship.

"Cadets, meet your commander," Mr. Nielsen announced with military formality. "Captain Thomas Scott Pangborn."

After a pause for drama, the captain began to speak. "Well, this looks like a capable group." His voice matched his heroic posture. Medium-everything, very masculine, but not deep or gravelly. Sort of a news-announcer voice.

"*Moghrey mie*," Robin spoke up. She smiled, her little butterfly smile, knowing he couldn't possibly understand the greeting. Little flirt.

The captain blinked at her impertinence. "Pardon? What's . . . 'morra mye'?"

"That was 'good morning' in our native Gaelic," she explained.

"She's talkin' to the birds," Ned quietly added, just enough to be heard. "Robin can make greetings in twenty-two languages."

The captain looked at him, apparently missing the resemblance, in coloring if not in the arrangement of features. "And you are . . ."

"I'm the brother," Ned said.

"I see. And how old is the brother?"

"Sixteen, sir, just last month."

"Ah. Old enough to know better, young enough to ignore knowing better. I remember those days. You have a name?"

"Ned, sir."

"Edward?"

"Sorry, just Ned."

"Pretty simple. What's your last name?"

"Menzie."

The captain pressed his lips and nodded. "Mmm. What's your story, Ned Menzie? Are you . . . Irish?"

Not having much of a story to tell, Ned fumbled out the best he could do. "We're Manx."

The captain's brows came down. "What's a Mank?"

Robin tucked her chin a little more, her big eyes wide. Ned came up to the challenge, though he had the feeling he was taking some bad bait. "The Isle of Man. West of England, east of Ireland, south of the mist and north of the moon."

"Mm . . . didn't know that place still existed."

Ned shrugged one shoulder. He never knew what to do with his hands, so they hung on the ends of his arms like plumb bobs. And his hair hung in his eyes and his clothes hung from his shoulders, as if still on a hanger, but humility and raggediness only carried a man so far. He met the captain's critical gaze and asked, "And where are you from, sir?"

Captain Thomas Scott Pangborn—a name which he seemed to carry like a royal title—raised his chin just enough to show the broad angle of his jawline. His eyes were fixed on Ned's.

"I'm Canadian," he declared.

Ned got the urge to ask, "What's a Can?" but snuffed just in time.

"What do your parents do on the Isle of Men?"

Robin shrank a bit, but Ned smiled at the captain's insult as if he'd never heard it before. "The Isle of Man, sir. It's named after Mannanan MacLir, son of the God of the Sea. It should be spelt with two n's, but one fell off."

Some of the other teenagers rewarded his gall with giggles.

"Our grandparents run a wool farm. Sheep and goats. We have six hundred head of four-horns and two hundred—"

"Four . . . horns?"

"Four-horned sheep. They're native to the Isle of Man." Shamefully, he couldn't avoid putting a little inflection on "Man."

"Sheepherders," the captain said, interested. "Shepherds. What do you do with your four-horns?"

"Wool."

"Wool? Funny . . . I thought that was replaced with synthetic fibers about two hundred years ago. I thought all sheep were grown just for lamb chops."

Ned offered only a passive grin. He hadn't really been invited to explain the success of the industry that supported his home. If ever someone ventured a direct question, he might give it a go.

"Mm," the captain moved on. "You'll come in handy. We're picking up a cargo of livestock. Of course, they'll all be in suspension."

"Easy to herd, then," Ned commented.

A flash of cold irritation hardened Pangborn's square face, but instantly vanished as he laughed heartily and clapped Ned on the back, a little harder than necessary. "Easy to herd! That's so true! I like a man who knows how to make light of a situation. How did you end up here?"

"Our parish priest put our names in the bin. I wouldn't take it up, but he was that joyous about it and I didn't want him disappointed."

The captain folded his arms and put a finger to his lips. "Ah—I think I remember now . . . the two of you are here on a special scholarship for the economically deprived. You basically won a random drawing."

Robin's chin tipped down and her eyes went up and batted once or twice, but her mouth corners turned up just a bit, making her cheeks into the butterfly-wings Ned had always found so funny. Since she was a baby, she'd had those cheeks. Ned absorbed the astonished stares of the other teenagers, each with its own interpretation of embarrassment or victory at another's expense. Then again, he knew what they were and they knew what he and Robin were.

"We don't say it right out like that," he offered, "but it seems we've been blessed by the generosity of others, and we've no shame in that."

"Well!" The captain clapped a hand on the knob of Ned's shoulder. "That was a damned grown-up thing to say. I respect that. Who else do we have here? Well, I'll get to know all of you in a day or two. From here on, now that your school year's officially over, the crew will introduce you to the ship's posts and how to operate them. You'll be manning important stations like the helm, docking, various scientific and mechanical posts, safety, damage control, and we'll eventually be doing emergency drills."

He paused, strode away from them a few steps, down to the end of the polished salon table, then made one of those stage turns and faced them again, making it seem as if he'd just decided what he wanted to say.

"As you all know, space is the most hostile environment in the universe. The *Umiak* is part of an innerspace fleet, serving established colonies, outposts, orbital stations, and new republics like Zone Emerald, Cargo City, RU490, and Ring Dome. We're now moving out on an elliptical course that will take us into open space for a four-month training and science experience. It's farther out than we usually go, so we'll have to stay on our toes. We have one scheduled rendezvous, but otherwise will only be engaging in your training. You'll get college credit toward your degree at Emerald University's elite Technical Academy. I commend your accomplishments. You'll be taking several class sessions on celestial navigation, theory, and operations of helm watch, as well as other watch positions for underway conditions, ship's maintenance, propulsion engineering . . ." He looked at Dana and made a gesture with one hand.

Dana took over. "Load configuration, small-engine operations, on-board operational safety, emergency management, damage control, the history of freight shipping—"

"And with completion of each session, you'll be given a certificate of accomplishment which counts toward college credit. Once you achieve all the certifications, you'll also receive a smart platinum-colored *Umiak* crew shirt like the ones Dana and I are wearing. Until then, you'll continue wearing your own clothing or you can wear the purple *Umiak* work shirt like Dustin and Luke over there. These shirts are badges of honor for your accomplishment so far, and accomplishments yet to come. I see some of you already have them."

Ned glanced down at the shirt he was wearing, a vine-green T-shirt with two bright competition motorcycles roaring down a stretch and the words "TOURIST TROPHY MOTOCROSS ROADRACE" splashed across the chest and "ISLE OF MAN" under the picture. Until now, he'd been proud of earning it, even though his sister claimed he looked like Peter Pan in his greens. Dustin and Luke, the two crewmen, were physically unalike—brown-haired Dustin tall and narrow, fair-haired Luke built like a brick—but in their purple crew work shirts they looked like a team. Indeed, they were.

He looked at Dana—yes, she was wearing the same shirt as the captain, but somehow it looked very different from his. On Dana, it was just a light-gray polo shirt with the name "UMIAK" on the left side, and an emblem of a ship's brass bell, and under the bell, the word "CREW." Hers was short-sleeved, as if meant for work, while the captain's was long-sleeved—perhaps that contributed to the image, Ned considered. On the captain, the simple shirt seemed more like a true uniform, stretched across his enviable shoulders and blocky pecs. He was not a huge man, but he was built of firm parts, well-proportioned enough to fill out his shirt in a military way.

"You'll be divided into watches just as you have been until now," the captain broke into Ned's thoughts, "and have a watch

leader to whom you'll report for the duration of the voyage.
You will not report to me or Dana. You'll report only to your
watch leader. If you want to ask me a question, ask your watch
leader first. He'll decide whether or not the problem merits
my attention. After we reach the apex of our elliptical course,
we'll loop back to Zone Emerald and you'll disembark at the
university spaceport. After that, your futures are your own.
Until then, they're mine." Pangborn scanned the faces of the
teenagers, then suddenly smiled and clapped his hands together
once, then rubbed them. "But we'll have fun!"

"Permission to dismiss to stations, sir?" Dana asked with a
tone that was so phony as to be comedic.

"Granted," Captain Pangborn said, "after you tell them
about my bell."

Ned was drawn to look again at the imposing man, almost
as if seeing the captain anew. He'd had never seen such a man,
so steeped in self-confidence, so heroic in his stance, whose
every pause seemed to be a pose for a picture on a brochure
cover. Between the statuesque captain and his photo-worthy
first mate, they made quite an impression on the gangly
young cadets.

But for this moment, the captain seemed on edge, as if he'd
been waiting to get this in, as if afraid the crew would forget
to talk about it.

With a blunted gesture, the young crewman named Dustin
directed the cadets' attention to a Greek-looking pedestal fixed
at the important end of the salon, almost like a shrine. On top
of it was fixed a sizable old-fashioned brass bell, as big around
as a cow's head, with an etching that said "RAVEN" and the
year "2092" under the word. The bell gleamed in the utility
lights, almost with prismatic effect. The colors of the reflec-
tions were slightly fanned in the bell's golden skin, making
soft patches of red, green, and white. The craftsmanship was

remarkable, with crisp impressions of ivy leaves running in a band around the bell's skirt. The housing that held the bell and allowed it to swing was formed into the bodies of two glorious mermaids. At the point where the mermaids' hands came together over the top, the bell was suspended almost as if in zero-G, floating despite its clearly considerable weight.

"The captain's bell," Dustin announced. "It will be polished every morning with special shining compound, using soft-bristled toothbrushes and shammies. There will never be allowed a single streak, a smudge, a fingerprint, or a hint of tarnish on the captain's bell. It's made of ninety pounds of bronze with a skin of pure brass. The bell comes from the captain's great-great-grandmother's command, an interstellar exploration ship called . . ."

He bugged his eyes at the cadets until they got the idea and a few of them chimed, "The *Raven*."

"Wrong! Gotcha! No, this bell comes from a steamship called *Raven*, and is over four hundred years old, back when they actually used bells on ships. The captain's great-great-grandmother bought this bell in an auction and it has served on ships of the Pangborn family ever since. Every morning, two of you will be assigned to polishing the captain's bell. The captain himself will inspect the work. Better be perfect."

Captain Pangborn interrupted again, if a captain can actually interrupt on his own ship. "Dana, have one of these cadets ring the bell."

"How about you, Robin?" Dana offered. "Ring the bell one time."

Robin stepped out of the line and went to the bell. Under the bell was a short bit of ropework made into a sennet with a glass ball inside a macramé cup at the end. Robin looked under the bell, as if checking under a woman's skirt, then took a grip on the bell pull somewhat tentatively, and gave it a tug. The bell knew its job. It almost sucked the clapper into the broad skirt, sending a loud *tang* of announcement through the living section of the ship. A beautiful sound—meant for the outdoors —set several of the cadets to a nervous flinch. For several seconds it produced its own echo in the companionways.

"Ah!" The captain gloried in the sound. "Nothing like it!" He closed his eyes and smiled as the bell tone rang, then opened them and nodded. "Well, I'm sure we'll have an interesting four months. You'll be on duty like regular spacefarers, doing jobs on the ship that need doing. We have a small crew because we're counting on the cadets to pick up the slack. These jobs aren't jokes. They're not practice. They're not games. You're real 'farers now, part of a noble tradition. Do it justice. Make it proud."

After a look of contrived ferocity to nail down his point, he nodded to Dana that she could take over again.

"All right, you cheeky monkeys!" she began. "Prepare to become intimate with the art of spit and polish. 'Dustbin' will divide you into teams of two. One team will be assigned to assist Spiderlegs in the galley. Every day, two of you will be galley hands. The others will disperse to various assignments. We devote one day a week to a thorough cleaning of the ship, and this, my little chickadees, is that day. Dustin—"

"Okay, I want two volunteers to learn to do the vacuuming," Dustin plunged right in. "How about Mary and . . . Dylan. Good. Thanks for volunteering. You two come with me. The rest of you wait here for further instructions. I'll be back in about . . . six-point-three-nine-nine-nine-seven-four-and-a-half minutes. Synchronize your brains."

"If you'll all excuse me," Mr. Nielsen said, "I'm going to go work on my lesson plans."

"And what plans would those be?" Dana lilted, giving him the ramp he needed.

"The cadets will each draw an assignment from a hat," Mr. Nielsen explained. "Each one will draw the name of a city, and then a twenty-five-year period in history. Each of you will have to do research on that city in that period, such as Alexandria, Egypt in 340 BC, or maybe Philadelphia in the 1970s, and you'll do a report on types of transportation that were used by people to move themselves. Not to move goods, but personal transportation. Then, later, we'll change cities and move up to how freight and wares were transported along trade routes and on water."

"Sounds monumental!" Dana chirped. "Why, I'm jealous that I myself won't have the time to do that work. Darned if I'm not green with envy."

Everyone laughed and groaned at the same time.

"I'm off," Mr. Nielsen said, and waved before leaving the chamber. "Do your work well, kids!"

Dustin took Mary and Dylan and disappeared through a hatch. Ned caught the glance of insecurity Mary flicked back at them, but Dylan, a short boy and the youngest among them, went off with confidence behind Dustin. Each of them would come back with a little experience to talk about.

The other regular crewmembers melted into various companionways, giving the teens a few minutes to absorb what they had just heard and to acclimate to each other. Ned turned to introduce himself to the five who he didn't know, but never got the chance. Instead, the tall boy with the shining crown of blond hair and the attitude of an aristocrat turned to Robin.

"'Hello' in twenty-two languages? Why? Everybody speaks English."

Robin was unintimidated by boys—one of the traits that set her apart from most girls her age. "Don't you think it's fun to have a secret language?"

"Sounds like extra work for no gain."

"Work is its own reward," Ned spoke up, coming to his sister's side. "We're blessed to have it."

The tall one drew a long breath through his nose and spoke as if he were making a forced effort to continue the communication. "This from a day laborer who volunteers to clean toilets."

"We work on a farm," Ned said with a shrug. "Nature's toilet."

Robin smiled, entertained by his brashness. She had the look of a fairy child, Ned had always thought, with her elvishly uneven smile and long dark hair falling softly around her ears. Her ears were shaped like shells, but there was a bit of a natural point that parted her sleek hair ever so slightly. She was no classic beauty, but she had a perpetual cuteness and a jade shine to her eyes that folk found appealing because it disarmed them of their tensions. All she needed was the butterfly wings, and off she would go fluttering to a Sidhe circle in an ivy grotto, with her long toes touching on the moss-covered stones and the moon kissing her twiggish arms as they floated out for balance.

She was his only sibling and they had been each other's childhood playmates. Possessing nothing ethereal to the naked eye, Ned was a typical farmer's son, stringy and strong, half wild, unremarkable, and more at home among the goats than the neighbors. His life had always been a blessing to him, it so perfectly fit his nature, a life of simple satisfactions, almost constant work that made the same demands day by day, grateful animals who came to his whistle, and devoted grandparents with good humor. He'd always considered himself lucky, but still, it was a surprise when the people came from the space-born City of Cargo to say he and Robin had won a scholarship meant for kids who had no hope of good careers.

No hope? He wanted to show them the braeside.

But his grans had said, "Go, boy, in good health. Never turn back a gift."

They were sweet and he was loyal to them. He saw in their eyes the joy that something had been offered him that they could never in a century provide, and with it the little fear that he might catch the bug and go off for a life in space, leaving them forever behind.

And I just might. This is a sparkling world, in space, with the stars a few steps closer.

All eyes still lingered on the cutout of air where the captain had been. He had left his impression.

"Not to worry," the tall blond boy said. "I'm sure he's the best of the best of the best. They all are, you know. Didn't you read the brochure?"

"Back off, Adam," the boy named Daniel suggested in his heavy Australian accent. "Be noyce and troy to get along, loik mommy says."

The other boy didn't face him, but dryly said, "You don't know my mommy. I most definitely have no intention of ever getting to know yours."

Dan responded with wide eyes and a fake flinch. "Eww, he hezz new intintin of ivver gitting to nyeww meen. Eww. Somebody worsh him off. Bloke passed through my fart."

The blond boy's heavily lidded eyes closed once, then opened again with perfect passivity, declaring that Dan's mockery had missed its target. His gaze, when he opened his eyes, was no longer on Dan at all, but instead floated to the odd-gal-out. The other girl . . . Pearl.

A moment ago the cadets had stared at the empty spot where the captain had been, now they shifted attention to the one among them who was truly not "among" them. There she stood at the far end of the long salon, her back to them, rocking back and forth on her locked knees, biting her cuticles.

As mousy as a person could be without actually being a mouse, Pearl was not just thin, but pin-boned. Painfully thin, with pencil-like limbs, long hands, and twiggy fingers, she moved as if the air itself might break her, unstable as an antique bud vase on a fragile glass stand. Everything about her was dun-brown from her clothes to her dusty skin to her drab hair to her saggy eyes. She held her shoulders forward, causing her chest to seem collapsed. Though only fifteen, she already had an old woman's hump forming on her back. Her tiny breasts already sagged inside the thin dust-blue T-shirt whose boat-neck and long sleeve only accentuated her dying-sapling physique. She was cursed with fragility, a bloodless little thing with a faint but lingering odor that reminded Ned of low tide.

She cast them, with her blushless face, only the most bleak of glances. Finally she put out both frail hands to steady herself and stepped through the companionway to begin the long awkward walk to the next hatch. She had a funny walk too, crossing her feet in front of each other, and her shoulders went forward and back, forward and back, alternating like machines.

As they watched her go, a single voice began to narrate the moment.

"I've heard of her." Again, it was the tall boy with the chin-length waves of sand-blond hair, the one who was so in control of himself. He spoke in measured tones, as if doing a voice-over for a nature special. "Pearl Floy. Genetic mutations like her . . . they usually die in infancy."

Ned deliberately interrupted the narration. "Mutations?"

"She's a freak. Nature got its wires crossed. The researchers had to give her a special classification. Birds attack her and peck at her in the spring. Animals react strangely to her. They sense something."

"Nonsense," Robin scolded quietly. "She's just a person. What a thing to say. How would you feel?"

"What I feel has no bearing on her," he said. "Fifty years ago, she'd have died. Sometimes medical science does a disservice to keep something alive when nature tries to correct its errors. Some things are meant to die and we should let them. She's had brand new diseases nobody's ever heard of before, but she's never had a human virus. Not one. Never had a cold, never had the flu . . . bacteria that reside on normal human skin just die on her. She has her own kind of bacteria." He shifted on his feet, casual and aloof. "There's a hypothesis that she's not really human. She's something weird. A throwback. They say she can't even reproduce." He paused for a few seconds, to let his soliloquy sink in. Then, with perfect timing, he added, "She even smells funny."

Ned grimaced as if he'd eaten a sour bit and twisted a look at him. The other kids seemed mesmerized.

"She's on the ship for a reason, right?" asked the girl with cornrowed hair. Leigh was her name. "She has some kind of skill that got her a bunk here?"

"Some pathetic talent," the tall boy accepted. "They let inadequates into this program sometimes. It's an egalitarian program to include lessers."

"Maybe she's not a throwback," Ned spoke up. "Maybe she's the next stage of humanity. That's how evolution happens."

The tall sophisticate turned a superior gaze on him. "How would *you* know? You haven't quite evolved, have you? Why don't you get a haircut?"

Ned gave him the disarming shrug and puppy-dog happy face that was the definition of his personality, blinking out from under the dark mop whose value had been called to point. "I'm Ned. What's your name?"

The elegant boy made use of his height by stepping closer to Ned, just enough to prove he could actually look down at him. His deeply set eyes and square face made Ned think of the portraits of eighteenth century nobles in a gallery, with their powdered hair and confidence of separation.

"You don't need to know my name," he said.

A few seconds passed.

Only after a calculated pause did the tall boy break off the withering gaze and stride out of the cabin, through a companionway that led to the aft section of the ship. Where he was headed, no one knew.

Ned stood there with his pride in a puddle—or at least the other kids thought his pride was in a puddle. In fact, he was unflapped. He knew that after this voyage he would never see that boy again, and he had no reason to answer to him.

He looked at the others and made a silly grin. "Guess he put me in my place, eh?"

"Aren't you embarrassed?" Dylan asked.

"Why?"

Stewart spoke for the first time today. "He thinks he's better than you."

Ned shrugged. "Maybe he is."

Leigh looked down the companionway. "That's Adam Bay. He pretends he's somebody."

"Doesn't seem to want to be here, does he?" Robin commented.

"'Oy'll tell yer, mate, 'e's a thermodynamics wiz," Daniel explained with his thick Australian accent. "Bloke thinks this expedition is a waste of his toyme."

Leigh added, "We all worked the two whole years to earn this, but he just automatically got in. On just the mention of his name. They sent a limousine to his house."

"If he doesn't want to be here," Ned asked, "why did he come?"

Dan said, "His father made him."

"Well, he should do as his father wishes."

Robin sidled closer and quietly asked, "After we clean the whole ship, then what?"

"Then we're going to a circus!" Dan declared. "You can 'ave cotton candy and royde an elephant!"

Leigh sighed in a disgusted way. "We're going to rendezvous with another ship and take on their cargo."

"Another ship?" Ned echoed. "Way out here?"

"Way out here," she said. "It's called the *Virginia*."

"I want the loose fastenings completely re-fitted. No more temporary fixes on those. Weld in new titanium plates to screw them down into. I also didn't like the turning quadrant to starboard when we tried to stabilize for orbit at the last station. Check those thrusters and improve that radius. We also need to get on the relief valves. They should've been done last week. And get Luke on that pinhole corrosion in the starboard flank bay. I don't like having a thousand little holes where there aren't supposed to be any perforations at all. He's been putting it off. I want them filled with the new polyester resin compound, then polished flush."

"Stuff smells awful." Dana followed Captain Pangborn into the charthouse while making notes on her portable office, the mate's handheld datapod.

"Breathing is optional," the captain said. "Getting the job done isn't. Luke isn't the one to be worried about smelling bad."

Uneasy with the talk about her shipmates, Dana shifted the subject. "This cadet program picks one student from a series of specialties, so these kids are the top of their lines. Adam Bay's specialty is thermodynamics. I hear he's quite an advance runner in the field. All the adults are jealous. And they were child stars themselves."

"Child stars always fizzle out early."

Inside the charthouse, the captain moved past the dazzling navigational theatre as if it didn't exist, and punched a code for hot beverages into the embedded dispenser next to the chart desk. "Coffee?"

"Hot chocolate, please," Dana accepted, though she really didn't want any. "They're an interesting bunch of kids. Lots of

different backgrounds. Leigh is an astronomy major special-
izing in nebulae and cosmic dust clouds."

"She's the Jewish one? The one with the cornrows in her
hair?"

Dana looked up. "Is she? Does it make a difference?"

"Not to me. She's blond, is all. Doesn't look Jewish."

"She has a strong personality, likes to cook, and she wants
to be a rabbi and study the Torah . . . or a cosmographer . . . or
a linguist in French."

"Ah, to be young and uncommitted."

"Mary's speciality is electricity. She wants to go into power
systems for non-terraformed outposts and colonies. Then
there's Pearl Floy . . . she's . . . different. But she apparently has
some unique talents."

"She's the ugly one with the eyes like an owl, and she's got
those eyebrows that hover as if she's always asking a question?
And the teeth with spaces between all of them?"

"Uh . . . yes . . . She's just at an awkward stage. She'll grow
into—"

"The Cobb coils!" He snapped his fingers. "I knew there was
something else. Don't let Luke do those. He's too ham-handed.
Put somebody else on it."

"Cobb coils," she murmured, and tapped it into her
datapod.

Pangborn leaned back on the chart desk, crossed his ankles,
rested his elbow on a folded arm, and blew softly across the
surface of the coffee. He scanned the working consoles, data
readouts, and happily purring banks on the nav theatre as the
ship streaked through space on pre-programmed auto-pilot.
The beautiful bank of color-coded screen frames and displays
was comforting.

"What 'unique' talents?" he asked.

"Pardon?"

"The weird girl."

"Oh, I'm not sure yet," Dana admitted. "She hasn't told me and there's nothing on her bio. I could read through it again and look for hints."

"Why don't you just ask Nielsen? He's the education officer. Doesn't he know?"

"Apparently not. Pearl doesn't speak much to the other kids and I get the sense that she really hates the other girls. She keeps looking at Adam Bay, keeps trying to stand next to him, or she just lingers behind him. But she never talks to him or tries to get his attention. If he ever looked at her, I think she'd wither."

"Sounds like a twist of bottled neuroses to me. I've been in space twenty-two years and I've never seen anybody with truly 'unique' talents."

The beverage dispenser hummed cheerfully and began to fill two hefty mugs marked with "UMIAK," sitting side by side in the cubby. They warmed Dana with the aromas of coffee and frothy chocolate, a scent of ski lodges and office work, transforming the chamber into something essentially human despite being so far from Earth.

Dana bobbed her brows in what she hoped he would take as passive agreement. "The Australian boy, Dan, got the Emerald scholarship for transonic acoustics. He's self-confident and cocky, but I've noticed he accepts criticism exceptionally well and doesn't take it personally. Stewart, the quiet, happy boy, is going into theoretical chemistry."

"That kid with the dopey smile all the time?

"He did a terrific year-long study on making ships airtight. He invented a new atomic-sized-powder nano-alloy bonding film. He plans to become a caulking specialist for spacefaring vessels and containers."

"Then he's on the right ship."

"Then there's the short boy named Dylan—he's a good sport. He's into magnetology for—"

"Thanks," Pangborn said abruptly. "Doesn't matter."

He became much more interested in watching the last spurts of coffee drop into the big blue mug.

Dana put the datapod down. This was the fourth time she'd tried to familiarize him with the cadets, and the fourth time she'd failed to keep his interest.

The captain took the steaming mug of coffee to the chart desk, where he kept his favorite condiments, and doused it with so much milk and honey that it really wasn't coffee anymore. As in ships since the beginning of seafaring, the charthouse was a mini-quarters for the captain and mate, their own bunks off the flanks on either side, right nearby. Hardly a glamorous place, the charthouse was nonetheless comfortable, warmly lit, and efficient, manic in its neatness. The usual clumsy mix of wood, metal, plastics and electronics, the small area was like the inside of a brain case, rimmed with little square monitors that represented every part of the ship, every compartment, and the inner guts.

Pangborn was comfortable here and spent almost all of his time here, reading in his private wardroom, which wasn't much bigger. Dana was happiest when Pangborn was reading. She trusted her own experience and training, but he didn't seem to. She knew it wasn't personal—he didn't really trust anybody to be entirely up to his standards. A maddening trait, since the crew was willing to do whatever he wanted and he always seemed satisfied with their work and didn't ask for more, but somehow he communicated that everything they did was just adequate. She was getting used to it and learning to ignore it.

Only when his coffee was flavored to his tastes did Pangborn reach back and hand her the mug of hot chocolate.

"This new trick better work." He sniffed, flexed his shoulders, and looked at his reflection in the dark liquid. "Elite teenagers and two proletariat charity cases . . . if I don't increase the ship's income on this passage, I'll have to apply for redesignation and go through a major refit. These runs are getting so safe that the rates've dropped like bowling balls. Too many free agents getting into the game, too many ships . . . now I have to stoop to this. Ferrying pre-pubescents."

Dana made a subdued eyebrow-shrug. "They earned their passage, Captain, fair and square. Years of scholastic achievement led to this. They've been given the chance to jumpstart great careers. They have full-ride scholarships at Emerald University which they completely deserve."

"Not all of them." He pocketed one hand, leaned back against the edge of the huge embedded fish tank, and inhaled the coffee. "Not the Manx shepherds. Those two are too troglodytic to know an opportunity when they step in it. I wish these voyages were long enough for cryo-sleep. I'd slap all those imps in crates for the duration. Then I'd go kill the publicity agent who turned my ship into a brat camp."

"At least we'll have something to do, teaching these kids. It's more interesting than cargo runs between established colonies."

The captain made a forced and mirthless grin, showing the slight gap between his front teeth. "A duty I'll joyously hand over to you and Nielsen, which I'm sure you will execute masterfully."

Dana paused and this time looked up, not sure how to frame the question she knew had to be asked. She turned her body to be square with his. Maybe her posture would do some of the talking. "You . . . won't be participating in any of the sessions?"

His intense eyes gripped her. "You expected me to?"

"Well . . . it's your call, of course." She tried to let the uneasy moment pass. It didn't. "You might think about reviewing the contract with Ultraspace. They chartered the trip and sponsored the contest that got the Menzie kids in. If I recall correctly, there's a clause in there about command participation. Lessons from a fully licensed ship's captain is required for their complete accreditation."

He gestured at her with his coffee cup. "You have your captain's license."

"Yes . . . but . . . I'm sure they intended that the captain of *this* ship participate. I would've inferred that from—"

"You check. Ultraspace can charter anything they want, spend its money any way they please, I don't care. When we're out this far in space, who's to say what happens and what doesn't? If we satisfy the minimum requirements, nobody can call us on it. You handle it. And also check that port quarter mooring cleat before we raft up with *Virginia*. I heard a shudder in the tilt-lock."

"Oh . . . will do." Dana turned away from him. Having him see her expression wouldn't help anything at all.

"Have you read this cargo manifest?" he asked.

"The animals? Yes, I've read it."

"Hell of a list. Clones, hybrids . . . whole farms . . . endangered species . . . new species . . . old species . . ."

While Dana pretended to busy herself with clerical minutiae so she didn't have to communicate with his eyes, Pangborn flexed his spine and warmed his hands on his coffee cup. He rolled the cup between his hands, so the word "UMIAK" kept coming in and out of his fingers.

"Too bad they'll all be asleep," he commented. "Might be fun to watch."

CHAPTER FIVE

Blood and acid. The smell permeated every corridor, every compartment. Traveled in the air or through holes burned through the decks. Walkways and scaffolding that only hours ago had provided arteries of access all around were now compromised by the caustic remains of shredded aliens, painted with the red blood and blue entrails of those who had died facing them. All this mess was fused with some kind of congealed resin.

The once-welcoming ship had changed. Power starvation dimmed the channels leading from chamber to chamber. Sound-dampening carpet reeked with soaked-in blood and urine, the fluids of torment. Scents were signals long ago assumed to serve only animals. Humans used them, or fled from them, but didn't need them. To live amid heavy odors was shunned as crass, unnecessary. The clean ship, once smelling only of soft lubricants and pleasant cleaners and fresh air was today choked with odor. Rot. Putrification. Like the bubonic plague. And somehow . . . the smell of panic.

The smell nagged at him. The stink that wouldn't clear, that kept feeding the fear spoonful by spoonful. No matter how frantically the ship's emergency ventilation systems struggled and recalibrated, the stink was in the upholstery, the carpeting, the clothing, the very metal. There was no getting used to it.

He carried the only weapon, a small sonic-pulse pistol he always kept in his quarters. It had always provided plenty of protection against the type of enemy he anticipated—humans . . . raiders, pirates, salvagers. In all its years, it had been used only once, to subdue a crazed passenger with mental problems. Even then, it had been fired to wound, not to kill.

The energy in the little pistol warmed his hand, showing him that it was ready. It was a loyal puppy.

The burden had fallen on Alley to control the panic. Control it, ease it, head it off—there wasn't a good phrase, or any one plan that worked. Sweat percolated from his face and neck and around his beltline. If only he could just worry about himself, he could make his own choice when to die. But he was the captain. If he got killed too early, would the others have a chance in hell? A suicide mission would put him out of his own misery, but would decapitate his crew and passengers. Their last hour would be worse for lack of that one eternal hope—that the captain would think of something.

But he hadn't thought of anything. His best plan was to round up the survivors and try to lock them down in the best-shielded place aboard—the engine room.

And he didn't even like that plan. But a lifeboat was a lifeboat. They would at least get in.

"Everybody," he warned, "stay quiet. We're almost there."

They had started as a group of forty-one, all he could gather from the original sixty combined crew and passengers. The first nine people had died within an hour of Jonsy's sending out the alarms, before even the basic emergency shutdowns and isolations could happen. Even with the security bulkheads down, the slaughter had begun. The creatures killing the people hadn't stayed together, but dispersed all over the ship, and begun the bloody spree. Several people were missing, unaccounted for.

Alley knew a suppressing assault when he saw it. The speed of the attacks gave the plan away—eradicate all life-forms other than themselves. No purpose, no sense of fear or defense—just aggression.

He hadn't even seen one of the animals yet. Not the whole thing, anyway. A flash in the darkness, a glossy tendril, a slashing claw, that warning hiss. Only those suddenly dead had seen what had killed them, if even they had seen it at all. He couldn't really know.

Fifteen minutes ago, the intraship communications system and computer conduits had failed from damage. Clyde said it was acid, burning its way through deck after deck, sizzling into the connectors, the grids, chips and network systems fritzed. Most of them fell offline. Alley's broadcast to the remaining crew and passengers had been cut off, but not before he gave orders to muster amidships. Those still alive tried to get there, and several had died trying. They were now down ten more people. There were only thirty-one left. Thirty-one terrified people, picking their way through the ship toward the engine room, the only place in the ship that could be fortified.

He didn't know what else to do.

"I should've listened to my instincts," Clyde uttered emptily behind Alley. "Something about that container was talking to me . . . I should've listened."

"Not your fault. You checked it. Jonsy lied. Who's in the back of this line?"

"Passengers."

"Where's LaMay?"

Clyde twisted around. Not too loudly, he called, "L'Dave?"

"Right here." LaMay's voice came back through the darkness.

"Who's at the back of the line?"

LaMay's disembodied voice was broken by the distance and effort to be quiet. "Couple of VIPs, I think. They volunteered."

"Clyde," Alley said, "go back there and take up the rear guard. Take Dave with you."

"Rear guard, aye," Clyde acknowledged, but there was distinct fear in his eyes. He was being sentenced to do the impossible—defend against what he couldn't see coming, what he had no weapon to fight, or be the sacrificial lamb.

Proud of his crewman's quiet acceptance, Alley appreciated Clyde's keeping the fear out of his voice, for the sake of the innocent people behind them both. As Clyde broke away from the wall against which they were all pressed, Alley glanced back at the faces of strangers. He didn't know these people. He had shaken every hand and welcomed them aboard, but they were privileged people who had chosen a new life on a distant established colony. He was the custodian responsible for getting them there. They were all adults, at least. He breathed a sigh of relief for that.

Their faces, fading off behind him into the curved corridor, were lit only by battery-powered emergency lighting on one-third power. The dim amber lights created an otherworldly underglow and cast the faces of the people as unnatural Halloween chalk drawings, lit from the wrong direction. The rows of little amber lights were enough to walk by, but dim enough to conserve power for a longer period.

How long? Would he and these people outlast the lights, or would it soon be unimportant how long the batteries held out?

The lights would last about four days.

Four days.

Nine dead in one hour. Twenty more by dinner time. Now it was, by the clock, night. It felt like night.

"I hear somet'ing!" It was Voola, five people back, huddled with each arm hooked in the arms of two other women. They looked like a singing group caught in a thunderstorm. Voola's faced was limned with worry lines, smeared with the blood of those she'd tried to save. They had only found two alive, but not for long.

Alley froze in place and held out a hand to make others stop moving, shifting. He listened.

A creak of confused metal. Drips of moisture. Spritzing lubricant. Snapping electricity. The amount of damage was a meter-by-meter shock. It had its own sound.

"Captain, I am hear somet'ing!" Voola choked. "Please!"

"Shh!" He snapped his fingers.

Behind him, the pasty faces of the survivors were like ghosts of some ancient shipwreck, shocked out of their sleep, out of their prayers and dreams, torn from the futures they had so carefully planned. They did as he ordered, and cringed in silence, only the smallest whimpers squeezing out.

No other sounds. He listened. Closed his eyes. Listened again. A grip of shivers ran through his ribcage.

Alley opened his eyes. "Follow me."

Was it in front of them? Blocking their way to the engine room? Whatever Voola was hearing, he couldn't find it.

Feeling the weight of all the people behind him bearing down on his shoulders, Alley stepped forward into the amber glow. The corridor ceiling seemed lower than ever before, the walls tighter. They crept past smelly damaged panels dripping with residue that burned their throats with its electrical stink.

Someone coughed—a cannon shot. Alley cringed.

He moved forward toward the curved part of the corridor. The curve betrayed him. There was no seeing beyond it for another ten steps. He'd walked it a thousand times. Now those ten steps were miles.

One . . . two . . . behind him the passengers shuddered so
deeply that he felt the ripples. He felt also the malevolence of
their tormenters like a fume penetrating the ship. He sensed
the wickedness, the pure evil goal, unimpaired with desires or
negotiation. There was no deal to be made, nothing to play on.
No edge.

Four steps.

He stretched what there was of his neck and wished to be
taller, trying to see around the bend. He wanted to be taller,
stronger, more imposing. They were following him anyway.
There hadn't been a single resistance. He expected that from
his crew, but these passengers could've challenged him. The
big man with the red hair who made a fortune in desert
plumbing. The woman who had built her own business in the
field of aerospace after inheriting a failing company from an
uncle. The landed heir to a British lordship. The aging retired
captain of a military supply ship. None had challenged him.
So far.

He didn't know whether to be honored or worried.

Seven . . .

A scream shattered the tension—Voola!

Alley whirled to discipline her for not keeping quiet, for
giving in to eruptions of panic, but he found all the other
people facing not Voola but a utility locker embedded into
the skin of the corridor. Voola pointed at the locker with one
hand, the other balled into a fist and crammed against her
front teeth. She was still shrieking.

The captain, Clyde, Dave, and two other men shoved the
women out of the way and closed on the locker.

"Move, move!" Alley slammed his way to the center. He
squared himself in front of the locker and grasped the handle.
The other men braced themselves, brandishing kitchen knives
and titanium bars.

The weapons were silly. They all knew.

Was the locker big enough to have one of those things inside?

The handle was hot. How could it be? The metal burned him like a skillet's edge—or was it just the sweat in his hand?

He gripped the pistol and aimed it high.

"Let me!" Clyde pressed at his side, reaching for the handle. He was whispering, but in ghastly intense desperation.

"No—no!" Alley protested.

"Yes!"

After a second Alley got the idea. Clyde would open the locker, giving Alley both his own hands to steady the weapon. Dave came up beside Clyde, and together they gripped the locker handle.

Alley hissed, "Heave!"

The two men put their combined weight into a single monumental heave. The door of the locker, with an almost animal shriek, was torn completely off its hinges. It clattered down the deck, striking the big red-headed man, who batted it farther down and braced to fight whatever came out after it.

Alley felt his hands squish on the pistol. Stunned only briefly, long enough to realize what he was seeing in front of him, Alley shoved his weapon into Clyde's hand and plunged forward, diving into the locker.

"Come out of there, you greedy stick-insect! Come out here! Come out!"

Bending backward and shoving one knee out, Alley twisted his hands into fabric and hauled back until the coiled lump unfolded into a spindle.

"I'm sorry! I'm so sorry! I'm so sorry!" Jonsy Coyne howled and cranked in Alley's hands.

The bosun was a sorry creature, unshaven, slobbered with saliva and blood. He recoiled from Alley, his arms cramped around a bundle of fabric he held tightly to his chest. Ignoring the petrified people watching, the captain wrenched him brutally out of his hiding place and slammed him against the wall, then followed him there and crushed him tight. "How many were in that container? How many?!"

Jonsy's eyes turned to crescents, his mouth screwed up in a terrible bow. His voice was a shatter. "It's just—I just—"

"How many? Talk!"

"Eight-eight-eight . . . eighteen . . . I'm sorry, I'm so, so, so sorry!"

"Eigh*teen*?"

"I—I—think—"

"How many got out?"

"Cook says . . . seven . . . didn't he say seven? Where is he?"

"He's dead, you sorry specimen!" His hands dug into Jonsy's collar. "There are eleven more inside? Eleven monsters waiting to develop? Give, goddamn you! Stiffen up and speak to me! What was your deal? Tell me what the deal was!"

Jonsy's soggy eyes blinked beseechingly. "I didn't want this . . . I didn't! Oh, God, Captain, help us . . . help us!"

"Help you?" Alley raged. "Help you? I'll help you to hell! Two dozen people dead in half a day! Living people shredded like discarded garments!"

Jonsy shrank in his hands. "We didn't . . . We didn't know . . ." He hugged his swaddled bundle and tucked his chin to it, his long fingers cramping into the soaked cloth.

Alley forced himself to lower his voice. "What . . . was . . . the deal?"

Cradling his bundle, Jonsy whimpered, "Rockie made the deal."

"Keep talking."

"We cleared the box . . . reconfigured the locking mechanisms and the shipping codes . . . they paid us ten times my annual . . . salary . . . I'd never . . get another . . . chance . . . There were supposed to be eighteen . . . embryos—but dead! They were supposed to be dead! Frozen!"

"Who was the shipper? Who's responsible for this? Who hired you? Give me a name!"

Weeping again, Jonsy squeaked, "I don't know . . . it was a blind ticket."

Alley exploded, slamming him into the wall again, then again. "You cleared a box onto this ship on a blind ticket? What kind of a bottomfeeder are you?!"

Hot with fury, he rang out with his right hand and slapped Jonsy flat on the side of his face. Jonsy wobbled and lost his grip on the bundle of rags. It went flying down the corridor, tumbling at the feet of Voola and the two other women. As it rolled, it freed itself from the wrapping of rags. When it stopped rolling, the sodden mass was staring up at them with Roxanne Coyne's eyes, shocked in the last moment before death. Or the moment after.

The women jumped backward into the people behind them, and the clutch of people flinched as if they shared a body. Rockie's severed head moved on the deck as if in a cradle, her long black hair pinched into bloody strings.

From back in the shadows, Dave LaMay uttered, "Oh, crap . . ."

Well, that pretty much summed it up. Nick Alley let his anger overwhelm his surprise. It was over for Rockie, just like the others.

Out of the amber glow, Clyde and Dave reappeared and looked down at the gruesome sight. They made no effort to hide the sight from the others. There was no blanching the nightmare anymore.

Jonsy stared at his wife's mangled head and wept openly. He pointed at it, like a child pointing at something frightening.

Alley reached out a hand toward Jonsy, though he was still looking down at the head, and dragged Jonsy toward him. "Are you telling me there are eleven fully developed creatures . . . still in that box?"

"But the box is locked up again," Clyde said. "The automatic security system closed it after three minutes because Keith and Gunny didn't open it with the correct protocols. Whatever's inside is locked inside."

Shivering and quailing, Jonsy sank against Alley's shoulder. "They were supposed to be already dead, frozen, in the—the—the—baby form—"

"You didn't notice it was a cryo box?" Alley barked.

"Well, yeah, but . . . y'know—"

"Is there any way—and you better tell me the truth, you stupid pus—*any* way the others can get out?"

"Not if . . . not if . . . security automatically closed it . . . if the box closed itself, like . . ." Jonsy's red-ringed eyes rolled between Alley, Clyde, and Dave. "They were in sta—stasis—so they wouldn't, y'know, grow up."

"Are they still in stasis?"

"I don't know . . . either way, they're held in the center . . . y'know, puffs of gravity . . . if they can't touch the sides, they can't break out—they can't, can they? Please tell me they can't . . ."

His face screwed up into a knot, his voice a squeak. Everyone watched him with a flood of pity and scorn. He had fallen prey to the oldest of human flaws—simple cheating. A bad bet that had cost him everything.

"Please, don't ask me," he pleaded. "I didn't know . . . I didn't . . . didn't know . . . didn't know . . ." Jonsy's eyes involuntarily crammed shut. He dissolved into open-mouthed sobs.

"Captain, shouldn't we keep moving?" Clyde urged.

Alley pitched Jonsy back against the bulkhead. Jonsy slid down the wall as if melting in his clothes. When his haunches touched the floor, he coiled into a ball and crawled across the deck to the bloody bundle of Roxanne's head. Still sobbing, he gathered it up, pulled the drizzles of torn cloth around his wife's gray face, and cuddled it to his chest.

"Just a minute," Alley said. "Just let me think . . ." He turned to Dave LaMay. "What's your take on this?"

LaMay was drawn and beaten. He'd had the first encounter with the creatures, surviving only because he was already in an EV suit. He escaped through a maintenance hatch. It had taken him two hours in his half-shredded suit, with its shattered com system and struggling life-support units, to find his way back into a working airlock in an area that wasn't compromised. He'd been too late to warn the first nine casualties. While he clawed his way around the outer hull of the ship, trying to get back in, the invaders had continued their rampage.

Running now on empty, LaMay put his exhaustion aside to do what was left of his job. "Well, Jonsy released a half-dozen or so of those things, and there were more inside, but the box was closed and locked again. So the ones still inside are trapped in zero-G by the air puffs, just floating as if in space. They can't reach the sides of the container to push off anything. They can't get a purchase to use their strength. The sensors will keep them right in the middle."

"Until somebody opens it again," Clyde added sadly.

Alley squeezed his fists, thinking aloud. "But it means we only have to worry about the ones that are already out. Seven, instead of eighteen."

LaMay's once-bright smile was only a ghost. He drew a shattered breath, then actually let out a little ugly laugh. "I was just thinking," he said slowly. "The Excepted Perils Clause . . . exempts us from responsibility for acts of God. Funny, huh?"

"You think these creatures are acts of God?" Alley uttered.

"Who else?"

Alley took the moment to hate seeing that expression on his otherwise cheerful and willing crewman.

He had never expected to be the captain of a battlefield. Somehow, though, all the training, the years of shipboard life, the ancient quasi-military existence, honed by untold millennia of tradition instilled in every sailor the idea of orderly defense. Any day, any sailor could end up defending his ship. Over thousands of years, the style of life aboard ships had hardened into one right way that worked all the time—an unbroken chain of command, a system of commands and orders, strict procedures that clicked into place even when minds were foggy or shocked. And he was ready.

If they were alive at this moment, it was only because of procedure. If they were dying, it was because their ship itself had become the hostile environment.

"Pick up this wretch." No longer sneaking, Alley raised his voice so all could hear. "Let's go. Come on, everybody, let's go."

His pistol now hung at his side. He strode down his corridor, his ship, taking possession boldly if only for his last few steps. Though the survivors were afraid, knew they could be leapt upon from any orifice, they only let him get about twenty feet ahead before they emboldened and followed, matching his pace.

"Come on, everybody inside." At the hatch to the main engine room, Alley smacked the controls, fed in his entry code, and pressed his thumb to the identification plate. The hatch slid open in a beautiful industrial way. He had no idea whether the compartment had been compromised, whether a handful of attackers was lurking inside. He made a bet. The ship's policy was that the engine room was constantly sealed, to be opened only by authorized personnel, and since none of those things had a thumbprint, he made the mental bet that the area was safe.

What difference did it make? Either it was or it wasn't. No place else was, anyway.

He stepped into the engine room and stood aside, using his gun to wave the others inside. "Come on, keep moving. Don't stop. That's it, come on in. Everybody sit down over there. Just sit down and breathe. Tell us if you're wounded. Otherwise just everybody sit down. Clyde, seal this hatch up."

He scanned the engine room. It was a dim chamber, rarely lit. Usually it operated in darkness. The engines of the *Virginia* were so dependable, so time-tried, that they required almost no attention other than basic maintenance. He'd often joked that Gunny's job was the easiest on board, with the most cooperative motive power in the entire merchant space fleet. A sudden urge to give Gunny a compliment for the excellent condition of the engines was crushed by a sharp recollection that Gunny was now little more than a flattened puddle with claw marks, somewhere in the port quarter.

He made a private vow to give somebody a compliment. Who? Didn't matter.

There was momentary silence, except for Jonsy's pathetic sobbing somewhere down the line of people.

"Clyde, Dave, spread out," Alley ordered. "Check the security of this area, quick." He paused and kept looking around while the passengers found places against a bulkhead to sit and gather their wits. They were bruised, dirty, unkempt. Most of them were in shock, mourning their own dead. None had been spared a loss. A husband, a wife, a friend, a traveling companion. Each had paid somehow. Many had seen the slaughter of their loved ones in person, managing to escape somehow, thanks often to the narrow hatches of the *Virginia's* cabins and common areas, hatches skinny enough to let a human through but would give one of those creatures a tangle that bought time.

There was no talking for the two minutes it took for Clyde and Dave to return from the corners of the chamber.

"All secure," Clyde reported.

"We locked everything," LaMay added. "Even the vent shafts."

Mercifully, he didn't mention what that meant—that there would only be air for a handful of hours before the room had to be allowed to breathe again.

Voola settled on her wide backside between the two other women and began tending the lacerated hand of the woman on her left. She glanced up at Alley and asked the most reasonable question.

"Do they eat?" she asked. "Vill dey eat us?"

"No information on that," Alley said. "We know they use other life-forms as incubators."

"They must consume something," LaMay ventured. "They can't gain mass without fuel of equal mass . . . can they? We know they grow—"

"They're also alien life-forms," Clyde told him, as if discussing any ordinary ship's business. "Who knows what kind of environment they evolved in?"

"Increase in mass could be locked into their biology. Maybe they're born with packages of hyper enzymes or hormones . . . something that gets triggered when they . . . erupt. For all we know, they may never eat. We don't know enough about them."

"Knowing might not help us," Alley said. "We're at war. That's what we know. We know they kill. If they see you, they kill you for no reason. If they leave you alive, it's to use you."

"What for?" the red-headed man asked. "'Use' us for what?"

Alley looked at him.

"You know, don't you?" the man asked. He stood up,

pushing his huge frame off the floor. He was all shoulders and chest, with narrow hips and short legs, but somehow, presented as a package he seemed huge. "You know what they are, don't you?"

"Tell us," one of the woman pleaded. "Be honest."

Realizing he'd slipped, Alley rubbed his aching hand across his face and around his neck. "Yeah," he admitted. "I think I know. Warnings have been sent out about a species of . . . aliens . . . that are highly destructive. Several ships and a colony have been compromised." He offered a small shrug with both shoulders. "They're . . . galactic heartburn."

"'Compromised'?" the woman challenged. "That's what you call it?"

Her painted-on eyebrows were clownish in their positions of worry. They were embarrassingly artificial, drawn on as if with a brown marker by a man with no artistic talent. They traveled from way over on her temples, in big poorly shaped arches, to the bridge of her nose, like tracings of a country road on some old map. They amplified her expression, which flipped between anger and terror.

"What's your name?" Alley asked, dumping all pretense that the captain knew everybody who ever rode aboard his ship. Her medium-length brown hair made a frowsy frame around her face. Long, small scratches in one cheek now defined a formerly pretty face. "Lena Dearborn."

Alley nodded passively. "Lena, we'll do our best."

Disarmed by his tone, she asked, "Where do they come from?"

"Nobody knows."

"But how did they get here?"

"They were smuggled aboard."

"What? You mean . . . you mean that loading show you gave us? They came aboard then?"

"Seems to be."

She began to cry fitfully, angrily. "How could you do this to us!"

He was willing to take her abuse.

"That's not fair, Lena," the big red-headed man said.

"Fair?" she wept. Sobs broke from deep in her chest. "My sister . . . my only sister . . . my nephews . . ."

Voola coiled a chubby arm around her. "Oh, merciful God . . . hear our prayer . . ."

"Put in a good word for the rest of us," LaMay said. He was annoyed. Alley appreciated that.

Clyde approached, and from his body language it was clear he wanted to speak privately. Alley bore off to the other side of one of the power cells. LaMay followed.

"How long can we hold out in here?" Clyde asked.

"Does this fit into the Space Perils Clause?" LaMay asked.

Alley screwed him a glower. "What is it with you?"

He shrugged. "I'm studying for my captain's license."

"Oh, yeah. That's some one-track mind, kid."

"It helps me keep going."

Alley broke into an involuntary smile. Everybody had his own recipe for bravery. "Under 'dangerous cargo.' I'd sure like to see the dock warrant for that box. If we live through this, I've got a customs officer to eviscerate."

He pushed both hands through his short hair and massaged his scalp for a couple of seconds, thinking under his hands. What was the next step? Were there people huddling anywhere else aboard, hoping for rescue? Could he even get to them? Or would there have to be a bigger goal than to save individual lives?

How had they come to this? Just this morning, they were enjoying a perfect run, with a ship full of people anticipating long lives on a golden planet. His career was secure. There would always be a need for experienced space captains and time-tried dependable ships. Soon his wife would've joined him and begun a life of living aboard *Virginia*.

He was glad she wasn't here. One lucky line they hadn't crossed.

He thought of Roxanne's head rolling across the deck, sorrowfully pursued by her distraught husband. Silence spread through the engine room. In its way, the silence was like an ooze, moistening their fears and causing their mental wounds to welter. They were confused, stunned. He felt their percolating panic. They were trapped, but even worse than being on some deserted island. They couldn't even swim away. Even the lifepods had been rendered inoperable. They'd lost three people trying to reach the pods, only to find both lifeboats ruined, one by physical smashing, the other by acid draining from the deck above.

Finally, aloud, he uttered, "This won't work."

LaMay looked up. "Pardon?"

"We can't outlast them in here. We're ten weeks out from the nearest outpost, flying on autonav."

"Doesn't the autonav have to be refreshed every few days by an officer?" LaMay asked.

"Yes, but it has an automatic failsafe. Deprived of refreshed orders, she'll reprogram herself to her last ordered course. The ship'll just keep going to her next point of rendezvous and carry out an autotransfer, and infect the *Umiak*. After that, she'll go on into space and connect with one unsuspecting ship after another."

He paused for thought, added up everything in his mind, and ran through a dozen scenarios, but they all turned out the same. The ship had its orders.

More to himself than anyone else, he said, "I can't let it happen."

The words helped clear his head. The decision was made.

Everyone was watching him. They could wage a fair but protracted battle here, hoping for some other ship to stumble upon them and help, or they could do something else.

"Okay, folks," he began, turning to the desperate faces. "We've just entered an elite phalanx of human beings. We're the *Titanic*. The *Lusitania*. The World Trade Center. The Nimbus Expedition. The victims of Velvet Brigade's Slaughter Dawn. The Yellowstone Supervolcano of 2103."

He paused, reading the realization in their faces, and gave them a moment to absorb the grim picture before continuing.

"We're the people who woke up this morning expecting one future and getting another because of forces out of our control. We're about to become that small group who make it into the history books. At this moment, we have to decide what history will say about us. Will we be victims or heroes? It's up to us now."

They saw it in Nick Alley's eyes. He didn't have to explain further.

"Out here, with no weapons?" Clyde wondered quietly.

"I wouldn't say that," Alley told him. "Take a look over here."

While the others watched, he led his officers past the inhibitor casings, and under the access ramp, which made a scalene triangle and created the little cubby he ducked into. "Right here."

Aware of the audience watching him—his surviving passengers who counted on him—he squatted before an untouched locker with a rolling shield of circular borium dragonskin plates. Alley engaged the lock with his personal code and raised the rolling shield.

Inside was a pretty fair arsenal, loaded into neat racks. Four RPG rifles, sixteen M-40 grenades, and five independent-targeting shoulder-held missiles.

"We're armed?" LaMay said with a lilt of hope.

"Hope for the best, prepare for the worst," Alley said, and pulled out two rifles. "Standard Marine assault weapons, with a couple of non-standards thrown in for spice."

He pulled out a stocky, unfriendly pulse-shot with a wide shoulder-rest and a heavy barrel the diameter of his wrist.

"What the demon is that?" LaMay asked.

Alley checked the propulsion charge on his old favorite. "It's a MacGregor Firebolt. My own personal contribution to repelling boarders."

"Just to be clear," Clyde began, "this means we go on the offensive and hunt them out?"

"Yes." Alley's answer was deliberately simple. "Our cargo's worth millions and our mission is worth billions. Our lives are priceless. Every hour makes us hungrier and more tired. In a handful of hours we won't have the strength to fight. Either we starve slowly or we fight them now, while we're still strong. We'll leave these people here and go out on assault. We'll kill as many of those hell-cats as we can. If we get lucky, maybe we'll get them all and survive."

"Which direction?"

Caressing his Firebolt, Alley thought about it. "First to the pilot house. It's the last stand for navigation. We have to destroy the autonav system so the ship doesn't go on to infect other ships. If nothing else, we have to do that. We have to stop this malignancy before it spreads."

He lowered his weapon and took a step back. He suddenly thought of his wife.

"Can we track them?" Dave asked. "Body heat? Motion?"

"We don't have that equipment aboard," Clyde said. "Why should we?"

Alley shrugged, feeling a little guilty for not loading everything possible for any wildly imaginable situation. "Nobody carries more weight or bulk on a ship than necessary. That's just reality."

"There has to be something we can convert," Dave said, his imagination cooking. "We've got medical sensors. Let's reprogram the suckers."

"They're all in the medical section," Alley said. "We're not. That's a whole other expedition."

"I don't understand," one of the passengers asked. This was a man, elderly and frail. "You're going to try to send a distress signal *or* kill the monsters *or* . . . turn off the ship so it doesn't meet with another ship?"

"If we could do all those things, that would be a good day."

"Can't you just turn off the ship from down here in the engine room?"

Alley tipped his head, helpless to explain in such a short time. "We can't just pull a wire and the engines turn off. It's wicked complicated." With his tone, he let them know the subject was now closed. He didn't remember when he'd developed that skill, but every captain eventually got it. "This is volunteers only. Who's going with me? And don't worry about wanting to stay here. These people are going to need leadership."

"I'm going," Clyde said.

Dave shook off a wave of exhaustion. "Me too, Captain."

"I'll go," said a third voice.

They looked back toward the main deck and saw the big redhaired man standing in a shadow that struggled to cover him.

"What's your name?" Alley asked.

"Henry Nagle, sir."

Alley approached him and shook his hand. "I know about you, Henry. You've had a hell of a career. You deserve better than this."

"Everybody has to fight some time, Captain. I'm willing."

"So am I," came another voice.

Behind Henry's huge form, Lena peered at them. "I won't die sitting here."

Somehow her volunteering didn't help Alley's sense of possibility. As a husband, he wouldn't want his wife to have to be in the vanguard, even though he suspected she would do just as Lena was doing.

"That's enough," he said. "The rest will fortify here and defend themselves. We'll try to get to the pilot house and at least send out a warning and a distress signal."

"A distress signal?" Lena asked. "You mean somebody could come help us?"

"What about the ship we're meeting?" another woman asked. "I'm Beatrice Foley . . . I'm supposed to transfer mail to the students on that ship. Can they help us? If they know what's happening? Can we call them?"

Alley glanced at Clyde, but offered only a vague answer. "We'll try."

He started handing out weapons. They emptied the locker completely, and came out packing. He loaded Clyde, Dave, Henry, Lena, and himself with all the weapons and rounds and grenades they could carry, then doled out the rest to the row of survivors, and one by one gave them instructions about the basic use of each weapon, about half of which involved how not to blow themselves up by mistake.

"Okay, this is it," Alley said finally, when there was nothing left to be said. He made eye contact with each of his assault team, and added, "Destination . . . the pilot house at all costs. Whoever makes it will have to shut down the autopilot and hit the distress button. It's just a big red button high up on the nav theatre. A monkey can do it. Are we set?"

One by one, they nodded. All seemed calm, except Lena, whose face was sketched with pure revenge. She'd crossed that line.

Might actually help her.

"How can dis be happening?" Sitting now on a utility bench, Voola uttered words slurred with disillusionment. "How God could create such demons? How he could make dis happen to us? Please, Holy Father of Grace, how dis can happen?"

"Voola, give me your hand." Alley stepped close and took the woman's cold, plump fingers. He held tightly for a moment, until she looked at him and blinked her eyes clear. Then he pried her fingers open, slapped a plasma rifle into them, and folded both her hands into the form-fitted grips.

"Stop praying," he ordered. "Fight for your life."

CHAPTER SIX

"I refuse."

Two simple words, and everything changed. They were unthinkable words, astonishing words on a ship. Everyone knew that defiance on a ship was different from defiance anywhere else, except perhaps the battlefield. But they were the same, weren't they?

Adam Bay's two little words set the main salon on edge. The table was set for breakfast, and all the cadets were seated around as Ned and the portly little cook delivered big bowls of spaghetti and sauce. Ned mixed powdered milk, but his attention was on the confrontation that didn't involve him.

"You're on port watch," the crewman named Luke was saying to Adam Bay. "Port has the soles and bowls detail today. That means cleaning heads. That means you."

Adam adjusted his narrow hips to a punctuating post and folded his arms casually. There was no defiance in his posture or tone. Just fact. "I don't clean toilets."

Luke, the no-nonsense young crewman with no sense of humor, squared off with him over a bucket and sponge. "You don't have a choice. We all do the work. That's how it is aboard any ship. The burden is shared."

Adam, with his taut young skin and teenaged self-confidence, also had the gift of a strange kind of wisdom for his age. He was completely unimpressed by the experienced crewman.

"I don't share burdens," he said.

The other cadets watched this from the dubious safety of the salon table, where breakfast was being served by Ned, who was today's galley slave.

Luke matched Adam's cool dominance. "I'm the angry one," he said. "You're not allowed to be angry. Angry is *my* assignment."

Ned reined in a smile, revising his assessment about Luke's lack of humor. Apparently it was soil under grass. He poured the milk he had just mixed up from a powder to Pearl, then his sister. Robin almost spilled her glass, as, eyes wide, she intently watched the confrontation.

They'd been soaring along for another week and things had gone generally well. They'd each spent time at technical postings, caring for the equipment and machines, learning the fussy maintenance, and going through the process of emergency drills. They were being taught merchant shipping laws and the elastic relationship between military and private expansion in space. Until today, Ned and his team on starboard watch had been cleaning the heads. But it was Sunday, the beginning of a new week, and the assignments were being rotated.

Adam Bay stood passively before Luke, broadcasting his refusal with willowy calm. He was the only pool of calm in the room. Everyone else was on edge. Defiance on a ship . . . very dangerous.

"You'll be cleaning the heads," Luke said, speaking firmly.

"Why should I?" Adam's long eyelids came down once, and back up.

"Because we're all equals here. You're not better than anybody else."

"Yes, I am. When's the last time the captain cleaned a toilet? Or Dana?"

"They're officers."

"You said 'we all.' Does 'all' mean 'all,' or not?"

"You have to take orders."

"I didn't enlist," Adam countered easily. "I signed no contract."

"Your parents did."

"Does the contract say, 'will do menial labor'?"

"It's implied. There's a cooperation clause."

"Show me."

Luke was a hardened crewman who had worked on spaceships since the age of thirteen. Ned got the feeling that Luke knew what he would do to make Adam work, but didn't have the authority to do it. Or perhaps it was only an image he was projecting, matching Adam's aloofness with his own nonchalance.

"Should I get the mate?" he asked.

"Why don't you get the captain," Adam challenged. "I'll be even more scared."

Luke sniffed, wiped his nose with his sleeve, wobbled his head, and stepped out of the salon toward the aft sections—the charthouse, the officers' quarters.

When Luke's footsteps on the corridor's deck faded, Dan choked down a swallow of the spaghetti he'd been holding in his mouth for the last two minutes. "Adam, don't make trouble!" he said with his thick Australian drawl. "This is like jumping from the sandbox into med school! We're gawn home as qualified space techs with made careers. Just getting *on* this ship is—"

"I know what it is."

Dan spoke even more passionately. "We get to skip all the pansy required classes and cut to the chase, mate! Don't ya care?"

"You're rocking our boat, Adam," Leigh interrupted. "After nine weeks, I'm going to Zone Emerald as a certified Grade One apprentice astronavigator. Do you know what an astro-navigator makes?"

For a short girl, she spoke tall.

Adam was unaffected. "Yes," he said. "I do."

Burned by his so-what attitude, Leigh shook her head and gave up. She went back to her salad.

Chris, the boy with strawberry-blond curls piled on top of his head, looked at Adam. "Okay, you don't care about us. Why would you endanger your own future?"

"My future's secure. So's yours." He pointed at Pearl. "Even hers. You'll still skip all the bullshit and you'll still get your big boost."

Seated beside Chris, the girl named Mary, a sturdy and sporty girl with a good sense of fair play, suddenly shrank a bit, just enough for Ned to notice. Perhaps she just didn't like confrontation or preferred to stay out of squabbles, but Ned noticed her change in posture and thought it unfair that she should be made uneasy.

Ned drew back his pitcher of milk and straightened. "Mind your language, please, around the ladies."

Adam Bay's incisive blue eyes rolled to him. "What 'ladies'?"

Ned simply stood there, behind the three seated girls—Robin, Leigh, and Pearl, across from Mary.

Adam flared his eyes. "Oh . . . you mean *them*. I thought somebody else had walked in."

"The captain's going to come," Christopher warned. "Don't you care?"

"Be realistic," Adam told him bluntly. "What's he going to do? Throw me overboard? He can't corner me in a round room."

"He can put you off the ship," Ned said, with just enough edge to be threatening.

Adam was unflapped. "If only. There's no place to put me off. We're too remote."

Feeling a responsibility to defuse the tension because he had ginned it up, Ned tried to make light of the moment. "We're no more remote here than on our farm. In fact, this is downright crowded. We come from a place so lost and lorn . . . Man is a cloistered island."

Untamed, Adam declared, "Godforsaken, you mean."

"I doubt I mean that," Ned said. "But I might."

Stewart, Chris, Mary, and Dylan laughed. Pearl made a pathetic "Ha-heh! Ha-heh-heh!" after the others laughed, trying to be one of them, which killed the laughter and rolled some eyes.

Adam waited to see whether he could get a rise out of Ned. When it didn't materialize, he held his head back and looked down his straight nose at the other boy.

"'Man . . . is a cloistered island,'" Adam repeated, musing. "Very poetic double entendre. I doubt you meant that either."

He turned away and moved down the salon toward the captain's bell, enshrined at the forward end of the chamber. The conversation was over. He didn't leave the salon, but moved away from them.

Letting a quirky smile rise on his face, Ned continued pouring milk.

Leigh turned to Robin. "Doesn't your brother ever defend himself?"

"No," his sister said. "He defends me."

"Doesn't anything get under his skin?" Stewart asked from across the table.

"Unprovokable, our granddad calls it." Robin smiled up at Ned, giving away the family secrets.

"Which one of you is older?" Leigh asked, looking at Robin and Ned in turn.

"Actually she's the elder," Ned said, "by six minutes."

"You're twins?"

"How come we never knew that?" Stewart asked.

"Because secrets are fun!" Robin said gleefully. "When they come out later, it's more fun!"

She and Leigh laughed.

Seated between them, Pearl looked around through her big ostrich eyes, then forced, "Ha-heheheh!" She sounded like a coughing dog.

Her oddball effort only dropped a wet blanket on the gathering. She noticed.

Robin's large eyes rolled beautifully to Ned, like a pair of black swans turning on a lake. She tended to hold her chin down, as he did also, while still looking up with those big lash-ringed eyes. The look gave her an aura of maidenly allure. Ned had muscled off more than a few boys who took the wrong download from those eyes.

He winked at her as they shared a moment of sibling communication.

"Do you like being pretty?" Pearl suddenly asked. She was fixed on Robin.

Robin, taken off-guard, glanced between Pearl and her spaghetti. "Oh . . . I never gave it much thought . . . not a lot of mirrors on a farm, and all . . ."

"I like your name. Robin. Like the bird. Did your mommy name you after a bird?"

"She never said. I mean, she died when we were one. Are you named after anyone?"

"I hate my name."

"Oh, why? Pearl's a lovely traditional name."

"It's witchy. An old-lady name."

That was some strange husky voice, Ned noted, and tried not to wince at the scratch of it. Even after all these days, he couldn't get used to it.

"You're imagining that, now," Robin said, attempting to concentrate on twisting spaghetti onto her fork.

"How do you talk to people?"

At Pearl's unprovoked question, Robin's shoulders tightened. She squirmed. "Pardon me?"

"I read a book on how to be popular."

"That's . . . good—"

"It didn't work. So I ate it."

The whole table froze in mid-chew.

Robin accepted her fate. "You *ate* a book?"

"It was the paper kind."

Eyes shifted all around the table. Everyone seemed to wish there were an adult here right now.

"Is that the truth . . ." Robin made her body into a C-shape as she tried to lean away.

There was a moment of silence.

Then—

"Can I touch your hair?" Pearl asked. She had stopped eating, not that she ever ate much, and stared with unblinking eyes at Robin, crablike in her fixation.

Ned paused and watched, tuned to his sister's discomfort.

Robin's unease was abrupt and alarming. "Well . . ."

Pearl's birdclaw stole up to Robin's hair, stroking and fondling, rolling the strands between her fingers. "I want hair like this. Give it to me."

Her fingers, braided now into the strands of Robin's long hair, knotted and yanked hard.

Robin's head snapped sideways. "Stop that!" she shrieked.

"Don't yell," Pearl rasped. "It's not fair!"

Slapping the rangy hand away, Robin cried, "You pulled my hair!"

"I want it."

"What?"

"It's *my* hair. Give it to me." Her hand, narrow and cold as cutlery, snatched out at Robin's left ear, snagging another hank of hair.

But Ned was already there. The pitcher of milk drove a wedge between his sister and the strange banshee going after her. Pearl was shockingly strong for her frame, her weight, apparently deficiencies made up by raw will.

"Girl, you're daft to act this way!" Ned shouted. "Off her, now!"

Robin wrenched away, but some of her hair stayed. She bent backward, half off the bench, and grabbed her hair to keep possession of it. Pearl's elbow cranked upward, nailing Ned in the rib. The pitcher of milk went flying.

As if in a dream, the pitcher turned in the air, its handle moving from starboard to port, then began to tip. Milk erupted from the rim in a single gout, then came down in a fan, dousing Pearl, Leigh, and the cook as he appeared in the forward hatch with a tray full of oversized sourdough rolls.

The cook was an abnormally short man, a hairy snowman with no neck, stumpy arms, treetrunk legs and a comically animated face. Right now that face pivoted upward like a big moon rising as he watched the milk go up . . . and come down . . . in his face and all over his tray of sweetly tended rolls.

The table of teenagers broke into a bank of pistons leaping out of the way. Ned had both free hands around Pearl's wrists—they were frail and narrow, but when she resisted he had to lean deeply in before he could control her. Where was all that strength coming from? She hadn't a muscle to call her own, yet he summoned all his power to push her away. She finally broke backward, as the final spurt in arm wrestling, and tumbled back into the captain's big bell. The bell swung away and rang loudly, and rang and rang again as it swung, calling its master and sending out its alarm. *Wrong, wrong, wrong . . . wrong, wrong . . . wrong, wrong . . .*

The cook's big Italian cartoon eyes blinked out from a mask of white. Milk clung to the thick single black eyebrow that went all the way across his forehead. "Oh, wow . . . oh, wow . . ." he droned, like the bell, "oh, wow . . . wow . . ."

"Mr. Spiderlegs!" Robin wailed, seeing what they had done. "I'm so tragically sorry!"

She snatched a napkin and began to sop up the liquid on the tray, but the rolls were already soaked through and beginning to shrink. Leigh, with cold milk draining down her cornrows and into the collar of her red camp shirt, had come to her own feet, but then held suddenly still in shock, gasping. Chris and Dylan came out of their own amazement and stuffed napkins at her. When she didn't take them, they began wiping her down, but in the way of young boys, had a difficult time knowing where to wipe and where not to, and therefore did little good at first.

"Aw, disgusting!" Leigh gulped as she defrosted. She swung around to Pearl. "Uch! You're *such* a plague!"

Pearl's two question-mark eyebrows were up on her forehead under the weird puff of a dark forelock. Indeed she could've been one of the sheep back home, Ned thought, when Kite nipped them into a pen.

"Now, now—" he spoke up quickly, holding his hand out to calm the chaos. "Everyone, quiet, quiet—it's just milk, after all. No harm done—"

"No harm?" Leigh shook the milk off her hands as it drained down her arm. "I'm a mess! And you're sister's been scalped! And—and—just *look* at the rolls!"

"They look good!" Dylan valiantly took one off Spiderlegs' tray and ate it, squishing milk down his chin. With his mouth full, he mushed out, "Goob!"

Adam chuckled. "The Hobbit speaketh."

Dylan ignored him and nodded vigorously at the cook, stuffing another doughy mass into his round face.

Spiderlegs Follo still stood in mid-stride, one foot on the other side of the hatch coaming, waiting for the universe to correct itself and the milk to reverse course and dive back into the pitcher.

"Let's work the problem," Ned coached. "Dylan, wipe up over there. Chris, here you go, a nice clean napkin. And Mr. Follo, I'll just take your tray and you go clean yourself up and don't worry about a single thing, by gosh, we've got it handled. There you go, a milk bath was the sweet reward for Queen Cleopatra. Can't do much harm, after all, can it? Makes the skin nice."

"'Cheerful' is not helping!" Leigh said. "Where's the door? I have to change!"

"Good plan," Ned encouraged. "You go that way," he said, ushering her to the aft hatch, then added, "And off you go forward, Mr. Follo," as he gestured Spiderlegs back toward the galley. "And Downunder Dan will go with you, sir, to help you, right, Dan?"

"Oh, no worries," Dan woke up. "Off we get!" He took Spiderlegs' round shoulders, a head below his own, and steered him out of the salon.

"Yup, yup," Spiderlegs complied. "Yup, okay."

"Everyone else, let's all have a seat ," Ned said. "Robin, how's the wig?"

Robin nodded vigorously and held her hands out in a placating gesture as she made her way to the *other* side of the table. "Fine," she twittered, "fine, just . . . fine."

"Brilliant. Have a seat, then."

"I will, thanks."

And then for the hard part. Ned turned to Pearl and reached out his hand, which immediately went cold at the prospect of touching her clammy claw again. But a gentleman couldn't shrink away.

"Come on, then," he beckoned to her quietly. "It's all right. You're one of us."

"She's one of *something*," Adam Bay said.

Blessed if Ned hadn't forgotten he was there!

The comment did its damage, but Ned forced past it. "Come on," he said again to Pearl. "We've wiped off the bench. No harm done. Could've happened to anyone."

"Anyone spastic," Adam added.

Ned turned, looked down the long salon, and asked, "Wouldn't you like to sit down for breakfast?"

Adam made no response whatsoever, nor any acknowledgment that Ned had spoken to him. There was no more than the smallest shift of his folded arms against his white polo shirt. He was wickedly amused by the proceedings, that was clear, and made no attempt to hide it. In fact, this was the first break in what he apparently thought was almost constant boredom.

Here, in the most interesting environment available to humankind, Adam Bay was bored. In every lesson, every study, every new task the crew tried to teach him, he grasped every nuance within moments, and almost immediately surpassed those who were teaching him. These experienced crewmen had only to give him the mere *idea* of something, and he instantly had it down. His mind worked on such a level that he could take over almost any station once he understood the basic use of it.

Ned didn't envy him. How sad, to have no mystery in his world.

Still, he was only seventeen, just a year older than Ned. There had to be something in the universe that Adam didn't know yet.

"Breakfast?" Adam said. "You have other things to worry about. We all do. Did you know that Pearl Floy was raised in a state institution? They don't call them 'asylums' anymore . . ." He spoke slowly, moving his eyes from one of them to the next, using his best campfire ghost-story voice. "She was kept there since she was seven years old, when they found her living off scraps in a recycling yard. By the condition of her teeth and fingernails and by analyzing her hair follicles, they figured out she'd been there for at least four months. They pieced together her story . . . missing persons reports . . . police files . . . testimony from neighbors . . . She'd apparently wandered away from her home . . . the same week her parents just . . . disappeared."

The room seemed to chill abruptly.

Ned let out a sharp sigh of annoyance. "I think we've had enough of that kind of talk."

"Shame on you, Adam," Mary scolded.

"You're making that up," Robin murmured.

Adam's deeply lidded eyes raised slightly, just enough to make a subtle communication. "Am I?"

Ned confronted him the way he confronted challenging rams in the herd at home. Never let an animal know you're not dominant.

"Pearl is one of us," he declared. "We're in a ship together, out here, alone. Like an island. It's different. Her life depends on us. Someday our lives might depend on her. We're going to respect her just for that."

He felt the eyes of the others, but his eyes remained fixed on Adam's, drilling in his point and making the best silent dare he could muster.

It was then that Captain Thomas Scott Pangborn made another dramatic entrance, punctuating the already tense mood.

Probably this wasn't actually a consciously dramatic entrance, except that every time the captain entered, it *seemed* dramatic. When he was in the room, all eyes were drawn to him, no doubt about that. Ned felt the magnetism and a deeply churning respect, dashed with fear.

Followed in by Luke, Pangborn had clearly been clued in about the issue at hand, because he ignored all the other cadets and immediately locked eyes with Adam. The captain matched the boy's self-confidence glare for glare. He came into the salon's aft hatch, and strode slowly forward, past the other teens, until he was only a long step from Adam. He put his hands in his pockets, taking his time, drew a long breath, tipped his head this way, then that, as if regarding an art work.

"What's your story, sport?" he asked.

Adam pressed his lips. "No story."

"You're refusing to do your work?"

"No. I'm refusing to do *menial* work."

"You're here to learn how to be part of a crew."

"I'm here to learn spacefaring skills. Navigation. Ship operations. Interplanetary commerce laws. You have a paid crew to do the cleaning."

The captain nodded once, and raised his brows. "I understand. Well." He turned in a direction that let him address all the cadets. "You kids wanted an adventure? This is the real thing. You're working. Adults work. They don't ride around on horses with their capes flowing, dueling with dragons. They get down on their aching knees and work, and while they're down, they thank God that they have work at all."

Without further discussion, no attempts to talk Adam into participating, Pangborn simply turned his back on the boy and faced Luke, still lingering at the aft hatch.

"If he doesn't work," Captain Pangborn said, "he doesn't eat."

Robin made a little gasp of empathy, but all the others were frozen with astonishment.

Ned held his breath. He'd never heard of such a thing. Not in real life.

"Confine him to quarters?" Luke asked.

"I think he'd like that," Pangborn said. "He doesn't eat, but he has to come to the salon for every meal and watch the others eat."

"What if he doesn't?"

The captain didn't look back at Adam, nor make any acknowledgement of him, but seemed aware of the attention of the other kids. "Then bind him and carry him."

The ruinous sentence was stated with absolute confidence that the hard-boiled crew could overpower Adam.

"Sorry about this," Luke said.

"Ah, he'll get over it." The captain rocked on his heels, allowing the tension to drop some. "We're on schedule to raft with the *Virginia* at 1300 tomorrow. I've received an automatic confirmation that she's on course and on time. All of you will be interested to watch the autoload. It's a fascinating process. Today and tomorrow morning, Dana will be teaching you about the autoload technology and procedures, so you'll understand what you're seeing. We're offloading our own containers from the last port and boarding all of *Virginia's* cargo containers, which we will then deliver to Zone Emerald at the same time we deliver you. I suggest you take a look at the educational pamphlets right over there in that cabinet and familiarize yourself with the basics and work up some questions. Any questions for me right here and now?"

During the little dance of glances and lowered chins, no one spoke.

"All right, then, carry on." The captain gave a brief look at the table of splattered plates and food, and paused over the puddles of milk in the spaghetti sauce. "Spiderlegs trying a new recipe?"

"Uh . . ." Chris began to say something—who could imagine what?

"Yes," Ned spoke up. "Like some?"

The captain didn't look at him. "I eat in my quarters. Hope it's good."

With his hands still in his pockets, Pangborn strode down the narrow salon as if beside a meandering stream, and looked at the students as if they were ducks scattering out of his way.

At the last moment before stepping out, he suddenly turned.

"You . . . uh, Mank."

"Sir?" Ned straightened as if a giant spirit hand had reached out and pulled his shoulders back. Being singled out set him right on the emotional edge. He'd rarely been looked at in his life, going to a small school, living on a farm, enjoying the solitude that suited him fairly well. Not that he was a solitary type—he enjoyed his family and a handful of friends at the Isle of Man TT motorcycle road race. He even had a sponsor, and a pit crew. That was his social life, and it was enough for him.

Right now he wished he were there, soaring along the miles and miles of open road on the little ancient island. He belonged there. Not here.

The captain's eyes gripped him. "How'd you like an assignment?"

Ned nodded valiantly. "Surely."

"You clean my bell."

About to leave the salon, Luke turned back. "He's not on that duty this week, Captain."

"Yes, he is."

Luke shifted, disturbed. "Oh . . . okay . . ."

The other cadets began to slip away, even though they hadn't finished breakfast, escaping for their own preservation. Ned caught their backs as they vanished one by one, and even Pearl somehow shimmied between him and the captain, turning sideways like an envelope going through a slot.

Ned found his eyes drawn magnetically to the bell, big as a watermelon and standing with its shoulders squared on its pedestal.

"I'll be back to inspect it," the captain said. "You have two hours."

CHAPTER SEVEN

Space is the ocean of the gods. There is no one plane of travel, no up, no down, and across is a navigation nightmare. Like a diver in deep water, a ship could turn upside down or completely around and never know the difference. Though there was artificial gravity inside a ship, the spacefares were without orientation in the vastness of the cosmos. Primary to survival was scrupulous attention to the instruments which told a ship where it was. Line of sight in such expanses just didn't serve. A shaving of a degree's mistake would be ruinous.

Inside the ship, even with gravity, the crew of a space vessel were more like divers. There was no single plane, no main deck. For every deck that went out in front and back behind, there were ten compartments, conduits, shafts, utility cubbies, access tubes branching out above, below, to the sides, at angles away and back. It wasn't enough for Nicholas Alley to lead his little assault team straight to the pilot house, concentrating only on going forward through the most direct routes. The direct routes were big, bright open corridors, perfect traps in which the first people had been killed. Keith had died walking down the main starboard corridor, carrying a tray of snacks for ten passengers who had died five minutes later. He hadn't even realized he was leading the predator to the prey.

Now the ship was conserving power in emergency status and the corridors, tunnels, ladder tubes, and veins were lit only by the amber or red hazard bulbs. Moving through them was like being part of an arcade game.

In Alley's mind, every artery laid itself out around them as sharply as a 3-D schematic. They were floating in the middle of a pool, with sharks circling from every direction. The monsters could be anywhere, rise or drop before them, or behind them, from the sides, or any angle.

He had stationed Dave LaMay at the vanguard, just in front of himself, with a meaty M-40 pulse rifle and two hand pistols stuffed in his belt. The rearguard was big Henry, never mind that Clyde had wanted to do it. Clyde was behind Lena. Would they think their captain was chicken, to put LaMay in front instead of doing that duty himself, and to protect Clyde with a passenger? Explaining would seem petty in itself. He had to stay alive, he or Clyde. They were the only ones who knew the complex shutdown codes that would disable the autopilot and turn off the beacons. To turn off a ship's beacons was tantamount to sitting down in a blizzard. It was suicide.

That was his plan. To cook the pig by burning the house down. He thought the others knew it, but left the blunt words unspoken.

In the middle of the short team, the woman named Lena gripped her weapon with unfamiliarity, but with zest. She was out for revenge. Grief was her shield.

Alley hoped she would get what she needed. He wanted some too. He let his mind burn with insult and rage. It helped.

"Doing a great job, Dave," he murmured to LaMay.

Dave's platinum hair stuck to his forehead as he glanced back and managed a sturdy half-smile. "I just want a big can of bug spray."

"If we're going to send a distress signal, why didn't we do it from the engine room?" Lena asked. Her pencilled-on brows undulated.

Alley looked sideways at her, and caught the pained look on Clyde's face. She still thought they were going for help.

"No way to do it from there," Alley said, preserving her hope.

He was halfway telling the truth. Only from two stations—the pilot house and the captain's quarters—could the ship's complex engine system and beacon broadcast be shut down, and only by an officer, which meant him or Clyde. They were each other's failsafes.

It was a mistake to bring him. I should've put him in charge of the survivors.

"Keep going," he said, to bury his thought. There was no correcting the error now.

Dave LaMay moved out again, heading aft in the ship. They were under the flank bay where Jonsy had loaded the blue container, heading back along the arteries of access that weren't really corridors, but work tunnels. They were uninviting utilitarian crawlspaces and tool alleys, veined with open cables, tubes, wires, hotboxes, and direct electrical accesses, each one loaded with storage places for the equipment required to maintain them.

Their target was the pilothouse. Alley calculated the odds that any of those attacking creatures would be in this particular crawlspace, but that didn't work. The answers were too random to calculate. Keith and Gunny had inadvertently released either seven or eight proto-morphs. He'd set the alarms off to warn everyone, but the half-hour they'd eaten up trying to iron out the truth, research the threat, and make a plan had been used by the proto-morphs to . . . morph. Through some unrevealed wonder of growth hormones or other natural magic, the little alien embryos didn't stay little for very long. They acquired lots of mass, seemingly out of thin air, and within hours became full-grown killers. The innocent crew and passengers of the *Virginia* were suddenly caught on a slaughter field.

The tunnel was its own kind of horror. He and LaMay had been here a thousand times in their years together, and Clyde had done a good job of making his life here a crash course in learning the systems in the short time he had been first mate. Alley felt bad for both of them. LaMay was studying for his captain's license, but hadn't held the right tickets for chief mate on a ship of this configuration, or Alley would just have promoted him to the post. To fill the gap for this voyage he had called on Clyde, a dependable friend from his former ship, and now here they were. Dave had taken it sportingly, just as he was now bravely leading the way along the sausage-shaped tunnel.

I should've left one of them behind, with the passengers. I should've left Clyde. That was a screw-up. We can't afford any more screw-ups.

The silence again . . . Alley wanted to shout it away. The ordinary hum of engineering and life-support systems was today a terrible drone, and seemed distant. There was no scratching of claws or hiss of animal noise. There was only the soundlessness of being stalked. Nothing was as silent as a predator on the prowl. Or lying in wait.

Was that it? Would they simply walk into a trap?

What choice was there but to make that bet?

He pushed his thoughts away and put his hand on Dave's shoulder, the other holding his own Old Reliable, a vintage MacGregor Firebolt that spat flame grenades.

"Where'd you get that old thing, Captain?" Clyde asked, as if reading his mind. Perhaps he saw the way Alley held the weapon to his chest, how comfortable he was with it.

"I grew up with this Firebolt," Alley quietly said. "Used to light up targets of straw in my Grandpa Breakspeare's backyard near Baltimore. When the police came because of the noise and flames, Grandpa took out a special permit and spent some serious dough setting up a safe shooting range for neighborhood kids. Three of them grew up to be cops, and two to be Colonial Marines."

"Wish they were here," Lena uttered.

"Yeah, me too."

Dave crunched over a spark tarp left on the floor to protect a circuit in need of repair. He glanced back. "Breakspeare?"

Alley's lips twisted into a little grin. "Family name."

"God, I wish I'd known that a year ago."

"Why?"

"I lost a year of ribbing you over it. Breakspeare . . . creator of *Momeo and Vuliet*."

"Nick!" Clyde's abrupt call snapped them back to reality. "Henry is gone!"

They twisted around. He realized what an error it had been to drop their guard even for a moment. Who could tell—maybe the enemy could smell levels of tension and knew when to strike! Anything was possible at this point.

"He was right behind me!" Clyde whispered frantically.

"Move!" Alley shoved Lena past him to LaMay and brandished his Firebolt back the way they had just come. As Clyde came to his side and formed up with him, he raised his voice just enough. "Henry! Speak up!"

"No—oh, no!" Lena choked.

"Henry!" Alley raised his voice another notch.

"Do we go back for him?" Dave asked, as if anybody had the answer.

"Yes!" Lena gasped. "He has six children! Captain, please—"

"Shut up!" Dave warned, and pulled her behind him.

Alley motioned them to stay where they were. He moved toward the empty spot where Henry had been.

He brought his weapon to his shoulder. His finger on the trigger made a faint squish with sweat as he sighted down the wide blue-gray barrel. The weapon began to warm itself, feeling the pressure against his shoulder, getting ready to shoot its fire bombs. He had always loved the old MacGregor because it could anticipate being fired. It seemed a little bit alive, a little smart.

"Henry, last chance!" he called.

His heart almost stopped when Henry stepped out from a slot in the tunnel wall that Alley thought had been sealed up months ago.

Lena shrieked at the appearance, then gasped, "Oh, thank God!"

"Sorry," Henry said, his face rosy with embarrassment. "I had to . . . I really had to . . . go."

"Christ!" Alley blurted. He lowered his weapon. "All you had to do was say so!"

"I'm sorry." The big man shrugged and closed his pants, then picked up his weapon from where he'd left it leaning against the wall. "When nature calls . . . it gets what it wants."

In the history of famous last lines, Henry would now have his own place of honor. The sheetboard above him peeled back like the skin of a fruit, and suddenly all they saw was his thick legs wagging. And they heard his screams.

Clyde opened fire instantly, having never lowered his weapon, but Alley held back, knowing his fire bombs would murder Henry first. "Move! Move!" he shouted at LaMay and Lena. He plunged forward and grabbed one of Henry's ankles, then threw his weight back. "Clyde, shoot, shoot!"

But Clyde was already shooting up into the new hole. The squawl of a xenomorph blared at them, hurting their ears, and Alley saw the snakelike gray trunk of a tail dip down for just a moment, coil around Henry's torso, and tighten its grip as it retracted into the hole, taking Henry with it.

Alley hauled hard on the one ankle, as hard as he could with no real purchase, using only his own weight. "Shoot! Shoot!" he kept calling.

LaMay plunged toward them, gritted his bright teeth, aimed upward, and rattled off burst after burst.

Above them, something cracked. The noise was sharp and loud, like cured plastic snapping.

Alley fell backward and slammed into the side of the tunnel. Clyde jumped away, taking Dave with him, as a shower of green sluice splashed down, draining over Henry's lower body, burning his clothing to rags. Acid!

Alley shouted, "Get back!"

He slammed his Firebolt into Clyde's chest and lashed out with his left arm—only now realizing that he hadn't let go of Henry's ankle. He still had it. The detached leg of the big man swung in his grip like a club and swatted Lena in the face. The woman gasped and disappeared from Alley's line of sight.

Alley let out a yelp and dropped the leg. Clyde was screaming—burned in the neck by acid. Dave dragged him back as the acid shower turned first to a mixture, and then to pure red blood as Henry's huge body was dissolved.

"Move! Run!" Alley grabbed Clyde and started running, heading toward the forward sections. "Dave, get her!"

Behind them the sounds of thrashing and sizzling were even more disturbing because there was no human sound, no screaming, no fighting. Big Henry probably had nothing left with which to cry out. Alley tried to block the image out of his head, but he couldn't do it. The image of what had gone on above their heads was pervasive because it was so obvious.

And he hadn't even seen one of the creatures yet.

Fighting off a pang of responsibility, he dragged Clyde onward down the tunnel, listening for Dave and Lena scrambling after him. A shaft of panic went through his chest.

"I've killed us all—" he gasped. Instantly he hoped Clyde hadn't heard.

Clyde was in no condition to listen. At Alley's side, stumbling valiantly, Clyde had his free hand pressed to the side of his face. His mouth hung open in silent, puffing breaths of exertion and pain every second. Acid burns . . .

Where did these creatures get all that acid? So powerful that it could burn through a ship's plating, but not burn through their own hides? What could they possibly be made of? Why would nature create a thing so one-sidedly destructive? Even a gazelle had been given the means to escape from a lion!

What did he have? What did the humans have to fight their aggressors?

One's down! We killed one! At least we killed one of them! How many are left? Six? Seven?

Suddenly it mattered how many proto-morphs had escaped when Keith and Gunny stupidly opened the blue jug. Every story was a little different. Gunny had said eight. Jonsy thought seven. Keith hadn't lived long enough to report.

"Keep moving!" Alley shouted. "Clyde, stay with me! Don't slip!"

Their feet set up a determined cadence on the narrow metal deck. Clyde was a mass of sweat-soaked clothing and rapidly weakening muscles. He clasped Alley around the back with his right arm, his left hand pressed to his face, but he was losing the battle and soon went down to his knees.

"Clyde!" Alley let him drop to the deck, stepped around, and changed his grip. "Clyde, I can't carry you!"

"We can carry him!" LaMay called, but he was already dragging Lena.

"No! Move on!"

Fortunately, Dave didn't argue, but followed the order and disappeared with Lena into the depths of the tunnel in front of them.

Clyde's eyes glazed by agony, wobbled back and forth.

Alley grasped Clyde's left hand and dragged it away from his face. The hand itself was halfway burned through, showing a palm of sinew and open white bones on the insides of the fingers. Alley suddenly thought of a Halloween glove, where one side was normal but the other side was a skeleton's hand. He was looking right at it.

And Clyde's face . . . the cheekbone was exposed, sizzling and dissolving into powdery liquid draining now toward his ear, eating flesh as it went. Now lying on his back, arched in terror and pain, Clyde abruptly choked.

"Oh, no," Alley murmured. He held Clyde's good hand. "No, come on . . ."

Clyde's eye focused for a final moment on his captain's. With a final shudder, his body gushed out one long irredeemable breath, and drew no more to replace it. The injury was horrific and ugly, but he probably died of shock. In the grip of grief, Alley felt his own lips peel back in misery and helplessness.

But there was more . . . the acid was starting to lose its power already.

Sucking his own breath in gulps, Alley summoned all his command strength and dropped Clyde's hand. He picked up the other arm and held the skeletal damage facing toward him. Against every revulsion crawling in his stomach, he stuck a finger into the acid-damaged tissue of Clyde's palm.

Only a faint burning sensation tingled on his finger. He was right—the acid was neutralizing.

"Clyde, I'm so damned sorry . . ."

Sorry for his mate's having to die in such a way, sorry to have learned something from it.

Alley forced himself away from Clyde's body and launched the long run to catch up to Dave and Lena.

This had been a grave mistake. They should've huddled in the engine room and fortified.

Or would they have simply starved to death?

He hardened himself to his first decision and stuck to the plan. Action was better than starving or waiting or hoping. Two more men down—only himself and LaMay left to reach the pilot house.

"Dave!"

"Here!"

Dave had dragged Lena into a slanted ladder shaft and begun to climb, as good a path to the pilot house as any. There were several options, a dozen possible routes, each one just a guess. Which area had been infiltrated? Were all the creatures bundled together in the upper space behind them, demolishing Henry's corpse, or were they solitary, spreading out all over the *Virginia*?

Alley threw the Firebolt's strap over his shoulder, grabbed the ladder's cold rungs, and began to climb.

How intelligent were those things? Could they anticipate which direction Alley and Dave and Lena were traveling? Would they try to head them off? Could he fool them by being clever or by knowing the ship better than they did?

He didn't know his enemy well enough to be able to make reasoned choices. Random choices were just as effective, or just as deadly, and he couldn't know. There hadn't been time for anything more than the most cursory of computer searches to get a glimpse of the past interactions between humans and these things. They could be killed, but they were better at killing. They could be blown apart, but had tough hides. They communicated somehow with each other in the same vicinity, but nobody knew how. Margin of error was small, decision time almost non-existent. They acted on some kind of enhanced instinct, not on calculation or consideration, so they couldn't be out-guessed or out-strategized because they didn't think that way.

But there was no time for more study. Anything more they could discover about the enemy would be revealed in the flames of struggle.

"Dave! Dave, do you know the shutdown code? Dave! Did Clyde teach you the code?"

But there was no answer.

"Dave!"

Again, no answer.

"Dave?"

Again.

CHAPTER EIGHT

"You can't use organic chemical-based caulks in near-absolute zero vacuum. They'd freeze to a brittle rock-hardness before they could be spread out . . . well, really they'd probably explode from the expansion of contained gases. Nano-alloy caulks are molecular-sized powders which . . . the moment they're in contact with the material they're supposed to be bonding, like maybe a ship's hull, they form a dense super-strong alloy film."

"A film? Like glue?" Ned asked.

"Um, yeah, kinda, yeah, but more like spray paint," Stewart replied. "The heat of the reaction melts them into a continuous solid film and adding more makes more reaction."

"Does it build up to what you need, or something like that?"

"Exactly. You just keep adding layers."

"In a zero-G environment? Right out in space? You don't have to bring it inside?"

"Nope."

"How do you make it . . . cure?"

"Good question! You get an 'A' in spray caulking."

"Well?"

"Huh?"

"What's the answer?"

"Oh! Nano-alloy caulk is sprayed like paint and activated by a gamma-ray burst from the applicator gun. It gives the nano-particles an electrical charge so they repel each other and can be shot from the gun, which is locally charged to the opposite charge to attract the nano—"

"Whoa, there, Cochise, you lost me bad. I'm lost, lost. I've a one-dimensional mind. No depth. I can only do one thing at a time and I have to think about it."

"Like cleaning the bell?"

"For the fourth time."

Ned let out an involuntary sigh on that last comment. He was indeed on his fourth hour of cleaning the captain's bell, having fielded three hours of failing to satisfy the captain. He had polished the already gleaming bell from shoulders to skirt. Not enough buffing on the skirt just above the lip. A touch of tarnish on the clapper. The two mermaids who formed the housing were unevenly buffed. No utility light reflection on the floor from the bell's copper underside. Streaks on the crown. Polish caught between the scales of the mermaids' tails. Not enough gleam on their flippers. Uneven cleaning of the letters of the word "RAVEN." The shine not raised to a high enough gloss. Fingerprints on the yoke. And he had learned the unhelpful subjectivity of the word "enough."

His arms ached from his ears all the way down. His throat burned from the constant assault of brass polish fumes. His fingernails were stained with green sludge, his palms almost black. He was now using a toothbrush on the raised frieze of ivy leaves running around the skirt.

Ned was glad of one thing this day—Stewart's company. The other boy was occupied by painting the undersides of the benches that provided seating at the salon table. Stewart was, of all the boys, the most like Ned himself, somewhat quiet but friendly, unaggressive but willing, and not bothered by manual work. They even looked similar, both dark-haired, but Stewart's hair was shorter and curlier, while Ned's was free-flowing and somewhat shagged, mostly because he tended to give it a clip here and there when necessary and rarely bothered a barber for a tidier look. And Stewart was a bit taller and Ned was a bit quicker. Stewart was normally quiet, even quieter than Ned, but when Ned asked him about his specialty—space caulk—he went off like a sparkler. Ned had enjoyed hearing about the unfamiliar technology for better than forty minutes now.

"Do you like it here?" Stewart asked. "In space, I mean."

"It's interesting, for sure. So much new."

"Like what?"

"All the technologies, pretty much," Ned admitted, digging between ivy leaves. "I'd never given much thought to space before."

"Happy on your island?"

"I always knew men moved in space, but I'm content in my life as a shepherd and sometime sportsman. I'm an Earth-born boy, I guess, and an old Earth at that."

"What's it like?"

"We live half in the past, because people like to visit the past."

"What's that mean?"

Ned paused to stretch his aching hands. "Means tourism. It's the mainstay of the Manx. It's in our vested interest to wear a cloak of the ancient. That means we hide our tech behind the cowshed."

"How do you get along without technology?"

"Oh, we've our share. We don't need much. Everything's a short buzz away across the Irish Sea. Universities, hospitals, shopping . . . Dublin, Liverpool, Glasgow, Belfast . . . we don't lack."

"You mean, you don't *want* much?"

"True enough," Ned agreed thoughtfully. "I like the solitude. I don't even carry a palm-com like the other kids at my school."

"Wow! I've had one since I was three."

"Yelling's just as good, when you're in spitting distance of everybody you care to speak with."

"Mostly your family or what?"

"That's it. Robin and the grans, along with the occasional invading cousin."

"Don't you have friends?"

"Plenty," Ned said, "but they're mostly motorcycling friends at the TT. The Tourist Trophy road race."

"Like that T-shirt you wear."

"That's it. We've had the occasional Beltaine bonfire at our farm, but mostly we meet on the roads and trails for a good ride, goin' hammers all over the island. Beats the city out of you, and you're back to tell the sheep all about it. They're good listeners."

Stewart smiled—he was usually smiling anyway, so it wasn't a far trip—and finished up doing his own work. He wiped his hands, looked at Ned and the bell, and asked, "Want some help?"

Ned shook off a feeling of dread. He made a little warning glance at Stewart. "Best not. That might go against the throw."

"Oh . . ." Stewart looked downcast for the first time. "I forgot."

To distract him, Ned asked, "Where're you from?"

"Me? Oh—I'm from Battle Creek, Michigan."

Ned smiled. "Sounds fiercely peaceful," he said, and they laughed.

They clammed up briefly as other voices sounded from the companionway.

"It's 'myriad' this or that, not 'a myriad of,'" they heard. "'Myriad' is an adjective."

"Are you sure? It's not 'a myriad of colors'?"

"No. It's 'myriad colors.'"

This would be Leigh and Robin, with Leigh doing the linguistics while she fixed the rubber band at the bottom of one of her cornrows. She was a short girl who would someday be a short woman, with a medium to thick build, intelligent eyes, and hair almost the same color as her skin. She was different from the girls Ned knew at home, and he liked to see her making friends with his sister. Leigh was no-nonsense and Robin enjoyed the senseless. Together they were an entertainment. Standing there with his buffing rag and his toothbrush, his filthy hands and his aching arms, Ned found a moment to grin at the sight of them.

Robin caught her brother's eyes and instantly got the expression of a girl looking at a beaten kitten. "Aww, Neddy . . . still at it?"

"Oh, it's job security," Ned dismissed.

"It's abuse," Leigh prosecuted, pointing at the bell.

Ned laughed, happy to be so defended. "What are you two doing here?"

"It's pulling on to lunch time," Robin said.

"Lunch? Did we not just have breakfast?"

"No," Robin said. "You've been cleaning the bell for an entire half-day. It's just not right. That captain's mortal cruel."

"Not to worry. It might've kept me from worse work. I'll just do my best and cuss the Irish. Where are the others?"

"Chris and Dan are with Mr. Nielsen, learning about redistribution of freight, preparing for off-boarding, and Dylan's doing something magnetic with Chelsea—"

"And Dustin," Leigh supplied.

"And Mary's, I think, on the helm with Dana."

Stewart stepped in with the girls as they began taking tableware from the burnished wood cabinets and distributing plates and cups around the big table, after Robin dealt out placemats to protect the beautiful trestle table. "What about Pearl?" he asked.

Ned glanced at him, wondering why he would ask.

Stewart suddenly realized his faux pas and quickly added, "And Adam?"

"No idea." Robin tried to be toneless, but failed. Then she lowered her voice. "Do you think the captain will really prevent Adam from eating?"

"I hope so," Leigh said. "Adam could stand to be silenced by weakness. Well, *I* could stand it."

"Oh, it's not good," Robin told her. "An empty bag can't stand, you know."

An uneasy quiet fell over them as Adam Bay entered from the aft companionway, characteristically unimpressed by his sentence to be here while the others ate. Clearly he knew it would be harder on the other teens than on himself, to eat heartily while one of their peers was made to go hungry. He stood aside, not taking a place at the bench. It seemed he meant to punish them further by standing and watching. He was not embarrassed in the slightest.

Through the forward hatch, at the same time, came Spiderlegs Follo, the little round cook, carrying two boxes of crackers and a tray of cookies. His animated round face, never quite completely shaven, went through several expressions. "Oh, hey, hey . . . this is good . . . somebody's here! Oh, hey, can I get, oh, maybe some help, maybe some hands in the galley?" He spoke in a hesitant, childlike tone, like a Christmas elf. "I got this . . . this . . . whole thing . . . this big . . . thing . . . to carry."

"How many do you need?" Ned asked.

"Oh! Oh! How about . . . maybe . . . uh . . ."

"We'll go," Robin lilted. "Come on, Leigh, let's be waitresses! I always wanted to!"

"Me too."

Ned looked at his filthy hands. "I'll need a moment to clean up—"

"Forget it," Stewart said. "I'll cover for you."

"That's well. Thanks!"

The other kids flooded out, almost in a panic to get away from Adam's hovering presence.

Ned found himself alone in the salon with just the other haunting personality. He squirmed a bit and winced. "My rib hurts," he finally said.

"That's where you got speared by Pearl the Weird."

Well, communication was its own blessing. Ned looked at him.

"I'm sorry for what's happening to you," he began.

Adam sniffed. "Sorry? For following the vaunted captain's orders?"

"He's just giving us a hint of the real thing."

"He's a fraud. It's an act. He pre-hated us before we ever came aboard. He punishes people he doesn't like. He goes out of his way to make us uncomfortable."

"Maybe he doesn't know he's doing it."

"Then why does he disguise it so well? He knows."

Troubled, Ned gazed at the other boy. Adam was tragically cynical for his age. Having grown up with his grandparents and not having that buffer of parents closer to his own age, Ned had learned to see teenagers through the eyes of the elderly, and his life had been one of deep contrasts—the aging friends of his grans at their church and in the towns, and over the water in Belfast and Sligo, Liverpool, and Cardiff, in contrast to his own friends. His grans had taken care to make sure he and Robin had playmates their own age, but to have the bumper of middle-aged adults around was a benefit they could not provide to the two children they were raising in their old age. And they had already been old when Ned and Robin came to live with them on the farm near Kirk Michael.

"I don't think the captain deals with guests very often," he attempted.

"We're not 'guests,'" Adam said. "We're customers. He's profiting from having us aboard."

"Still, he shouldn't keep you from a bowl of stew."

"He won't," Adam said smartly. "A person can go without food for two weeks. All I need is water. 'Captain lets teenager starve on ship full of food' is not the headline that'll do his reputation any good."

"Maybe he doesn't care about his reputation," Ned warned.

"But he cares about his license." Adam had an answer for everything. "And everybody cares about reputation."

Ned shrugged and went about the business of wiping his hands on a clean piece of paper towel. And another. And a third. "What's wrong with that? He's getting paid for us to get experience in the way a ship runs." He looked at his fingernails critically and added, "May have to sandblast . . ."

"Just leave them dirty," Adam recommended. "They can be your trophy. Prove you were here."

Ned shook his head. "That it will."

Annoyed that his niggling was getting no response, Adam pushed off the wall against which he'd been leaning and stalked toward the middle of the salon. "Doesn't it bother you that Pangborn hates us?"

"It doesn't," Ned told him. "Let him hate me if it does something for him."

Adam gave him a disdainful glower. "How did you *get* like this? What a buffoon you are. If you don't care about your own reputation, why do anything? Don't you have any hope? Any plans?"

"I plan to grow into these arms, is one."

They moved apart as Captain Pangborn abruptly appeared in the forward hatchway, materializing as if he had always been there. Had he? Was he eavesdropping on them?

The captain paused to look at both boys in turn, making them uneasy by saying nothing—well, Ned, anyway—and finally turning to study the condition of his bell.

Ned's whole body turned cold. He wasn't sure why. He crunched his hands into the wad of paper towel he was still holding.

The captain said nothing. He tipped his head to look at the back of the bell.

A moment later, Mr. Nielsen came in, then Luke, closely followed by Dustin and Roscoe, one of the engineers, then Cathy, a medical and dental technician, and Zimmer, a caulker. They were an ordinary looking group, as average as people could be, and Ned imagined that they represented the bulk of the merchant fleet working billet bank, people with skills but few command ambitions. The teens didn't know them well, but had been taught at some point by each of them about the execution of their duties. The assumption was that, as the weeks passed, the adults and the teenagers would merge into a cohesive body of professionals and apprentices, and that with time the skill gap would shrink. It was already shrinking.

For all but Ned, who was now an expert in polishing the bell.

"All hands, amidships," the captain commanded.

Dustin touched a com link that broadcast throughout the ship. "All hands, muster amidships."

Ned knew it was a show, because all the other hands had already been notified and were flooding into the salon. Pete, Nitro, Luke, Spiderlegs, and the other teenagers. The cook and cadets were carrying heat-retaining trays of food, but they were covered, so there was no guessing what the meal would be—which Adam Bay would be missing.

They milled about for a minute or two. More of the working crew poured through the two hatches—Maxwell, who was the boatswain; Cheater, the cockswain; Patty, Antoine, and

Noreen, all some form of engineer or maintenance crew which Ned hadn't managed to get clear yet; and three others whose names he didn't even know. As they came into the salon, some through the galley, others through the aft hatch, Ned realized that they had not integrated with their cadet crew as he might have expected. They hadn't been eager to say so much as hello. Why? Who had set the tone for such segregated behavior?

But he knew.

"Everybody here?" Captain Pangborn glanced around, counting heads, and continued speaking while Spiderlegs and the cadets prepared the table and laid out the food. "We're about to engage in a beautiful mating of ships. The whole process is completely run by computers, so we get to watch the remarkable show of human ingenuity. It's likely we won't even have to communicate with the captain and crew of the *Virginia*, other than formal greetings, which are done mechanically, so we can legally log the meeting. The merchant fleet is in the process of going to full-automation, so we tend to avoid contact, other than a few text notes, because we're all still in the experimental stage. That means this autoload is a test case. We're helping perfect the process for the future. I mean, occasionally, if there's time, we might have dinner, but that won't be happening this time. We're on schedules that take us down to minutes of specific delivery time. The cargo we're accepting, much of it, is time-sensitive. There are containers full of seawater with living sealife, segments of coral reefs, and highly sensitive support systems which can't be frozen. In the cryo-containers, we have animals which are rare, special, hybrid, and stressed in their current static condition."

Ned caught the captain's eye, though he didn't mean to. Should he look away? Or was it best to meet the gaze?

Before he could decide, Pangborn released him and continued talking to the others.

"Sending them in that condition is a risk, and part of our contract involves a hasty delivery. It's the main reason the *Umiak* and the *Virginia* will spend no social time hanging out here in space. We don't have it to spare. In space these things are carefully planned and executed by computers. All right, dismissed for lunch, but make it fast. Everybody to the midships observation deck in twenty-five minutes."

As Spiderlegs began serving pieces of a huge slab of lasagna in a deep tray, the captain stepped past Ned on the way to the hatch.

The captain paused, looked at Ned, looked at the bell, and gave it an uneasy ten seconds before speaking.

"After the autoload," he said, "you can come back here and finish."

He left.

Ned stood there with his hands and shoulders aching, his elbows stiff, and his throat raw from the fumes. He looked at the beautiful bell, its deeply polished brass shining, its copper mermaids' tails burnished, and its broad skirt reflecting the red, white, and green bands of the salon lights. He saw the etched ivy leaves, bright and clean, without the slightest edge of tarnish. The mermaid's hands, as clean and fresh as his sister's. The thin copper inlaid band around the top of the bell, which he had never noticed before, but now knew intimately.

Finish?

Only at this moment did he realize how truly exhausted he was. He closed his eyes tightly and gave his neck a twisting stretch. More of this?

With a raw sigh, he accepted his fate and turned toward the table. At least there would be lunch, and a break to watch the loading.

As he turned, he found two people watching him, for completely different reasons. His sister, and Adam Bay.

CHAPTER NINE

Seafarers and spacefarers knew any voyage could abruptly turn deadly. While routine was the critical way of life from the time of the earliest explorers, when "because" was a good enough reason, the wilderness always had something else in mind . . . to break the routine with bursts of excitement.

Now there were better reasons than "just because," but risk was still the 'farer's bunkmate. And here they were.

Nicholas Alley forced himself to work through the spiny panic chewing at his innards as he climbed the access ladder to the next level, the level where the pilothouse waited for his orders. There, if he made it, he would stop the ship here, deep in space, without a tracer signal, so it wouldn't go off and meet the *Umiak* and infect them, and so it could probably never be found. He would, if he had time, put out a warning and distress signal, but that was secondary. If he had time.

Those people in the engine room . . . were they dead by now? Had the invaders broken through? He felt bad about lying to them, telling them his mission was the distress call more than saving the lives of other ships and colonies. The *Virginia* was now Typhoid Mary. She had to be stopped. Their lives were all forfeit. Unless miracles happened—and he knew they could.

Every suicide jumper changes his mind halfway down.

He stopped calling out Dave LaMay's name, though he burned for the sound of a human voice, even his own. They must've gotten well ahead of him. *Good boy, Dave! Don't look back! Keep moving!*

In his mind he paced out the number of steps to the pilot house. Other than a short curved corridor, two hatches, and the tool alley, the pilot house was almost over his head. He kept climbing.

Three-quarters of his way up the ladder, which had never until today seemed so very long, he stopped with one hand hovering in front of him, not quite to the rung. He heard something.

"Aaaaaahhh . . . ahh . . . ahhh . . ."

Mechanical? Had one of the lube tubes sprung a leak?

"Aaaahhhh . . . aaaaahhhh! . . . aaaaaahhhhh!"

No . . . that was air. It had the same weak-strong-weak noise of air flowing unevenly, trying to fill a space before it ran out the other end.

"Aaaahh . . . aaaaahhhh! Aaaahhhh!"

That was human!

"Dave!" Alley called.

"Aaaaaaaaaahh! Aaaaaaah!" The pitch grew higher, more insistent.

Alley started climbing again, faster. "Dave! Where are you?!"

The terrible cry came again and again, unevenly, desperately.

Wild imaginings of torture blew through Alley's mind. He tried to banish them, to concentrate, focus, climb.

"Aah-aaaaaaaaah!"

Definitely a human voice, but not an inspired scream. He couldn't figure it.

"I'm coming—coming, coming—" Soaked with sweat, he leaped to the top of the ladder and crushed the stock of the

Firebolt into his shoulder and rounded the curve and jumped through the first hatch.

And there he met his enemy.

Sub-human or superhuman?

In the cloistered niche of the tool alley, the otherwise friendly and useful place where the crew stored racks of maintenance equipment in lockers, the wicked witches were lit horribly from below by suffering amber footlights. Still half in shadow, the insectoids turned their eyeless head cases and greeted him with their renowned attitude. From their smiling mouth parts clear liquid resin drained, puddling the floor which was already awash in blood. On the deck, Lena's petite body lay face-down, cleaved almost in half the long way, cut from the back of her neck to the crack in her bottom. Her white spinal column was completely exposed, slightly humped and bent in a strange S. Her face was burned in coagulating resin and a pool of blood.

Between the two aliens, clasped in their long claws hands, was Dave. His once-infectious smile was now a permanent grimace.

But it wasn't Dave, Alley digested as he blinked sweat out of his eyes. It was half of Dave. Below the thorax, Dave's pelvis and legs were completely missing. Part of his left arm was gone, except for the denuded bone which went from elbow to wrist, ending in a skeletal thumb and forefinger.

Part of Dave's skull had been bitten off. His brain case leaked gray matter into what was left of his wonderful platinum hair.

But his eyes were moving . . . terror-fraught, and he was crying out, "Aaaaaahh! Aaaaaaahhhh!"

"Dave!" Alley gasped.

The invader behind Dave had its hand up inside Dave's ribcage and its mouth parts embedded into the back of his neck, somehow forcing air into his body. The other creature stood slightly to the side, its hand pressed to Dave's chest, pushing the air out of his lungs through his voice box as the other creature blew it in. They had turned Alley's shipmate into a grisly puppet.

They knew something about humans. They knew Alley would answer the call.

"Stop it," Alley wept, dissolving. "Stop making him do that . . . stop doing that to him . . . that's not fair."

With its arm up Dave's thorax, the alien in back raised its head. Dave ceased his baleful cries. The last foreign breath gurgled from his mouth. His lips quivered. His demolished head sagged forward.

"He's coming with me, scarecrow!" Alley choked. His weapon came up and he opened fire.

A bolt of knotted flame streaked from the muzzle and smashed LaMay in the chest and went through him as if he were a snowman. Behind the torso, the puppeteer looked down at its own chest. The chest was gone.

Acid blew onto the bulkhead and burned through to bare circuits. A fan of white sparks drenched the two creatures and for an instant confused them.

Before Alley could move the barrel for a second shot, the other one was on him. Its tail coiled around his buttocks and they pivoted in a bitter dance with the Firebolt caught pointing upward between their bodies.

"Hah!" Alley shouted. "Eat fire!"

He snarled in that way men do when they've given up on their own lives and suddenly there's fresh strength. He used his pelvis to shove the Firebolt's muzzle up under the creature's chin and found a notch in the curved underside of the cucumber-shaped skull-thing, and he pulled the trigger.

The huge head came clean off. *Clean off.*

There wasn't even any acid. He was left dancing with the stupified body, its claws digging into his arms, still tearing at his flesh. Dead, and still fighting.

"Yeah! Shove off, Icabod!" He twisted his shoulders and fell out of the embrace.

The alien collapsed at his feet. He stood over it, yelling down.

"Damn interstellar post-nasal drip! Are you proud of yourself? You're nothing but gangsters! Your mama should'a slapped you early! Vulgar leeches . . . just keep dying. I'm going in here. You just . . . just stay there and . . . just *die*."

He extricated his feet from the remains and strode, proudly casual, through the hatch and into the pilot house. A force struck him in the side of his face—but it was only the side edge of the hatchway. He'd run right into it. His eyes weren't working very well. The space around him swam and wavered as if he were under water. He shook his head, but that didn't help. In fact, the delirium was suddenly worse.

Didn't matter. He was here. Maybe he should close the hatch. No time. Get to the code. The nav theatre wobbled in his gaze.

"See? See, stupid? See this?" he shouted back. "I just punch in the code and you're stuck here in the middle of bumfuck eternity! How'd you like that! You know what the abort code is? Six-four-six-A-Z-tilde-nine!"

He moved to the starboard side and forced his blurring eyes to find the keyboard. He reached for it.

"You don't even know what a tilde is, do you? You're so stupid . . . messed up my ship . . . turned my shipmate into a bagpipe . . . six-four-six-A-Z-tilde-nine. Here goes. Here it goes . . . this is it! This is the part where I win! Six . . . four . . . what—what the hell—what—the—hell—"

His right elbow was working. He felt it work. But the keyboard just blurred with color before his eyes. No numbers came up on the screen. No questioning voice of the computer system asking him to confirm. Why? Why weren't the numbers going in?

Was it unplugged? Was the keyboard not hooked up?

He dipped his head to look at the side of the keyboard, to see if it was still hooked up, but his eyesight went crazy and a sudden nausea flared up in his gut. His stomach rolled and he felt abruptly weak.

"Oh, man . . ." he murmured. "Okay. Six-four—six . . . what the hell . . . is this?"

He tried to push the buttons. Six. Four. Nothing happened.

With his left arm, he tried to wipe the sweat out of his face. Instead, he ended up smearing his face with wet strings. He shook his head and looked at his left arm. But there was not an arm there. There was wet bone. Wet white bone. A tangle of bloody ligaments. The broken-boned hand of a skeleton.

Just like Dave . . . they'd taken his flesh and sinew. They'd left him only bone.

He turned the filleted limb before his fading vision. "Just going into shock, that's all . . . I'll just fight it." He raised his voice. "Hear that, gangsters? I can fight it! Yeah . . . fought you, didn't I? Yup . . . I'll just do it with my other hand. Six . . . four . . . what the hell?"

The keyboard turned red in front of him as if he'd spilled paint on it.

"No, no, come on!" he shouted at it. "Six! Four! Six!"

He stabbed at the keyboard again and again with his right hand. Again, again . . . again . . .

The display screens above on the nav bank flickered in confusion, registering all sorts of letters and numbers as he poked and hammered at the keyboard. Finally he realized it wasn't the keyboard at all. He raised his arm to look at his right hand.

"Not now!" he cried out. Before him there was only a torn and bloody stump of a forearm. The hand was completely missing, sliced off at the wrist. "Not now! No, no, not now!"

Falling to his knees, he gritted his teeth and aimed the vulgar stump at the keyboard, stabbing again and again as his mind, deprived of blood, began to spin.

"Nah! Nah!" he screamed. Defiance made him insane, furious. Sinking into the barbarism he needed to try one more time, he leaned forward and tried to punch the numbers with his tongue.

His knee slipped and he fell sideways, jamming his chin on the console. His head reeled as if a prizefighter had punched him. Sliding sideways, further and further from the keyboard, he felt his strength flow away as the blood drained more and more from his wrecked arms.

"Six!" he called. "Four! Six! A! Z! . . . come on! Tilde! Tilde!"

But the computer wasn't set up to abort by vocal command.

As he slid deeper and deeper into the blanket of weakness that would be his last sensation, Nicholas Alley thought about the irony of that. It was for safety. So nobody could just talk the computer into stranding the ship.

He wanted to talk to the ship. She was real, she was alive, and she was moving through space to her poisonous date with the innocents of the *Umiak*.

And there was nothing left in the universe that he could do to stop it.

CHAPTER TEN

The autoload was all the captain promised it to be, and more.

What sounded like a mundane industrial process turned out to be a stunning tour through human ingenuity. The *Virginia* had come toward them out of open space, right on time, without a hitch. The two ships, working on autopilot and run by computers, had made a marvelous linkup hanging right out here in space, without even a scratch of each other's hulls. The technology was a marvel indeed.

And then, having rafted up, the two ships began the process of transferring the cargo, without the interference of the human crew. A thousand things had to happen, yet the ships performed this feat with casual efficiency. It was a beautiful thing indeed, Ned thought, when a machine knew what to do and just did it as simply as that, not even aware of the wonder it was accomplishing. There wasn't even any communication. The *Virginia* approached in silence, computers making all the courtesies necessary, even to giving pre-programmed signals of salute from the captain and crew. This was the precursor to the days when humans would no longer need to risk their lives in space for the sake of cargo. They could leave such chores to machines, and go on to better destinies.

Ned put aside the screaming of his hands and shoulders to enjoy the sight of the ship making its own transfer happen. From behind the broad airtight observation windows, he sat between his sister and Leigh—a happy place for sure—and watched in fascination as the captain and Mr. Nielsen narrated what he was seeing. The ship, which had before this been so tomblike, had jumped to life. The big flank bays, two giant holds on either side of the ship's middle body, previously dim and lit only for safety, were now bright with scene lighting, like stadiums before a game.

Overhead, boom davits on huge stanchions worked robots' turnbuckles on and off mooring cleats, moving enormous containers of bulk freight hanging from X-shaped cargo bridles, which held massive magnetic disks, big around as garage doors. The magnets could be turned on and off, and when they were on they held the huge containers by their tops and swung them along. Robotic arms telescoped out to adjust chafing gear as needed, looking like the arms of giants carrying rags. Deck-winch drums rolled purposefully. Long girders called "strongbacks" ran down the centerline of each of the two long holds, along which the containers flowed one after the other. Then things called "devil's claws," which the captain described as super-strong split-hooks, reached out at the right moments from different places along the route, snagged the links in the chain cables, and took possession of the containers one by one, moving them to their places in the stacks. The high-industrial quality of the operation was very similar to a factory, fully automated servants doing their pre-programmed duty, and somehow making decisions about the weight and stacking and trimming of hundreds of containers, each the size of Ned's barn back home. They carried everything a working city would need—goods, tools, clothing, condensed food, and wares of all types, but the most interesting part was the animals, the herds and flocks, pods and gaggles, swarms and prides in cryo-sleep for the voyage.

"The standard containers are one hundred and forty-five feet," Mr. Nielsen was narrating for the cadets. "They actually come in different sizes, but the sizes have to be compatible for stacking configurations. They're all the same width, but can be different footprints and different heights. And the average weight, regardless of size, is about ninety tons. Some of them might be smaller but are carrying more dense cargo. The boatswain's loading computer will decide by length, height, and weight where to stack them so we keep the ship in trim and to fit the cubic capacity of our holds. In space, being 'in trim' is different from on the ocean, because it's a 3-D environment, but it's still important to the navigation accuracy that we have certain equations of balance."

"How can the magnets carry so much weight?" Dylan asked. "The ratio doesn't seem right to me. Dustin told me that the magnets carry about twenty thousand pounds max. But if the containers are ninety tons—"

"Think about it," the captain challenged. "Why are there no life-forms allowed in the bays during loading?"

Dylan's round dimpled face worked in a shrug. "Don't know."

"Gravity," Adam said. "It's turned off."

"Correct," Mr. Nielsen said. "The containers only weigh about four tons under the diminished gravity. The gravity's not totally off, but reduced so that the containers remain in place when they're stacked, but light enough to be moved around by the electromagnets."

"That's what the spray metal was for!" Dylan exuded. "Those spray guns full of liquid metal, right?"

"Right," Mr. Nielsen said. "The containers aren't metal. They'd be too heavy. They're carbon-fiber-reinforced plastic."

Dylan was brimming with excitement. "And you just spray the top with liquid metal, just like paint! Cosmic!"

His enthusiasm sent laughs of delight through the viewing bay.

Ned glanced between Stewart and Dylan. "So the metal is like paint and the nano-glue is like paint . . . at least you know your artwork will both stick and last a long time!"

There were more laughs, which seemed to irritate the captain. He raised his voice to bring them back to the operation at hand.

"After they're loaded," the captain finished, "we turn the gravity back on so we can move around in there and do our work."

"What kind of work?" Stewart asked.

"Maintenance, mostly," Dana explained. "And it's very important to monitor the condition of the contents being shipped inside the various containers, since we're carrying living things. The cryo systems have to be checked regularly, because a mistake or a malfunction can cause death inside. Oh—a perfect case in point—how I love it when a perfect example floats by—look at this container coming up right now."

They craned forward to watch as an astonishing container came by—it was the size and shape of all the others, but the walls were completely transparent, and they could see what was inside. Marked with giant "OPEN WATERS" emblems, the huge container was an oasis of beauty. Inside was a contained coral reef, lit brightly with interior lights of its own. Shoals of fish, reefs of coral, banks of kelp, and all the creatures of the deep sea that lived in such places, from jellyfish to octopeds, moved about in happy oblivion.

"Jee-ach!" Ned gasped as he watched, fascinated.

"Beautiful!"

He sprang from his seat and pressed his hands against the viewing window, just as a giant octopus came to the side of the container's clear wall. It spread its thick arms and flared its tentacles, then curled its arms under itself to morph up a strangely human face.

The cadets and crew laughed at the antics.

Stewart said, "Nice mirror, Ned!"

Ned laughed and pretended to fluff his hair as if the octopus were his alter-ego. The octopus apparently saw him, for it flared its arms and reconfigured itself, puffing along the side of the moving container so that it stayed with Ned.

"It's got a crush on you, bloke!" Dan howled.

The container was a gigantic aquarium, god-sized versions of the mesmerizing salt-water aquarium in his schoolroom back home. Imagine!

Ned loved that aquarium. He had been drawn to it again and again, to watch the brightly colored clownfish dart among the anemones, and the baby moray eel poke its thumb-sized head out of its hole in the resin rock, gulping steadily in a perfect imitation of its parents, mouthing over and over, "I'm big. I'm big. I'm big." It always reminded him of a little boy walking around in his father's shoes.

Now the octopus, the biggest of its kind, was saying the same thing. *Take me seriously! I insist!*

"We have several of these aquaria aboard," Mr. Nielsen explained. "Obviously these animals and corals are not in cryo, because they wouldn't survive it. So we just transport a whole contained environment, with the coral and the sea bottom, and all. And the sides are clear so that the light from outside penetrates and there's a sense of natural conditions. They tried just lighting them from inside, but somehow the animals didn't thrive. They're still trying to figure that out. So far, it's just been best to transport them in transparent boxes.

Sometimes they set them up on display, just like you're seeing them now."

Ned bade goodbye to his octopus as the container floated on past the viewing bay, and his line of sight was interrupted by the huge letters OPEN WATERS.

"What do the markings and emblems mean?" Chris asked. "Logos?"

"Just like on trucks and planes," Captain Pangborn interrupted. "You've seen trucks and planes before, haven't you? You're not an idiot, right?"

Chris absorbed the put-down. "No . . ."

"The markings are temporary identifications. Those marks will change as the containers are hired by different companies to move their goods. You've bought products all your life. Don't you recognize advertising?"

Dan spoke then. "I can't see where the boxes are coming in from," he asked. Ned got the feeling he had asked to get the pressure off Chris.

"Well, look at the loading flow," Pangborn said, irritated. "If you pay attention to the far end of the flank bay, you can see the accordion chamber that links our hold to the *Virginia*'s. That's our method of engagement, where the containers are funneled in. They're coming in on the lifting gear on those two king posts all the way forward, and being floated into the flank bay by the winches on strongback strakes overhead." Then Pangborn lost his thought for a moment, stood up, and moved to the observatory window, his eyes fixed on one of the cargo bridles.

"Mank," he spoke sharply.

At first Ned hadn't understood the utterance and was busy watching a beautiful aqua OPEN WATERS container fly past him.

"*Ned*," Dylan whispered. "*Ffft!*"

Ned flinched out of his trance. "Hm? Pardon?"

The captain was looking at him. Only now did Ned digest the word that had been used instead of his name. He scolded himself for not being attuned to it.

He vaunted to his feet. "Sorry!"

"Have you got a good memory?"

"Oh, I . . . suppose I do . . ."

Seated on the end of the observation deck, Pearl throated out a laugh. "Memory. Hah-hah! Heh!"

"Pearl," Mr. Nielsen quietly reprimanded. She shrank immediately, but he reached over and patted her hand as if calming a mentally deficient person, but she snatched her hand away and warned him off with her eyes, like a bird.

Everybody looked at her for an uneasy moment. What a beyond-strange little person . . .

But Ned's attention stayed with the captain. He was on the hook for something—what?

Pangborn shook off Pearl's oddness and looked at Ned. "Can you remember some instructions for Dana?"

"I'll sure try."

"Tell her I want a wear survey done on several job components. I want the woven roving checked in sections nine, twelve, thirteen, fifteen, and . . . twenty. And twenty-two. Lube points I want serviced are the tilt-lock levers, clamp screws, throttle bearings, starboard side relief valves . . . winch transmissions . . . auto-gimbals . . . and check the turning quadrant on davit Charlie-Alpha. It's shimmying. And I want to replace all the Cobb-coils during their three-hundred hour checks. I'm also not happy with the flow along the inboard strongback in the starboard flank bay. It's causing hull vibrations."

Ned's brain almost went into a seizure as he tried to collect the data running past. These terms were unfamiliar, and since they meant little to him, he had trouble logging them away in order. Nine, twelve, thirteen . . . and what after that?

He glanced helplessly at the other cadets, who sat with eyes wide at his predicament. Perhaps some of them would help him remember. Leigh gave him a little covert thumbs-up. Was she encouraging him or promising to recall some of this when he reported to Dana?

Loaded with responsibility which he was sure he couldn't carry, Ned weighed the pros and cons of admitting right now that he'd forgotten more than half of what he'd just heard. He glanced helplessly at Robin, whose delicate features were screwed in empathy. She was ticking off items silently on her fingers, trying to remember for him.

And the captain was talking again. "Also tell her the air-cooled dasher blocks are due for replacement."

Foolishly, Ned nodded as if he understood. *Tell him. Tell him now, before it gets worse!*

"Now, you see how those devil's claws work?" Mr. Nielsen went back to his narration. "They only come out when they have a protocol to seize one of the containers and take it off the line, to pull it back into a stacking area. After the load is over, a scaffold of walkways and ladders will rise from their storage areas in the deck, and we'll be able to walk all over the holds and get to any given container. But the chances of having to do anything with them are pretty small . . ."

His voice trailed off. No one was listening anymore.

Everyone was looking now at Pearl, who was on her feet. She took a small step forward, then another. A third brought her to the viewing window where she pressed her long bony fingers in two teepees against the tempered glass. She stared, fixed as a cat, on a battered blue container with giant yellow letters as it floated by, one among many. It appeared from the accordion bay far down the hold, moved smoothly along the strongback toward them, came around a curve, and passed by the window with its broad blue side scuffed and tired.

Pearl's eyes never left that one container, until finally it was plucked away by a devil's claw and disappeared into a valley of other stacked containers, three levels up from the hold's deck. She continued to watch the space where the blue container vanished behind the stacks of others. Though other containers floated by to obscure her view, it was as if they weren't there at all and she could see right through them to the one.

Perhaps she liked the colors.

Ned watched her, fascinated. How did her mind work? What did she see that drew her so boldly out of the crowd?

Perhaps it was something out of her past, he thought. Something she had done that gave her pleasure or made her feel like one of the group. Everyone deserved a memory like that, to feel belonging and a sense of family. Did she have a family? A sister?

But the object of her attention was gone now, sunken into the depths of the hundreds of other containers, and it would take nothing short of a professional ship's loading master to find it again in that maze of colors and emblems.

Mr. Nielsen watched the girl too, patient enough to let her run through whatever emotions she was experiencing. The others took their cue from him. His patience was exemplary, and Ned hoped that each of them would be the recipient of it, each in turn, as needed.

As Pearl continued her hopeless vigil at the window, no one spoke. Thus there was only a thick silence as Dana appeared in the companionway and stepped halfway into the observation deck.

"Captain?"

Pangborn turned to her. His face bore no expression at all. "Yes?"

Dana glanced at the cadets, self-conscious and obviously hiding something. "We've received a long-range."

"From the *Virginia*?"

"No, not yet."

"Then who's it from?"

"It's from a . . . legal concern."

"What's that supposed to mean?"

Dana shifted in a way that revealed her annoyance at his forcing her to be specific. "It's from a lawyer."

CHAPTER ELEVEN

"I didn't want to tell you in front of the cadets. Ultraspace sent a coded communications relay and bounced it off the Boyer Satellite at Outpost 966. It was their last official notification to all their creditors."

"Creditors?" Pangborn's jaw hardened. He didn't like the sound of that.

Dana steeled herself to continue. Now that the two of them were alone in the charthouse, she wished she had brought somebody else with her. Dustin or Cathy, or just somebody else to help field the captain's reaction and to witness whatever he was about to say. Something told her she should've protected herself with a witness.

She felt like a doctor giving news to the family of a loved one's sudden death. "Ultraspace is out of business. There's not going to be any remuneration for the cadet experience."

Pangborn took the news stoically, but his mind was working. His eyes abruptly tightened and his lips flattened. He instantly digested the enormous implications of what she had just said.

"Like hell there won't," he declared. "Those kids' parents are going to owe me their passage."

Dana shook her head. "The parents and sponsors have already paid Ultraspace. You'd have to sue Ultraspace's shareholders, but you won't collect. They've protected their assets by filing bankruptcy."

He turned away from her, pacing the circular nav theatre as the lovely displays put him in silhouette.

Dana quietly attempted, "You still have income from the cargo transfer."

"It's not enough," he said. His tone was brutal. "I have debts too. You and the crew talked me into trying this cockamamie angle, bringing children aboard and treating them like little dauphins . . . 'Oh, we can teach them, Captain!' 'Oh, yes, Captain, they'll be lots of help!' 'It'll help pass the time!' 'An educational program will give us prestige!'" He stopped mocking and coldly announced, "Of all the people who should pay for this, it's not me. You can all bear this burden with me."

A chill went down Dana's legs. She tried to read his tone, his expression. "Meaning what, specifically?"

Pangborn rolled an idea around in his head, then spoke his decision. "The crew gets no pay for this voyage."

Dana straightened. "Captain, I can't sanction that!"

"Who's asking you to?"

"You can't just unilaterally nullify their contracts!"

"Who says? You?" He made a crude sound with his lips. "I'm not going back to that ghetto life, scraping by, watching every penny, making payouts to scuzbags before I pay myself . . . I'm tired of being a church mouse."

The tension was interrupted by a subtle beep and the flashing of the proximity lights on the beautiful nav theatre. Dana stepped forward and keyed in the response code that would free up the data.

"It's the *Virginia*. The autoload is complete. In another hour the accordion tunnel will be retracted and they'll bear off. We'll be on our own again."

She stepped toward the hatch.

"Where are you going?" he snapped.

She looked back without actually turning back. "You know where I'm going. You just informed me that you'll be denying the crew their salaries for this voyage. That legally obligates me to inform them immediately, while we're still in the vicinity of a transport option. You know the regulations better than I do, so don't act so shocked."

Even she was amazed to be talking to him this way, and almost tried to snatch back her words. Or at least her inflections.

Pangborn's square jaw tightened. He made a painfully fake grin.

"Go ahead," he dared. "Inform away."

"Who's 'we'?"

"Dustin and me, and Roscoe, Pete, Maxwell, Nitro, Noreen, Cathy, and Zimmer."

"That's . . . two-thirds the deck crew."

"That's right. And a couple of others are thinking about leaving. We'll take your shit, but not for no pay."

The confrontation wasn't entirely unexpected. Pangborn gave them his best poker glare, but there was little that hadn't already been given away. "You're leaving me high and dry in the middle of a voyage? Hanging here in space with a ship full of children? What kind of worms are you? We're *months* out."

"We're transferring over to the *Virginia*. We have clearance by automatic boarding pass. They've got the bunk space."

"Who authorized that?"

"It's an automatic authorization according to the Space Rescue Clause."

"Did you talk to Nick Alley? Does he know you're jumping my ship?"

"We got an *automatic* clearance," Luke said again. "He knows that maritime law requires him to take on anyone without a criminal record who wants transport for . . . what's that called?" He turned to Dustin.

"Irreconcilable differences. Just like a divorce."

Luke nodded. "We're all done with you, man."

"We're paying for our passage," Dustin firmly said. "Their passenger system sent us ticket confirmation. We're going home."

"Better life," Luke said. "Less you."

"What am I supposed to do hanging here in space with less than half a crew?"

"We don't care."

Dustin appeared more reasonable, if not more sympathetic. "You can hover here until you can have more crew shipped out to take over. Or you can turn back to Cargo City."

"You realize that loses the income from the shipment."

"Yeah, we realize."

"Maybe you can find more suckers to hire," Luke said, "until we spread the word about you."

Pangborn met their betrayal with icy disdain. "You disloyal irritants. You'll never get a space-time letter out of me."

Luke's anger burned to the surface. "You don't have the right to deny us our space-time credit!"

"A crew in mutiny?"

"It's not a mutiny," Dustin said. "That's an unfair characterization."

"How about this characterization? A stinking, disloyal muscle-flexing by low-class proletarians. Sue me."

Luke took one step forward, but Dustin stopped him. "We will."

Pangborn leaned forward. "And you'll get your paychecks when you can beat them out of me."

When Dana entered, having heard the last several sentences of this conversation, her appearance stopped Luke from trying to do just what the captain dared him to do.

"Okay, thanks, you two, we'll take it from here," she said.

"We're leaving," Dustin said. "Our gear's already transferred."

"I know." She made a quick motion for them to leave. "You're cleared to off-board. The *Virginia*'s leaving. You'd better shuttle over right now. You've only got about four minutes."

She offered her hand, which they both took in a business-like and regretful way. In a moment, she was alone with the captain.

"A significant portion of the operational crew is gone," she said. "The *Virginia* will be bearing off in eight minutes. I'll do whatever you want, but there are only a couple of choices."

"I appreciate that you stayed," he forced himself to say.

She made a verbal shrug. "Doesn't change anything. Do you want to heave to and wait for relief crew, or do you want to turn back to Cargo City?"

"I haven't decided. They just hit me with this."

She set herself for the harder questions. "How do you prefer to handle the cadets?"

"They're not 'cadets.' They're just stinking-rich stowaways."

Pangborn spoke with a dangerously measured tone. He had a temper, she knew, but she had never seen him lose it. His temper manifested itself in other ways.

"They're not stinking rich and you know it," she challenged. "Most of their parents are average people with average jobs. These kids *earned* scholarships and sponsorships. They deserve—"

"Freeloaders. The law has conditions about non-paid, non-paying personnel. I have discretionary power."

"Well, I'm not sure how you could possibly use it," she told him. "The situation is what it is. If it's just you and me running the whole ship with a diminished crew, all we can do is take them back to Cargo City. It's still the closest outpost, other than Duarte Station, and you'll get your hide sued off *and* your license suspended if you drop them there with those lone-wolf rapists."

She paused, hoping a moment of silence would help. It didn't, but his lack of response proved to her that he was past the initial anger and was thinking hard, changing course, analyzing his options. The prospect was bizarre—completing a major leg of a voyage without a trained crew.

She changed her tone. "Look, Tom . . . they're good kids. I know you don't like them, but they're super-smart, and they've learned a lot about the ship's systems. I'm sure if we ask nicely, they'll help out till we get back to Cargo City."

But the captain had stopped listening. Dana recognized the posture. He was slightly turned away from her, so she couldn't see his face, but saw the wedge of his jawline as he gazed upward thoughtfully, freeing his mind of the plans they'd assumed were set, weighing his options, cooking up alternatives, using his imagination. He had a good imagination. She'd seen him come up with creative solutions before, though truthfully she didn't see any different possibilities now. Without an experienced crew, the ship wouldn't be able to function.

Dana knew Pangborn to be an excellent technical commander, but not hampered by truth or loyalty. She had accepted that because she knew it going in, and had adjusted. She never expected loyalty, and she checked whatever he told her. He could be creatively flexible, and she could shift gears quickly. They had found a middle ground that worked.

But now she was nervous.

Pangborn touched the controls for the exterior visuals. Two screens fritzed briefly, then settled on the view of a beautiful mural floating past, shockingly close to the cameras. Dana was amazed to see not the *Virginia*, but the ironclad *Monitor* sailing past the *Umiak*. The famous mural of the Battle of Hampton Roads, known throughout the space fleet.

Together they watched as the final moorings retracted and the *Virginia* was free to go on her way. Though seeming to move very slowly, the *Virginia* bore off from the *Umiak* and in less than sixty seconds she seemed to be suddenly very far away. The aspect of her retreat was disturbing.

"I hate this part of a rendezvous," she said quietly. "It's like being left behind."

She was snapped back to reality when Thomas Pangborn drew a long breath through his nose and sighed it back out.

Then he turned to her, with a completely new musing on his face.

"Who says I don't like them?"

"We have a problem."

Captain Pangborn was businesslike and calm, but Ned detected the slightest tension in the captain's shoulders and a stiffness in his legs, and his face was dusky. If the captain had been one of the rams on the farm, these signals would've indicated meeting a threat.

Ned watched him carefully as he spoke to the assembled cadets around the salon table. Lunch was over, and Spiderlegs was collecting the leftovers, but all the cadets had been told to sit still and not help.

They were the only people in the salon. Even Mr. Nielsen was missing. All the ship's crew had been tacitly ushered out. Only Dana remained, standing over to the port side, opposite the captain, making like a hole in the wall.

"I've had to let several members of the crew go," Pangborn forthrightly said. "I can't pay them. I got stiffed by your travel agency. These things happen, just not usually in the middle of a charter. The shortest route is to take you back to Cargo City where you boarded. For me, this means no pay for the load we just took on, because I'll fail to complete delivery to Zone Emerald. For you, it means no certificates, no scholarships, and no Emerald University."

He took a pause for effect, and it worked. Mary clapped her fingers to her lips in surprise. Chris fell back in the chair and made a terrible moan of surprise and grief.

"No way!" Dan drawled. "No way . . . no way . . ."

Pearl grinned her gappy grin and uttered, "H'heh! No university."

Pangborn cast her an annoyed glare and moved on. "For those of you with parents who can afford the exorbitant cost of passage, it's still probably another thirty months till there's another charter out to Zone Emerald. You'll lose your jump on everybody else your age. After another year or two, you won't be prodigies anymore. You'll just be smart adults, and there are plenty of those. They don't impress anybody. You'll have lost your time to glow."

He paused again to observe the puddles of teenager melting around the table. Leigh's head was completely down in her arms. Dan was making shooting motions at his own head with his hand in the shape of a gun. Robin simply gazed, wide-eyed, but more in empathy for the others than for herself and Ned.

They had come just for the ride.

When the agony had been maximized, Captain Pangborn began talking again.

"But there's another option. We can help each other. We all have the same goal: get to Zone Emerald. We can make a deal."

"What deal?" Dan asked, pausing in mid-fire.

Pangborn pulled his hands out of his pockets, put them on end of the salon table, and leaned forward as if to be intimate and confidential with them. "You—all of you—be my crew. I'll give you full credit, titles as members of the crew, not cadets, official space-time letters when we're done, and proof that you were trusted with a valuable ship and its cargo. That looks good on any resume. Instead of a fake, sterile fantasy, you get to do the real thing. You won't waste your time being treated like a bunch of prissies, where we just pretend you're important. You really will be important. Working your own passages is a time-honored tradition. We'll make a couple of pickups and deliveries, and I'll have you at Zone Emerald in six weeks. Maybe less, if we get lucky."

Adam, sitting there with no plate in front of him, was the first to speak up. "I want a mate's position."

Everyone else flinched at his rapid reaction. He had digested everything faster than the rest.

Pangborn straightened and folded his arms, and looked at Adam with a nod of respect. "Okay, Sparky. You know what you're worth. That's good. You can be second mate. You've got the brains. We'll see if you have the maturity."

He held Adam's unflinching gaze for a few seconds longer than necessary, then turned again to face the entire complement.

"Is it a deal?" he asked. "Will you be my crew?"

The teens exchanged tentative glances, each hoping another would make the decision. They ultimately ended up mostly focused on Adam, since he had displayed himself as willing to match the captain dare for dare. They were waiting for him to speak.

Ned, at the end of the row beside his sister, parted his lips to speak.

"We'll do it," Adam abruptly said, stealing anyone else's chance even to ask a question. If he hadn't been elected the leader, he had elected himself.

Was that so bad? Ned wondered. How many good leaders in history had simply stepped up?

He relaxed back a bit. At least they had a plan that satisfied everyone's goals. The captain had tangled with a difficult situation and conjured up a course of action that worked for everyone. That deserved respect.

"I'll inform Mr. Nielsen that your formal lessons will be suspended and his capacity as education officer will change to some other assignment. Of course, if you have any questions that don't affect your duties, you can still address them to him. Dana and I will work up a station bill, probably pairing most of you with what's left of our crew. We'll decide whether two watches or three will serve better, and you'll be assigned. You'll find that things will go pretty much as normal once we get into a regular routine. All right, cadets . . . dismissed."

Half-stunned, the teens rose slowly, and then more quickly. Soon they were filing out, anxious to get away, to think, to talk among themselves and digest the situation. Ned saw fear in some eyes, intrigue in others, resilience in a few. Too bad he didn't have a mirror to see what was in his own.

He was the last through the hatchway into the galley, where some of them would help Spiderlegs secure the galley. He lagged slightly behind, half expecting the captain to call him back to "finish" the bell.

But he made it over the coaming intact.

As the teenagers clogged up the companionway, Ned was forced to pause as the line backed up. Behind him, in the salon, the captain was alone with Dana in their cloud of unease.

He alone heard the comment from their captain to his obligated mate.

"Let's see if our little pests have the stomach for some real adventure."

Ned lingered, shamefully curious, and chided himself for hearing as Dana followed the captain toward the aft hatch.

Dana's question to the captain sent a shiver up Ned's spine.

"What . . . pickups and deliveries?"

CHAPTER TWELVE

Adam Bay came into Ned's periphery so slowly that Ned almost didn't notice. Only when the other boy crouched at his side, then slipped down to sit on the salon's deck near him did Ned really register the presence. People had been coming and going from the two salon hatches all afternoon. Ned had left only once, to use the head. This was his seemingly perpetual assignment. Or curse.

"Ned Menzie . . . Bellmaster," Adam began dramatically. "If only the duty were as glorious as the title."

Still polishing the bell through half the afternoon, nauseated by the cloying odor of polish, Ned blinked his burning eyes and coughed. "Where's everyone else?"

"Working. He's got us at posts all over the ship. He floats around like the lord of manor, putting us on positions and giving us the hour's goals, then moving on. Dana comes around and checks on the operation. She looks nervous. She doesn't like having us at these important stations. What if something goes wrong? What if we push the wrong button? What if our remarkable skills are being wasted on some unfamiliar—"

"Is there a point you'd like to make at all?" Ned interrupted, mindlessly buffing.

Adam bent his knees and rested his arms on them, and looked at him with a frank glare. "How long are you going to put up with this?"

"As long as it takes." He continued to buff the bell housing with the tenth chamois cloth he'd wrecked. "I'm not being hurt any."

"He's not out to hurt you. He's out to break you."

"There's nothing to be broken. All things end in time."

"He thinks there is. He took a dislike to you from the start. He doesn't think you deserve to be here."

"I don't."

"Huh!" Adam made a mirthless laugh. "How charmingly self-effacing."

"That's me. Whatever it means."

Lowering his voice to an ominous tone, Adam warned, "You know what he'll do."

"What?" Ned snapped.

"If he can't get to you by holding you down, he'll get to you by holding your sister down."

This hit a nerve. Ned paused and glanced at the other boy. "Oh, he wouldn't."

"Of course! Denial. Always constructive." Adam leaned back and flexed his shoulders, gazing contemplatively at the salon lights. "Have you really convinced yourself there's anything Pangborn thinks he *can't* do out here in the cathedral of space? It's our word against his. So all you have to ask is . . . what do you think he'll do to her? What ugly, filthy, bone-breaking duty is there aboard a ship like this? What sort of job would ruin those perfect lily-white hands of hers? Shrink that happy spirit? What kind of torment can a man like Pangborn conjure up? I agree with you—it's worth waiting for. I'd sort of like to know myself." Appearing casual and contemplative, Adam rearranged his legs. "Don't you think he's perfectly named?

Pangborn . . . Pang . . . born . . . Thomas Scott Pangborn . . . just enough simplicity to be striking, with a sting of uniqueness. You can be sure no one else in history has ever or will ever have that name."

"Can't be sure of that at all," Ned droned, pressing his thumbnail into the fin of a mermaid and pretending there was something to dig out.

Adam looked at the gleaming bell and the mermaids' fins and scales, the sinuous ladies' hands and their long locks of bronze hair, cast in perfect swirls, and their frozen faces. "Do you really think you can actually get it clean enough to satisfy him?"

"Haven't you something to do?"

"I'm the second mate. I'm doing my job. Supervising the common crew."

"What else has he got you doing?"

"I've been at the helm. Supervising Leigh's astromapping and monitoring the navigational system."

"Lots of supervising, then. Sounds like a good job for you."

Adam paused, and frowned. "Is that a dig?"

Ned just sighed. "Not intentionally." And he kept working.

"Yes," Adam continued to muse, "I'd be worried about your little backyard bird if I were you. After all, we're out here in deep space, nobody to look after us, a captain who may or may not be an evil genius, with or without a moral guide rail . . . we really don't know, do we? And your sister is such a fetching little temptation—"

With the speed of a snakebite, Ned latched his dirty hand onto Adam's throat. Blackened brass polish smeared under the boy's chin as he flinched back, banging both elbows on the wall.

Ned felt his own eyes burning, but now with the limits to which he'd been pushed. "Now, that's *enough*. Keep your tongue civil. Or keep it in your head."

The slight clench of his jaw sent its own message.

Adam's aristocratic blue eyes were icy, but communicative. He tipped his head back, submitting to the pressure of Ned's hand. His eyes, though, never wavered. Had he been put in his place? Or merely postponed?

No way to tell.

When someone stepped through the forward hatchway, Ned moved one finger away from Adam's throat. A moment later, the rest. By the time his sister and Leigh came all the way in, he had withdrawn his grip entirely. His fingers felt as if they were about to fall off.

He looked up at his sister, filled with unpleasant thoughts of what might happen to her out here if things went wrong. Then he tried to squelch those thoughts, knowing that ideas had been put in his head by the calculations of Adam Bay.

"I told you he'd still be here," Leigh said to Robin. The two girls looked down at the two boys.

"You tell him," Robin said.

"But I'm not *that* sure."

"You sounded sure when you told me. Heaven's sake, have a bit of confidence."

"Well . . ."

"Yes, what news is it that we can't do without?" Adam challenged.

Leigh met his glare firmly. "You don't impress me."

Robin poked her. "Tell!"

"I think something's going on." Leigh lowered her voice. "I've been working with the astro-navigation system. I've been checking the astronomy around us. I think the captain's lying to us."

Ned stood up. "What do you mean, lying, Leigh?"

"He told us he wanted to make a couple of local pickups— local—then go straight to Zone Emerald as soon as possible. But we're going in the wrong direction."

"He didn't say anything about local meetings," Adam said. "He said we'd make some pickups and deliveries."

"But I heard him tell Dana that those meetings would be at the apogee of Planet 4 in the Tycho star system. I think he just wanted to get her off his back. We're heading on a completely wrong trajectory. If he wants to get to Zone Emerald, why are we heading the other way?"

She told him with her eyes the rest of the story—that she was afraid, that she had discovered things with her astronomical charting skills that perhaps the captain didn't realize she had figured out. That there might be danger if he knew.

They heard more noise through the hatch. Ned quickly raised his finger to his lips, and Leigh backed off, glancing only at Robin in a way that would keep their secret.

Ned looked down at Adam, still seated comfortably on the deck, and hoped his glance was adequate warning. But he knew he couldn't stop Adam from saying anything to anyone.

A moment later Dana came in, leading Chris and Dan, and trailing the little aberration—Pearl Floy.

"Where's everybody?" Dana asked. "We called all hands for the cadet crew. We have a new station bill for the next three days."

"I'm here," Adam announced, and got to his feet.

He had to stand aside as more cadets poured through the forward hatch. Dylan, Mary, Stewart . . . and behind them, Captain Pangborn himself.

When he saw the captain, Ned grew cold in the gut and quickly began, "Oh—Dana . . ."

"Yes, Ned?" She turned to him, but before he could address her, she shook her head and pulled the blackened chamois out of his hands. "That's enough of this. I'm taking you off this duty. Don't even clean up. I'll get somebody else to do that."

He glanced at the captain. Pangborn watched the interaction with practiced reserve.

"I have to make a . . . a report . . ." he began. "I apologize that I've not seen you until now . . ."

"No need to apologize," the first mate said. "Make your report."

He squirmed and summoned every bit of will and recall. "The captain wanted a survey . . . on the weaving roves in sections nine, twelve . . . and twenty . . . and thirteen . . . and he wants the tilt-lockers and screws . . ."

He began to sweat around the neck. Behind the captain, he saw his sister mouthing numbers, but couldn't make them out. Leigh, even farther away, was making little hand signals. "Two" with one hand, "one" with the other . . . what did that mean?

The captain knew what he wanted done, but he simply folded his arms and let Ned sweat it out.

"And the transmissions and the turning davits . . . after three hundred hours . . ."

"Three hundred?" Dana asked. "You mean this morning or tomorrow morning?"

Pangborn shifted on his locked legs and sniffed, saying nothing to help Ned.

Stewart's eyes were wide under his brown bangs. His lips were tight, teeth together, sending mental waves.

"I, um . . ." Ned quaked for another five seconds, then knew he was finished. He used his wrist to brush a lock of dark hair out of his eyes.

No, nervousness wasn't helping. He'd failed and he knew it. Time to be a man and own up.

He squared his shoulders and looked at the captain. "Pardon me, Captain, but I'm not able to fulfill this assignment. I don't recall enough of the details. I don't want anything on the ship to go wrong because of my failing."

Dana pressed her lips tight at the sight of his aching hands and could tell by the way he held them that he was hurting and exhausted. She awarded him with a smile of admiration. She put her hand on his shoulder and patted it.

"Ned," she said, "you're a trooper."

Everything suddenly stopped. The hills opened and the skies began to sing. Angels began a chorus of alleluias. Ned's hands and shoulders and his back and knees were healed. Thankless work was no longer thankless. He knew he would have worked all night more for that compliment, and for the gazes of respect from his fellow cadets.

Then something new happened. A new voice began speaking.

"Check the woven roving in sections nine, twelve, thirteen, fifteen, twenty, twenty-two. Lube points he wants serviced, tilt-lock levers, clamp screws, throttle bearings, starboard side relief valbs, winch tran-missions, autogimbals. Check turning quadrant of davit Charlie-Alpha. Shimmying."

They all turned sharply. It was Pearl. Her dried-prune voice continued its otherworldly monologue.

"And I want to replace all the Cobb-coils during their three hundred hour checks. And not happy with the flow along the inboard strongback in the starboard flank bay. Hull vibrations."

The room changed as she spoke. Those standing near her had backed away—Stewart and Mary. Pearl now stood alone at one end of the salon, with the rest of the cadets, Pangborn and Dana bunched at the other end. Only Adam actually moved forward, driven by fascination, to the front of the bunch, but not all the way to Pearl.

Her round eyes fixed on him. Her brows went up in wonderment.

"And replace the air-cooled dasher blocks."

Finished with the report, she closed her mouth and scratched her knee.

In unintended chorus, spellbound, both Ned and Dana uttered, "Thanks . . ."

Intrigued, Captain Pangborn took charge. He strode toward Pearl. Halfway there, he paused at a cabinet with a special magnetic lock, and punched in the code. When the cabinet sprung open, he pulled out a handheld compad and used it to pull up a data screen. He flipped the screen over and held it in front of Pearl's face. Then he pushed the button that would scroll information at a rate too fast to read.

"Take a look at this, Pearl," he said.

Pearl's eyes fixed on the screen. Ned could only imagine the numbers and codes flying past her. The lights and colors flashed on her pasty face. Page after page, line after line.

"Captain," Dana began. She stepped forward.

He cut her off. "Wait."

She stopped.

The lights flashed on Pearl's face. Her eyes didn't move, and she didn't blink. Only her mouth corners turned up in a Mona Lisa smile.

Captain Pangborn snapped the compad away from her, turned it to face himself, and ran several pages, then stopped randomly on one. "Where's the Larkowski Nelson Bailey container number 94 A?"

Pearl picked at her own fingernails, digging and peeling. "On the left side . . . port side . . . row three hundred and six, twelve up, nineteen deep. Clearance code nine-nine-T-Z-Z-X. Lock combination and passwords seven-seven-three-dash-Medusa-orange-Lucy-amoeba-Tommy."

The ship's company reacted—some with a nervous laugh, some with, "Wow!" and "Oh!" and "Crap . . ." and others with astonished silence.

Ned pushed forward to Adam's side, amazed.

Adam felt his presence and moved even more forward.

"Pearl, what are the odds of a collision between two Earth-sized planetary bodies if the Swan Galaxy were ever to pass on an angle fifty degrees to the plane through the middle of the Milky Way?"

"Fourteen thousand quintillion point nine to the twelfth power."

Robin gasped and pressed her hands to her mouth.

Adam took one more step toward Pearl. "What will be the day of the week on February 29 in the year 45,067?"

"There won't be one. It's a leap year."

"Did you know that?" Ned quickly asked Adam.

"It was a trick question. I had a one in four chance. Pearl, what's the weekday of same date the following year?"

"Tuesday."

Ned pushed forward, stepping past his realization of how smart Adam also was. "Pearl, how many hairs are there on my head?"

"One hundred nine thousand fifteen."

"Oh, my lord—" Dana gasped.

Pearl pointed her waxy index finger as if casting a spell at Robin. "One hundred twelve thousand two." Then at Leigh. "One hundred forty thousand nine hundred seven." And most passionately at Adam— "One hundred fifty thousand two hundred . . . three."

They stared at her as if they'd opened up a lunch box and found a Caliban in there.

"Pearl," Adam challenged, "what did your father say to your mother at 6:30 P.M. on the Saturday night before they disappeared?"

"Nothing. He wasn't home."

"At 8:30, then."

"'Get this mutt off the couch. He's shedding.'"

Dan, standing behind Dana, uttered, "Crikey . . . it's sorcery!"

Mary, standing with her usual quiet caution on the other side of the salon, gripped Chris by the arm and gulped, "Jesus . . ."

But Adam wasn't finished. He bent slightly forward, glaring at Pearl. "What happened to your parents?"

In Ned's periphery, Mary began to tremble. Chris clasped her tightly against him. Robin and Leigh closed the space between them and huddled together. They were terrified.

"Stop that!" Ned stepped between Adam and Pearl, but faced the other boy defensively. "She has a right to her privacy."

But Adam was already on to the next point. He ignored Ned and blurted, "This explains it!" He clapped his hands once, sending a collective flinch through the salon.

"I have to go," Pearl said, not exactly asking. "I have to play with my birds. They're waiting."

The captain lowered his brows. "Your birds?"

"My baby birds are waiting for me."

"Oh, sure. You go play with your baby birds."

Pearl made a funny laugh and square-pegged her way out through the aft hatch.

"Birds . . . ?" Dan echoed when she was gone.

"She's pretending," the captain assured. "Like a toddler." He turned to Adam. "What explains her?"

"She's an ultra-savant!" the boy told him. "There's only one born every couple thousand years. Maybe a hundred of them in all of human history, including the ones who were killed as witches!"

Leigh gazed in wonder at the space where Pearl had stood a moment ago. "You mean she's smarter than all of us?"

"No, she's not smarter." Adam raised his own finger to make a specific point. "It's a skill, not a talent. And it has costs. She probably can't make leaps of logic or understand abstract concepts any better than a small child. She probably can't assemble plans or think too far into the past or future, even though she remembers everything she's ever seen or heard. Even peripherally. It also explains why she's so uncoordinated. Her brain is busy with other things than muscle control."

Leigh's quick mind was also working on this new idea. "Are you saying she's a human databank?"

"No, there's more to it than that. Even computers can't do everything she does. Computers can only do what they're programmed to do. This is probably why Emerald University wants her at this new establishment of intellectuals and science—"

"What else can she do?" the captain interrupted.

Adam paused and thought about that, sifting for an answer, and he seemed both bothered and fascinated that he didn't have one. "It's possible nobody even knows yet. And we won't know . . . until she does it."

"Why are we headed in the wrong direction?"

Dana followed Thomas Pangborn into the charthouse. Feeling overloaded, she had pursued him halfway across the ship, asking the same question.

But now that they were here, in private, in officers' country where no one else could possibly overhear, she had a new question for him.

"Are you trafficking in contraband?"

Pangborn drew a long breath through his nose and sighed it out. "Lot of nerve asking me that."

She ignored his feigned indignation. "Do you have a golden goose aboard this ship?"

"No, of course not. That's interesting, about that douche-bait henbane girl, isn't it? She really does have a reason to be here after all. 'Ultra-savant'—"

"Goddamn it!" Dana slammed her fist against the display casing. The visuals on the two closest monitors destabilized and were shot through with static. "Tell me the truth!"

Pangborn calmly went to the beverage dispenser and keyed in the code for his coffee. His shoulders tightened, then relaxed as he decided what to say. He paused, picked at his teeth with a fingernail, and leaned his buttocks on the console's cushioned rim. "It's not contraband."

"Oh, shit!" she spat. "You left me out of information like this? Not contraband, my ass! It can't be anything else!"

"It's no more contraband than having your little Manker shepherd stowaways aboard among a band of specimens who at least earned their way here," he insisted. "It's top-secret copyrighted technology and part of the contract is a no-peeking clause. I had no choice or we wouldn't have gotten the shipment—"

"Like hell you didn't," she seethed. "The first officer aboard a ship of this class is a qualified captain in the fleet and is supposed to be informed of every—*every* command-level interest. Everything on this ship is considered need-to-know for me and you know it, and so do the people who hired that shipment, and it includes every aspect of the freight! What are we carrying and who *exactly* is coming to pick it up?"

"I don't like your tone."

"Does Captain Alley know about this?"

"His ship is his own business."

"Meaning no! He didn't! I know Nick Alley! Who's working against him on his own ship?"

"I don't know and I don't care."

"Who's coming, Captain? Who's coming to this ship? We have innocent children aboard! You're not allowed to open this vessel to boarders of any kind without complete clearance and an open regulation book in your hand!"

"They're friends of mine."

"Is that supposed to work?"

Pangborn turned away from her and pretended interest in the navcoms. "You're making too much out of this. The regulations don't run this ship. I do. We're out here, this is happening, and there's nothing you can do about it."

"What are their names and clearances?" she demanded. "I want to run background checks."

"They don't have 'backgrounds.'"

Dana flopped her arms. "Oh, perfect! Smugglers!"

"Look," he said evenly, "you'd better accept whatever I tell you to accept." He turned to her. His calmness was shocking. "These people know me. They don't know you. You don't have enough crew here to mount a mutiny, and if you do anything to neutralize me, they'll wipe out every living thing on this ship. If you're smart, and you are, you'll let me handle these people. Trust me—you don't want to deal with them. I already gave them authorization to board the minute they arrive. They'll just come here and walk right in. See how easy it is to do business? They're only here to pick up one box, and they'll be gone into the night. It's no big deal unless you make it a big deal. Just go about your own business and keep those brats out of the way. By morning it'll all be over. Quit having a hissy. Be flexible."

Dana almost threw up. She sank back, astonished, and let her arms drop to her sides as if he'd slapped her. She shook her head slowly in dismay and disappointment.

"This stinks," she snarled.

Pangborn didn't look at her. He clicked on the proximity display, and there on the deep-distance scopes was a blip. A red blip of approaching body. Another ship on an approach vector.

"Then plug your nose," he said.

Pretty dark. Tip-tip toes. Don't fall. It's always bad to fall.

Always break something, tear something, some muscles, some bones. Patella. Femur. Ilium, ishium, lunate, malleus, ossicles, coracobrachialis, condyloid . . .

Such pretty bones, with all the muscles running around and around. Cubital fossa. Zygomatic. Nasal. Maxillae, palatine, lacrimal, sacrum, coccyxlunatetrqiquetriumpisiformTrapezi-umtrapezoidcapitatehamate—

"Oh, birdies!"

See? No falling down. All the way here, no falling. Tip-tip on the walkway, way up high, and way over and way in.

"Birdies! Hello! Can you hear me? I know you're in this blue thing. I can feel you in there. We can all fly pretty soon. Would you like that? I feel so tiny standing here. Are you tiny too?"

Oh, there's the lock. Millions of codes and numbers and letters and jumping things and typing things and talking things. Disambiguation.

Easy.

Poke, poke, number, number, number. More, more, more, more, more, diddly, diddly, diddly, easy.

"Open, open! Oh, good job, Pearl! Smart girl! Can you do it again? I can do it, Mommy. Don't send me away again."

Boy, there's lots of hissing! Sucking and hissing and steam.

Door opening! Better get out of the way.

Sounds coming from inside. Little animal sounds.

"I hear you, birdies! Come out! Come out and fly away! There you are . . . aren't you cute? That's right! Run away and learn to fly! Fly, birdies! Fly!"

CHAPTER THIRTEEN

"Who called all hands?"

Ned's question met with blank and quizzical expressions from the other teens. Nobody seemed to know.

They were in the crew's quarters, a strange place for them to have been called. The call itself caused a lightning bolt of dread to shoot through each of the cadets. What had happened now? What had changed? Had the captain been angered or frightened by the revelations about Pearl? Or was the *Umiak* just far enough out in space that the captain had no reins on him, legal or otherwise?

Ideas spun in Ned's head. He was too good at conjuring up scenarios to rest easy at this sudden call for a meeting. He'd always had a good imagination. Too good, it seemed, today.

Ned looked around. Everyone was here—all the cadets. No adults. No crew. No captain. No Dana.

Robin and Leigh, now perpetually together, showed that friendships had been forged over the past days. And there were Chris and Mary, together more and more, and Dan and Stewart, whom Ned had learned to trust. And Dylan, who always had a jovial willingness that anchored their doubts.

"Where's Pearl?" he asked, counting heads.

"Doesn't matter." Adam stood at the far end of the crew quarters, almost cloaked in the blue curtains which hung from the bunks. There were two rows of bunks, stacked on top of each other, and part of the courtesy and maintenance of the ship involved the curtains' always being drawn, even when no one was in there sleeping. It was a good plan and kept the ship tidy, which made it more livable day by day. Ned understood. The farm was the same way. If routines weren't established and rules kept, the goats would be in the kitchen with their heads in the fridge.

Adam looked quite princely standing there in his white shirt, his chin-length wavy hair catching the lights from overhead and making a red-gold halo around his face.

"What's this?" Ned asked.

"I have something to show all of you."

Without taking a step, Adam reached out with his right hand and drew back the blue curtain on the bunk at his shoulder.

There, lying as peacefully as a child, more peacefully and more relaxed than Ned had ever seen her, was Dana. Her face was without tension, her eyes closed, one hand flopped over her chest, her mouth slightly open. She didn't look asleep. She looked unnaturally still.

"Oh, dear God!" Robin burst, and flew forward. She shook the woman by that flopping arm. "Dana! Dana! Wake up!"

"She won't wake up," Adam told her.

Robin spun to him. "You've *killed* her?"

"Killed her? That would be too easy. Not to mention imbecilic."

"What did you do?" Ned demanded. "Be specific!"

"It's nothing. It's a special coma-inducing cocktail to put them in a hibernation state. They're just asleep and they can't wake up for a while."

"How—could you do this?" Mary blurted. "How do you know how to do something like this?"

"Because I *know* how. How else?" Adam folded his arms and leaned back against the wall. "I spent hours every day in my dad's lab, developing this formula. It's going to be used on severely injured people in space to hold them for treatment. It's more soothing and stabilizing than cryo-sleep alone. She'll wake up feeling wonderful."

"When?"

"Not for quite a while."

Leigh stomped forward, quite intimidating for her stocky stature. "You wake her up!"

"I can't," Adam said. "It has to run its course."

"What's the course?"

"It's different for every individual. She'll have to wake up on her own."

Chris, standing toward the back of the group, grasped his strawberry curls and gulped, "Oh, *man* . . . unbelievable . . . wild!"

Shocked, Ned broke through the crowd of likewise astonished cadets and tore aside another curtain. "Mr. Nielsen!"

The counselor and education officer was in a bunk, but he wasn't supposed to be here at all. Both he and Dana had their own quarters, not in the same bunk areas as the deck crew. Adam had warehoused them here.

Ned tore aside another curtain, and another. Cheater— Patty—Antoine—the only members of the crew besides Spiderlegs who had stayed with the ship when news of the bankruptcy had come through. All asleep!

He whirled on Adam. "Why've you done this?"

"Why not?"

"We can't do this!" Leigh challenged.

Adam blinked at her. "Why not?"

Robin's voice squeaked a bit. "We can't be our here without adult supervision!"

"*Why* not?"

"This is some kind of mutiny!" Stewart exclaimed, looking as if his head were spinning inside his skull. "Why would you do this?!"

Adam folded his arms. "I almost mutinied at band camp. I was only there a week."

"Wait a minute, wait a minute, mates," Dan drawled. "We can do this. He's right. We can be on our own . . . don't we know the basics?"

"The basics is just the basics," Dylan wisely said. "The child's play part. You know? Child's play?"

Stewart dropped to sit on the edge of Dana's bunk. "We're mutineers!"

"We're not mutineers," Adam calmly told them in a buttery tone. "We're expatriates."

"Yeah!" Dan chimed. "I always wanted to be an outcast!"

"The outcast from the Outback," Adam congratulated. "You get the idea."

"What are we going to do?" Leigh asked. "Where'll we go?"

"Why don't you tell us? You're the astro-navigator."

"I'm not even sure where we *are*!"

"You'll figure it out. Desperation does that. You'll accept the challenge. We have our own ship now. We can go anywhere, or nowhere. We can live free, make our own decisions, set our own schedule—"

"Schedule?" Leigh slapped her hands on her thighs. "We have futures! We have plans! There are scholarships waiting for us! You did this without consulting any of us? So you can play God and play grownup and run around pretending you know what's best for everybody?"

"We'll get in trouble!" Mary declared.

Adam huffed. "Oh, we'll get in trouble!" he mocked. "Oh, no! Somebody's going to come and spank us! Oh, my! They'll send us to bed without supper! Sorry. That's already been tried on me. Doesn't work. You just wait 'em out. Haven't you figured that out yet, Meeereee?"

"Wait—" Dan interrupted. He held out both hands, thinking fast. "I think we *can* do this! Crikes, I think maybe we can . . . we know how to maintain the ship, and the ship pretty much runs itself, roight?"

"Right," Adam said. "You do your jobs, and I'll make the decisions if anything comes up. It's not that hard a job."

"You're seventeen years old!" Stewart uncharacteristically spoke up.

Leigh shook her head and wagged her hands. "I'm not hinging my future on you!"

Completely unaffected, Adam said, "Lord Horatio Nelson commanded a ship in the British Navy at the age of nineteen. It happens all the time. Eighteen- and nineteen-year-olds are sergeants and lieutenants in wars, making command decisions every hour, every minute. A sixteen-year-old can get a private pilot's license. A couple of weeks ago, I was a passenger. Then I became a cadet. Then I became a second mate. Now I'm in command. Happens all the time."

"Command?" Straightening slowly from where he had been checking Mr. Nielsen's pulse, Ned squared off in the middle of the narrow bunk area, looking at Adam. "Where's the captain?"

"What captain is that?"

Horrified, Ned felt his chest contract with anticipation. As if he were an old-time gunfighter he held his hands out at his sides, poised for an action he couldn't predict. "Adam . . . what've you done with Captain Pangborn?"

Adam smirked, very pleased with himself. He drew a long satisfied breath, stepped to the port side of the cabin, and drew back the curtain on the aft-most bunk.

There lay Captain Pangborn, trussed up like a pig on its way to the spit.

Adam held the curtain back, leaned on the bunk support strake, and merrily declared, "Ding-dong, the witch is dead."

"Oh, God help us!"

Robin slunk forward, her hands clenched at her chest, and peeked into the bunk where Captain Pangborn lay. Ned crowded behind her, and was startled when she gasped and pulled back against him.

The captain was looking back at them, awake, his mouth covered by the kind of mechanical muffler that was used on prisoners with gag orders or unruly rioters. Ned had seen those before, but only on the news. Why would there be one aboard this ship?

The captain's hands were also shackled with magnetic cuffs, and his ankles were hobbled by the same kind of metallic arrangement, but of the kind that had rotary linkages that would allow him to walk, but not run.

Ned grasped his sister by the shoulders and moved her aside so he could bend for a better look. "He's not dead?"

"Does he look dead?" Adam disrespectfully reached out and pulled a lock of the captain's hair. "He's just shackled. Aren't you, Captain, oh, Captain, my Captain?"

"Why did you leave him awake if you drugged the others?"

"Because I want him to see everything we do. I like having an audience. I also always wanted a pet. I'm looking forward to leading him around and showing him how much we don't need him."

"Where'd you get these . . . manacles?"

"They're his." Adam nodded at the captain, whose glare was calm, but not accepting.

Stewart then asked, "Where's Spiderlegs?"

"In the galley," Adam said. "What does he know? From now on, I'm not missing a meal."

Ned pointed at the captain and said, "Unlock him."

"No."

"Adam!"

"No. I'm not afraid of *him* . . . why would I be afraid of *you*? Neddy?"

"We'll figure out how to unlock him."

"No, you won't."

Ned reached out and dragged Dylan into the middle of this. "Dylan's an expert with magnets. Those are magnetic locks, right? He'll figure them out."

"Maybe," Adam acknowledged saucily, "in a week, ten days . . . don't you think these locks have been designed with all the Dylans in mind? Besides, do you really want to uncuff him and find out what kind of retribution a man like him will use on us?"

Chris suddenly came forward. "That's right—we don't know what he'll do! We need somebody else to make this decision. Let's contact the authorities! Somebody'll come!"

Ned wouldn't have gone for that, except that he saw instantly that the idea was growing in the minds of his fellows. He looked at Pangborn.

The captain's glare was bloodcurdling. What, in fact, *would* he do? Even Dana had not been able to balance him. What would a smart and ruthless man do?

And what choice was there? Ned knew that none of them could open those locks. Even Dylan, as Ned glanced at him, seemed perplexed at he stared at the mouth mask and the manacles and the leg irons. Perhaps it was too much to ask. Adam had jumped off a cliff and taken all of them with him.

"This can work," Dan was babbling, off in a corner now, mumbling to himself. "Could be it . . . could work . . . no worries . . . just a trip to the back country . . . no worries at all . . . just a . . . an adventure! Just like the captain said! This a real adventure!"

"I don't care," Mary broke in. "It doesn't matter who runs the ship as long as it runs, does it? It's almost fully automatic, isn't it? Isn't that what they've been telling us all along? I mean, how many decisions actually have to be made?"

"Pity's sake," Ned droned. "The ronnag's on 'em."

He met Robin's eyes, for she was the only one who would understand his comment. Wanderlust . . . restlessness . . . they'd been seized by it.

Captain Pangborn glowered at them, not even trying to fight his bonds. They were his own stock, so he clearly knew better.

Robin beseeched Ned with a long baleful stare. Ned felt the responsibility shift, but he wasn't sure how it was shifting. Would they follow Adam? Was he the natural leader he seemed to be? Or was something else happening?

Even lying in that bunk, trussed up, Captain Pangborn was psychologically powerful, still held them in some kind of thrall. They were still afraid of him, and in the way of young dogs, still respected him and wanted him to be in charge. Except for Adam, and maybe Dan, and moment by moment Mary.

"Oh, and I have a surprise for Ned," Adam lilted. "Come through here, everyone. Chris, Dan, pick up the captain and bring him. He'll be very interested in this."

Chris and Dan quickly moved to follow Adam's directions. They were much more comfortable being told what to do than standing against any kind of authority that asserted itself. Ned didn't blame them—they were all teenagers here. Their worlds had been run by adults all their lives. Every teenager ever born

wanted to race to adulthood, but when it was suddenly dropped
in his lap and felt heavy, the story was different. Only Adam
seemed ready and willing to dismiss the need for experience.
Was it an act?

Robin looked at Ned. Ned just gave her a nod to follow, to
go along for now. What else could they do?

Adam led them, with the captain surprisingly non-resistant—
possibly he wanted to get out of that bunk—to the construction area of the ship, where the crew made things they needed.
It was a mini-factory, with a smelting furnace and a machine
shop, a carpentry shop, computer and small engine repair areas.
The *Umiak* was almost an independent city, ready to support
all sorts of work and repairs. The construction room was a
repository of tools and diagnostics, with walls of parts-bins
and storage.

"Right this way, gentlemen. And ladies."

Adam led them to the smelting furnace, more or less a kiln-
sized cauldron used to melt old parts down to their constituent metals and use them to cast new parts. It was always
on, always bubbling with volcanic fluids, and heat from it
was funneled through the ship to keep the crew chambers
warm.

"Put the captain right over there. Ned . . . Merry Christmas."

Adam pulled up a spark tarp which had been draped over
what everyone assumed was just a small motor or bundle of
parts. But when the tarp came up and was flung aside, Adam
revealed not a mechanical item, but the captain's bell.

The bell stood alone without its mermaid housing, disen-
gaged from its pedestal or any of the majesty which it had
enjoyed in its long life.

Pangborn made another protesting sound and pulled
forward, but Dan and Chris held him back, despite their own
amazement at what they were seeing.

"No!" Ned shouted, but too late.

Adam seized the bell in a bear hug, heaved it up off the deck, banged it on the edge of the smelting furnace by accident, then simply rolled it into the bubbling cauldron.

Pangborn made an agonized and angry wail.

"Neddy!" Robin dragged Ned by the shirt, because he had almost followed the bell into the cauldron.

The beautiful brass bell, turned on its side, gulped the silver liquid metal.

"Good God!" Ned shouted. He whirled on Adam. "What've you done?! Why would you do such a vile thing?!"

"Because vile deserves vile," Adam told him.

"He's done nothing to deserve this!" Ned gestured to the captain, who was watching the bell turn like an ice cube melting in a hot drink. It turned only a few moments, made a slurping sound, and abruptly sank.

Adam's voice burned in Ned's ear. "Yes, he has."

"This is your retribution for a bit of harmless tedium?"

"It wasn't harmless tedium. It was drudgery by force."

"Auch! You've a big song, haven't you!" Ned turned in the other direction, to the captain who was being forced to watch his family heirloom rendered down to a golden puddle. Pangborn's mouth was of course held silent in the mechanical band that allowed him to breathe freely but made speech impossible. His eyes, though, did his talking for him. Everything was there, from bitterness to rage to unshrinking defiance.

Adam stood proudly beside the cauldron, his face glazed with radiant heat, watching the last of the bell's brass melt like butter and blend into the silver base.

The other teens were simply stunned, each to his own level. They circled the cauldron and watched the arcane ritual play out as if they were watching some kind of ancient human sacrifice. Ned suddenly felt as if he were back at home during the fires of Beltaine and the revels of Halloween.

The bright liquid metal reflected the worklights, which then danced freakishly on the faces of the teenagers and their cheerless captain, who shuddered with rage in his bonds.

"Wretched," Ned murmured. He looked from the cauldron to Adam. "Shame be on you for the beast you are."

Adam only made a noble snicker and smiled with confusing warmth at him.

Bing! Bing! Bing! Bing! Bing! Bing!

"Faith!" Robin jumped, physically startled by the sound of the warning bell. It wasn't the danger klaxon—they'd heard that during one of the safety drills. This was something else. The ship was trying to alert them about something.

"What's that?" Adam asked.

"You've taken command!" Ned snapped. "Do you not know *everything*?"

"It's a proximity alert!" Leigh said. "Another ship!"

Stewart yelped, "Maybe the *Virginia's* come back!"

"Oh, Christ, we're in such deep poop!" Dylan moaned.

The captain made a sound of struggle, drawing their confused looks, but it was Leigh who acted. She stepped to a com link in the wall and called up the information from the charthouse navcom.

"It's not the *Virginia*," she said. "It's got a . . . an I.D. signal . . . no name . . . the identification only says C904."

"What's that mean?" Dylan asked. "What kind of ship doesn't have a name?"

Leigh shook her head at what she was seeing on the alert screen. "This can't be good . . ."

Adam wasn't about to let this turn of events disrupt his moment of glory. He gestured to Dan and Chris, then pointed at the captain. "Bring him."

They dragged Captain Pangborn away from the cremation of his bell and headed down the companionway. Mary and Dylan, Stewart and Leigh followed, until only Ned and Robin lingered behind, in the company of the deep sleepers who offered no salvation.

"Sweet mountain air . . ." Robin murmured.

Ned nodded sadly and met her eyes. "Mutiny in Neverland."

CHAPTER FOURTEEN

The captain's hobbled legs could only move so fast. The captain was nobly silent. He made no struggles. Ned, struggling plenty on the inside, shuffled at the back of the group with Robin, neither of them with their hearts in it. Ned had the feeling they were heading full-long into a catastrophe. He would've washed his hands of it, but for the sakes of the ladies.

Who was in that ship just coming to their side? He tried to judge by watching the captain's face, his eyes, his demeanor, but he gave away nothing. Did that mean he knew these people and thought things would go his way? Ned couldn't divine.

They stumbled down to the starboard hold, where the loading bay was, and sure enough the accordion tunnel was extended, linking *Umiak* to another ship. Whose? Why?

Adam boldly peered down the tunnel, with the other teens behind him. Ned hovered at the middle of the group, and they edged bit by bit forward, trying to see past the hissing steam venting from both sides of the just-securing tunnel. If the steam was venting, then no one had come inside yet.

There were two other passageways leading off from the tunnel's sides, but Ned didn't see anyone peeking from

them. They were only utility passages, which had ladders
leading to the upper scaffolding. No one should be up there
either.

Or had they already been boarded? How did these things
work? Could strangers just walk aboard?

He wished he had spent less time polishing the poor
dissolved bell, and more learning the ship.

Adam suddenly stopped and backed up two steps. The whole
gaggle of cadets bumped backward into each other. Beside
Ned, Chris and Dan still held the hobbled captain, who made
a disgusted grunt.

There were people walking toward them through the tunnel,
through the veil of steam, which now turned yellow as it vented
the last residual gases. The tunnel was huge, big enough to emit
a stream of the enormous cartage containers, but even so the
small group of humans somehow looked big and imposing.
Perhaps they just *walked* big.

The steam softened to reveal seven people, brimming
with weaponry, dressed in horrid mismatched clothing that
demonstrated personal statements of ruggedness and threat.
They had nothing in common in their dress or deport-
ment, no sign of unity for crew or cause. They dressed to
be frightening—and they succeeded in that singular goal.
They were all types of people—a big-boned, clearly pregnant
woman with her hair done in three colors. A dwarf man with
muscular arms and teeth filed to points, and his face tattooed
with tiger-stripes. Flanking him were three more men with
thick boots and jackets of synthetic leather, each with his own
style, except that two had the same craggy, jaundiced face.
Twins. It was easy to see why they were jaundiced . . . they
both had thick homemade cigars clenched in their teeth, and
smoke writhing about their bald heads. The third man was
actually wearing a skirt or maybe a kilt, and his socks were

bunched around his ankles. If it was a kilt, he was wearing it all wrong.

Another woman was dressed like an American Indian, with deerskin and fringes and beads, but who also was clearly not Indian at all, but Nordic, with long straight blond hair and crystal blue eyes. Behind them all, as if bracing the rearguard, was a giant man of indeterminate race with a wide black handlebar moustache. Dressed in bright red from head to foot, he towered over the others by at least a head and clearly meant to strike fear with his sheer enormity. He was big, and he liked being that.

They might as well each have had one eye and a club and been roaring, "Death to Caesar!"

Behind Ned, Robin uttered, "Oh—*pirates*!"

Ned hoped the new people had not heard her.

"Who the hell are you?" the dwarf called out. He had a strong, shocking voice. "Where's Pangborn?"

"Identify yourselves first," Adam countered.

"Blow me. Where's Pangborn? Where's our shipment? It was supposed to be right out in the open, ready to go."

The thick-bodied pregnant woman said, "I don't like this, Detroit. This smells."

"There's Pangborn!" the giant said, pointing his broomstick finger at the captain. "What the hell, he's bound up! Some kind of game?"

Pangborn stomped one foot, but that was the extent of his actions.

Detroit tipped his blocky head, surveying Pangborn and the cadets. "Where's the regular crew?"

"We're the crew," Adam declared.

Four of the boarders laughed. The others were less amused by what they heard.

"Where's the real crew, junior?" Detroit demanded. "And what's Pangborn doing tied up?"

"The crew abandoned ship. Captain Pangborn threatened to kill us. We were scared. Can you help take us back to our parents?"

Ned shook his head at Adam's ploy. What a stock of nerve he had!

"Parents!" Handlebar Moustache snorted.

"Hey!" The pregnant woman hauled off and smacked him across the face with her gloved hand.

"Quit hitting me, Tina!" he wailed. "Always hitting me!"

"Respect!" She held up a warning finger, then pointed at her belly.

He groaned an apology and tried to regain his enormity.

"C'mere, kid," Detroit snarled, and began to waddle forward with a strangely imposing set to his walk, despite his dwarfism. His beefy arms rolled forward and back, his fists clenched. The others came along with him, creating a bank of bulldogs.

Adam didn't step back, but began slightly to lean back as if he were about to take a step.

"Ohhh—" Mary moaned, pressing backward into Leigh and Robin.

Ned murmured. "Don't retreat."

Adam half turned, as if he didn't hear. "What now? Throw them some meat?"

"Stand your ground!" Ned hissed. He pressed his hand to Adam's shoulder as if to support him.

"They're going to kill us!" Chris gulped, keeping his voice low.

"We'll find out what they want and give it to them," Ned quickly said.

"Right!" Dan said through tight lips. "No worries then, eh?"

"*I'm* worried!" Leigh argued.

Robin, pressed up behind Ned, peeked over his left shoulder. "Invisible . . . invisible . . . invisible . . ."

The troupe of boarders—were they pirates or smugglers or what?—thundered closer and closer.

Suddenly Mary let out a quick shriek and jumped as if she'd been struck. There was a form now between the cadets and the smugglers, an unexpected appearance, out of the yellow fog, as if conjured by a spell.

Pearl!

The skinny girl knobbed out from the nearest passage in the side of the boarding tunnel. She looked at the cadets with a very odd smile, nodding in agreement with some thought of her own. She flat-footed out of the nook between the two groups.

Behind her, the smugglers stopped in their tracks.

"Hi!" she husked to the cadets. "Hi, everybody! We have some new friends. You'll like them. They're big and strong and they have wacky hands!"

Ned extended his hand, but shamefully was too shaken to take a step toward her. *Take a step. Take a step toward her, you coward . . .*

At least speak!

"Pearl," he began, unsatisfied with his voice, "come toward us, now. You belong with us, not them."

Pearl's brown eyes dropped in disappointment. "But they're sweet."

"Indeed they are." Ned stepped out forward, finding the stomach to do it. His hand, outstretched before him, white and pasty, looked like an old-fashioned envelope on its way to the post in a Sherlock Holmes story. He felt detached from it, as if it floated free between him and the oddity.

She was already closer to him than to them. He had only to widen the gap, to get her before they got her.

He felt the cold moist sprinkle from the yellow mist, beading on his fingertips.

Unable to figure out which hand to hold out, Pearl put both her hands out in front of her, palms down. Two steps got under her.

And then there was . . . something else. Moisture.

Not the soft yellow mist, but a thick, clear drainage percolating from the area above Pearl's head, from the sounds of tearing in the skin of the accordion folds of the retractable tunnel.

Collectively all eyes were raised. Tearing, ripping, and zipper-like sound, and the skin of the tunnel began to peel back. With every inch came more clear spurtle brimming as if from a waterfall, puddling around Pearl's black orthopedic shoes and splashing on her drab clothes. Her callow face rolled upward and she cried, "My birds!"

And down came the birds.

Perhaps there were two, perhaps three. In the yellow fog, there was suddenly a twist of scales and claws, elongated heads shining in the utility lights, lean ribs, and some kind of legs and slashing constrictor tails. And teeth—teeth.

Ned spread his arms wide to hold back the others, and leaned back, but couldn't find his feet. Open-mouthed, with all the others open-mouthed around him, he looked, hypnotized, upon the mouth of hell.

He had never seen in life a thing such as he saw now. Only in the thorny grip of a fever after hearing too many tales of the Sidhe had his mind conjured such images of wickedness. The creatures were perfect formations of tooth and claw and whipping gray tail, with slashers on five ends, and they understood the theatrics of terror. They piled onto each other, tangled and hissing, crouching, swirling, and turned their eyeless black heads toward the humans on either side.

Only a step or two from Ned, Captain Pangborn made a roaring noise through his mouth-bond.

Shouts—a scream—the chokes of the astonished broke out in a chorus with the unearthly shrieks of the creatures themselves. Then Ned saw, very clearly, three alien heads and three snouts, hunched shoulders and brandished sets of claws, all turned toward him and the other cadets. The creatures let out screams through their bared teeth, one scream on top of the next.

And there were more teeth inside. Snapping extra jaws.

The dogs of hell, not of Earth, not of Heaven, not of the Veil. Jack o'lanterns!

The breath left Ned's body as if he'd been punched. He felt the air pump from his mouth and not come back in. Like prey before a cobra, he and his clan were held still in shock as death rolled before them. He wanted to grab out for Pearl, to drag her back, but the seconds shot by while he was bound by fright. Without willing it or thinking about it, he held his ground before a squall line of demons.

Shrouded in gassy stink, the creatures twisted, never still, pitiless in their posture, and they hissed and screamed, rising before poor Pearl, tiny thing that she was. Her shoulder blades came toward one another as she looked up at them.

The creatures hissed again, and one of them retracted its center jaws, then all three pivoted their pod-like heads around toward the smugglers.

Handlebar Moustache, huge man that he was, giant among giants, Hercules and Samson and Mannanan MacLir, stared for a moment of detachment at the drooling creatures before him. Whether possessed by dementia or blunt reality, he fixed his eyes on the nearest creature, digested what he was seeing, reviewed in his mind all the rumors and legends and fact, then raised his sawed-off rifle and blew a hole in his own head.

Mary screamed as the body fell to its knees, and that triggered the slaughter. With blinding speed the three creatures blew toward the smugglers. In the same motion, Ned lashed out and grabbed Pearl by the shirt. He twisted in midair and shoved her at the other cadets, who were bunched in a knot and scared stiff.

Screams, human screams and the whistles of the demons erupted from both sides as a fan of blood and tissue sprayed across the deck. Ned slipped and fell to one knee. Adam fell beside him, and near them the other teens could only raise their hands to protect their faces.

A human hand, torn from its owner, skidded past Ned and struck Robin in the leg. She looked down, saw it, and erupted in a scream. She turned, looked back over Ned's head. And there went the beads and the deerskin, lashed with intestines. And there went the red leather. The creatures were ripping up Handlebar, though he was already dead.

As if caught in a nightmare, Ned turned his face up to Robin and saw the wedge of her chin, her mouth open, her stupefied eyes, and the gross, unthinkable scene as his sister reached out with her two beautiful arms and caught a sloppy mass of blood and blue tissue against her chest. She held the mass in her arms and looked down at it. Her lips curled around a silent scream. Ned tried to reach up to her, but couldn't balance himself to do it on the slick floor.

Beside him, Adam was also looking up at her, his face almost a painting.

Ned seized Adam by one arm and shouted, "Go!" and gave him a heave.

Above him, Robin somehow disappeared into the hold, in a flurry of arms and legs and running feet.

Casting one look back at the ghastly scene, hardly able to interpret what he was seeing, Ned forced his body to find balance almost as if floating above the floor. He took Pearl in one fist and Captain Pangborn in the other, and he tightened his grips, and he ran. And he ran.

CHAPTER FIFTEEN

They raced through the open hold, between the sheer cliffs of stacked containers, running blindly, without care. They might've run into anything, more of those creatures, more smugglers, into a blind alley or into a trap. Their minds weren't in charge. Like deer before lions, they just ran. They ran through a half-dozen hatches, leaping and tripping over the coamings, dragging the captain. Thank goodness Chris and Dan had come to enough of their senses to reach back and help Ned with his burdens.

They stumbled until they were gasping, and finally tumbled into heaps inside the galley. The galley was clean, spotless, gleaming, buffed to perfection by the last galley crew. Almost hospital perfect, and much too bright. Right now, they wanted to hide in a hole, not under lovely lights.

Ned pushed Pearl over the coaming and turned back, his skin crawling, to drag the hatch shut and crank the big locking mechanism. He spun and staggered into the galley.

Chris, Dan, Dylan, and Leigh . . . Stewart . . . the captain . . . Pearl and Mary . . . and over there was Robin, crouching to the floor behind the serving island, her back to him, shoulders shaking. Ned swept a quick headcount without really thinking about it. He counted colors of hair until he was satisfied he saw them all.

Mary sat shivering on the deck, clasping her knees to her chest, hollow-eyed, mindlessly gasping, "Wha—what—what—wha—what . . . what . . . wha—?"

Though she couldn't even push out the first word of her question, they all heard it complete in their heads. *What are they?*

Ned turned to the captain. For a moment they simply glared at each other in a strange depth of understanding.

"You know, don't you?" he asked. "You know what this pestilence is."

The captain lowered his chin. His brows went up. Slowly, he nodded.

"So you'd better unshackle me. I'm your only hope."

And those were his final words.

The past five minutes had been a black plague of bad news, telling them how dead they were if they didn't set him free. His litany of cold facts left them shuddering. The cadets were crumpled about the tiny room enfeebled by horror, and plucked to death by the captain's description of what they were facing, like children around that campfire, listening to that ghost story, and believing every word. For they had seen the befoulment before their own suffering eyes.

The captain knew all about the assailants. He held back nothing, for all Ned could tell, nothing. Would that he had, for the truth was that freakish. Acid for blood . . . to break prey down to their constituent parts . . . that was the job of acid. Some kind of drool that hardened into resin . . . they made their hives with it, some thought . . . little was known . . . much was rumored . . . facts were scattered, myths blooming. What were they? How smart were they? Were they ants or lions? Were they dogs? Not as smart as a border collie but smarter than Irish setters? Or were they as smart as dolphins, but acted like vultures? Cretaceous raptors or some advanced form of nature from a future yet undiscovered? The one consistency was unremitting slaughter and power beyond ken.

Shaking to the bone, Ned wiped his face with his hands and his hands with each other, trying to find some normalcy in the moment. He had kept waiting for the story to have some glimmer of hope, some key to salvation, but no such luck. Pictures swirled in his head of the barbarism they had witnessed and those the captain had described. Ships infested, destroyed. Colonies demolished, taken over, turned into malformed hives. Caves dripping with decomposition. Saliva turned into hardened resin, pressed into service as cells for living bodies used as incubation chambers. And then, what happened to those living ones. Queens and warriors and soldiers and swarms. And so much yet unknown, while the known was bloodcurdling.

"If we unshackle him, he'll feed us to them. Look at his eyes." Adam's warning came from where he was pressed back against the refrigerator, both his hands palm-flat on the cool door behind him. Sprayed with blood and panting like a racehorse, he still kept some kind of cool despite all this. "How do we fight them?" he asked.

"Fight them?" Chris blurted. "We don't fight them! We hide or something!"

"Or we escape the ship!" Leigh gasped, sucking each breath. "The life craft!"

"Do you want to go back out there?" Dylan countered. He shook his head wildly. "I'm not going! Not me!"

"Walk through the whole ship to the pods?" Chris echoed.

"Not me," Stewart mumbled, "not me, no way, not me, not me . . ."

"You can't hide from them," Pangborn said. "They've broken through every barrier ever put in front of them. You can't camouflage against them. They already know we're here. They sense body heat and movement. We're the only warm bodies aboard. No matter how smart you think you are, you can't turn into reptiles and you can't hold still enough. You have to unlock me right now. I have to fortify this ship. I'm the only one who knows how. I can save all your lives."

"He's not interested in our lives," Adam warned. "He's out for himself."

"Stop it, Adam," Ned said. "Hold your luff."

"My *luff*?" For the first time, a tint of anger colored Adam's tone.

The captain maintained his dignified sangfroid. "If any of those people are still alive, they're well-armed and trained in the use of their weapons. We need to find them and put up a united front."

"You mean you'll unite with them," Adam said. "What does that mean you'll do with us?"

"With *you*? I haven't decided. These other kids haven't done anything. They're innocent. You're the one who took this upon yourself. All of you others, you're not in mutiny . . . not yet. Not if you untie me and let me get about my business of defending my ship. What do you say, ah . . . sport?"

He held his shackled hands out to Stewart.

Stewart, ever complacent and cooperative, was clearly drawn to do as the authority told him.

"Stewart," Adam broke in, using a special tone, "he's stirring up trouble among us. A good leader doesn't do that. He doesn't even know your name."

Pangborn let his hands drop. "You're a piece of work, boy."

"If there are armed people still alive," Dylan quietly uttered, "then they'll be on our side against those things."

"Or they'll be on his side against us," Adam countered.

Chris spat, "That's crazy!"

"No," Ned said, "it's not. Think about it . . . why would we have not heard of these people until now?"

Mary held out a hand. "Do we know *everything*?"

He ignored her. "Leigh, there was no itinerary for this meeting with this other ship that had no name?"

Leigh nodded her head, with a loosened cornrow starting to unbraid right over her eyes. "True . . . Dustin was teaching me the nav computer and the rendezvous with *Virginia* was on it, but nothing else. They're coming from down there." She pointed with the confidence of accuracy at the deck and a few degrees to her side.

"How do you know that?" Ned asked.

"I can see space in my mind, in three dimensions, as deep as astronomy has mapped it. If I know the relative attitude of the ship, I'll know where everything else is."

"Really . . . " He moved toward her. "Where's Earth?"

"There." She pointed backward, and slightly up, as if her finger could extend through the ship, through space, past every spatial body in the way, through every cloud and nebula, through all the stellar dust, to the one planet to which they were eternally tied.

"Zone Emerald."

"There." She pointed up in front of her, at the ship's chronometer embedded in the wall.

"Alpha Negris," Dylan challenged.

She pointed over Ned's shoulder. "I'm never wrong," she said without a bit of arrogance. "They've tested me. I just look at a topographical design and I'm all set. They put me upside down in a deep diving bell and I still knew where every city and navigational marker was on the whole ocean around me. I knew the underwater rock formations and the trenches and everything. They put me in the Andes and I guided them out without a map. I've known the universe since I was twelve."

"Is that the truth . . ."

"The ship?"

"Yes." She said it in a way that made Ned understand that she could go through this ship as accurately as a rat who had been living here all its life. She knew every conduit and duct, every ladder and crawlspace, because she had simply looked at the design diagrams on the computer.

"Say so . . ." he murmured in admiration.

Adam, tired of the brain tour, held out an accusing hand at the captain. "Haven't you figured out what the smugglers were here to 'pick up'? Those things are here because of him. This is his little extra 'delivery.'"

"What's that mean?" Stewart asked.

"It means hired guns," Adam said. "Mercenaries. Killers."

Ned buried a shudder and took a leap. "Means smuggling."

Dan appeared in the middle of the argument. "Smuggling what?" When Ned and Adam simply glared at him, he came to his own conclusion. "Aww—aw! Those things? We're on a bloody ship smuggling bloody space wasps? Aw!"

He whirled without destination.

On the floor under the counter, Dylan banged his head against the metal counter. "We're in *such* trouble . . ."

"Is that true?" Mary gagged. She looked at Pangborn. "Did you know they were here?" She began sobbing again. Her face dropped between her knees, showing only the blood-crusted blond hair at the top of her head.

"Adam—" Ned turned to him squarely. "Tell me again that we can't wake up Dana. We need to wake her up so she can make the decision."

"She'd be with us!" Stewart said. "He pushed her around more than anybody else!"

"But she's an officer," Dan protested. "She's sworn to chain of command."

Chris shook his head. "How does that change when we tell her about those things and those people?"

"Maybe she knew!" Mary raised her head, wide-eyed. "Maybe she was with him all the time!"

"You don't need any other adults," Pangborn said. "You only need me. It's time to let your captain take over."

Adam rolled his wavy head toward Ned. "If you wake her up early, you could kill her."

"How long does your hibernation last?" Ned pressed on.

"Different for each person. Body mass, metabolic rate—"

"There's no way to reverse it or cure it . . . accelerate it?"

Adam paused to think. "I . . . don't know."

"Sure you don't!" Leigh bitterly accused. "Gosh, there's a shock! Something he doesn't know!"

"It's not approved yet," Adam told her.

"Perfect! You fed narcotics to the people taking care of us and you don't even know whether it'll ever be approved for human consumption?" She stood up abruptly, whirled on him, and with her short powerful body kicked him in the shin.

"Hey!" Adam crumpled in pain. "Why do you need somebody else to make a—"

"Because this isn't our ship!" Ned erupted. "It's not our call! We haven't the authority or the . . . the training . . . or any experience!"

"Look, *Mank*, I know you came here with no talents, but don't lump the rest of us—"

Ned drew a sharp breath in frustration. "Must you be so against the throw? Always putting a poor mouth on things!"

"Arrogant!" Leigh shouted. "Ned's right, Adam! Your talents, my talents—what good are they now? Against those — those hornets!"

"Hello?" A timid voice came out of a cabinet and nearly set the group to quaking.

"Oh, God!" Leigh bolted out of the way, shocked.

They froze as the cabinet door opened. Crammed into a pantry, out peeked the cook's funny face, capped with a soup pot on his head.

"Spiderlegs!" Mary gasped. "You're all right!"

Along with Chris and Dylan, she pulled him out of his hiding place. He elbowed his way out, because his hands were occupied. In one he held a huge rendering cleaver, the old-fashioned kind that Ned had seen used to butcher deer, and in the other he held a canister clearly marked "BAKING SODA." The round little man blinked his black-dot eyes at them. "This is terrible, just terrible! I saw 'em. Did you see 'em? They dint see me, but I saw dem! They got acid inside dem! Like real stomach acid, like the bad kind of stuff, eats through everything! Did you see 'em?"

"We saw 'em," Adam mumbled. He seemed annoyed that the disturbance was only the cook and not something more important.

Spiderlegs trundled around the galley, holding his cleaver and his baking soda can, agitated and waiting to be told what to do. "Good kids, good kids, don't worry . . . captain's here . . . Captain, you here?"

"I'm here," Pangborn said.

Spiderlegs looked at the manacles. "Playing a game?"

"Yes," the captain enticed. "It's a game. We're trying to see who can unlock these shackles."

"Oooh! I could try!"

"Yes, you could."

"Not yet," Adam broke in. "It's not your turn."

Spiderlegs wasn't exactly happy, not being childlike enough to forget what he had seen, but he was agreeable. "Oh, okay . . . Whose turn is it?"

Realizing this could be an unknown factor in the captain's play for power, Ned stepped between Adam and the cook. "We're still deciding. Do you have any snacks for us?"

"Um, sure . . . what's your name again?"

"Ned Menzie."

"I'm so bad wid names! I'm so dumb!"

"You're not at all. It's just a funny name."

"Nedmenzie, Nedmenzie . . . Uh, sure, I got graham crackers and I got some fruit and I got some plum preserves. Maybe I got wheat bread . . ."

Ned took the moment to rub his arms. He'd taken a sudden chill out of nowhere, even after the running and the rush of his blood through his veins. He knew the creeping cold was pure fear and couldn't banish it. He thought himself a perfect coward to be so craven and shuddering. Yet, what more could be asked? They had been pitched into a pot with their tormentors, and now the tormentors ran the show.

What could be done? How could such a pestilence be fought?

He heard then a tiny noise, a small whimper as thin and different to this place as the call of a curlew way on a hill. It cut through his foul thoughts and brought him back to himself. Where was Robin? Somehow he knew to look for her.

She was there, in the corner by the ovens. Perhaps there was residual warmth from the last meal.

"Robin?" He moved toward her.

She was softly sniffling, huddled about herself with her back to him, her legs bent under her and off to the side, as if she were one of the mermaids holding the bell. The little mermaid on the rock at the water's edge.

He came slowly around her, kneeling as he moved, thinking to comfort her with empty hopes and reassurances he couldn't support. Would he be able to protect her from the fear? And from the coming struggle and its dim end?

But another sound startled him and he flinched and blinked. A tiny, breathy sound, like a newborn lamb. Imagine his surprise, his amazement, to find his sister holding not a lamb, but a tiny bloody baby.

A human baby, meek and sweet, sucking on its nut-sized fist. Its umbilical cord was still attached, torn half-way down into blue shreds and the remnants of the amniotic sac still entangling the little bunched-up legs. He had seen it a thousand times—on farm animals.

"Souls . . . what am I seeing . . . ?"

Robin's gentle eyes turned up to meet his, soggy with tears and heavy with their new burden.

"They struck her about the throat . . . she tried to protect herself, but they ripped her open like a spit . . . all of a slap she was almost in half . . . and they threw the poor wee thing. They just lashed him out . . . it was terrible in this world to see . . ."

Ned's soft murmur rang in his own ears. "Oh, my soul . . . a changeling."

He stared at the moist wiggle, and watched his innocent sister grow a decade older before his eyes.

Soon he sensed other presences, and noted that the cadets had begun to gather around them, to bunch around and look at the unexpected and bizarre miracle in Robin's arms. With the wonderment immediately came the realization that they had another very big, very small problem.

And over there, the captain shook his head and seemed troubled for his own reasons.

Ned put his hand on Robin's shoulder and gazed down in abject wonder at the child who seemed so peaceful in his sister's arms. It was a little boy, growing more rosy and pleasant by the second. He had lovely black curls and might have been of some darker race. Ned couldn't tell.

A handsome child, conceived in the velvet folds of space, born of the ship of dread.

CHAPTER SIXTEEN

"Jee-ach . . . that was mortal . . ."

Exhausted, Ned slipped back to sit on one of the little stools. He fought valiantly to digest everything that had transpired in the last few minutes, for the universe had turned on its side. Everything that could change somehow had changed. There had been confusion, mutiny, invasion, death, and birth. Shakespeare, move aside, for we are here.

"You know what this is?" he muttered. "This is a teen slasher flick. I'll go to the attic, you go to the basement, and you girls strip down to your underwear."

Leigh pressed her hot face with her hands, but she was miserably laughing behind them. Dan shook his head and Chris dissolved into a mix of chuckles and trembling sighs. Mary's eyes were ringed with red, but she gazed at him and swallowed away her sobs.

Dylan, hunkered under the counter, reached up and slapped Ned a low-five.

Adam looked at Ned as if the words were a marvel in the wilderness. Somehow Ned had taken them to the next plateau, beyond initial shock, and to something else, a new stage of realization and grappling, to a point where they began to think about what to do, not what had been done. Ned had seen in his life many animals frightened nigh to their own deaths, only to suddenly move past their fright, rather to die in the grapple than to submit. Humans too. In all of history the story was told again and again of overcoming and rebounding. Could they rebound? Or were they trapped in a bottle dungeon with no rope?

"It's a medieval passion play," Adam contributed, "complete with dragons." He paused, looked at Pangborn, and added, "And ogres."

Ned almost said something to Adam, almost spoke, parted his lips to begin to speak. Instead, he pushed off his stool and paced, trying to keep things moving. "How can we fight them?"

"We can't," Leigh deduced wisely. "We can't. No way. We can't fight. Not those things."

"Nothing can fight those things!" Stewart gulped.

"Nothing can fight them," Pangborn echoed.

From where she stood with her miscreant frame braced against a vegetable crisper with both hands on the handle, Pearl said, "I hear a noise."

Leigh, her superior mind absorbing all the facts and dynamics and everything she had heard, glared at Pangborn. "How could you do this?"

"It was just a matter of shifting containers," he said. "Just a business deal. I don't pass judgments on what I ship. That's for the authorities and the politicians and the priests. The xeno-morphs were supposed to be embryos in cryo-stasis. Completely non-animate. There was no danger at all. Somebody must've opened the container."

"Didn't you factor in that possibility?"

"We never open containers. Why would we?"

"Pointless conversation," Adam commented. "It's done."

"Aye, it's done," Ned said. "The sun's gone down on it and we have to think what our options are. How many dragons are here? Can we track them?"

"There's a funny noise," Pearl insisted.

Dan spoke at almost the same time, bowling over her attempt. "You mean to fight 'em?"

"Every living thing must fight for its own life," Ned told him. "We can't live for each other nor can we die for each other. But together, we can fight full fetch."

He paced to the freezer and back.

"They're animals . . . nothing more. Fancy ones, aye, but animals nonetheless." He turned to Captain Pangborn, to the man he truly did not know whether or not to trust for anything—for help, or for answers. "Can we track them? Have they ever been tracked before? How can we count them? How can we know what we're up against?"

Pangborn sniffed and gazed at him. Would he answer?

He then swallowed as if he'd just taken a drink, and relented. "The ship is rigged with motion sensors. They're top-of-the-line. Brand new. They're a safety feature to find injured crewmen or . . . illegal boarders."

"That's smashing!" Dan cheered. "We've got something!"

Glimmers of hope shined in many eyes.

"I hear a noise."

"And how do they track us?" Ned persisted. "Has anyone ever known?"

"They got no eyes!" Spiderlegs declared. "Nothing up there . . . nothing! I din see no eyes at all!"

"Does that mean they're just big insects, working on sensors?" Leigh contributed.

"Why don't we have these on Earth?" Ned asked, but he was only thinking aloud. "Why aren't there giant insects on Earth?"

"Because of the gravity," Adam said. "Nature decided a long time ago how big things could be. Giant bugs would be crushed by gravity. They're not built for it."

"Big help," Chris grumbled. "It's not like we can use that . . ."

"They display animal traits," Ned said, staying with the only line of reason that made sense to him. "They're ruled by instinct, not reason. We can deal with them on that level. We can win against them if we play by their rules."

For a moment there was silence, a contemplative pause while every person in the room rolled that idea around inside the mind.

Adam, still limping, moved closer to Ned and peered at him through narrowed eyes. "How do you play by an animal's rules?"

Ned turned to him, but as he turned something came into his periphery. Pearl. Her expression was dithery, but not quite the human vacancy she was assumed to be.

Had she said something?

Yes, she had.

Adam started to move. Ned put up a hand and stopped him. Instead he stepped to Pearl and asked, "What did you say?"

Her crackpot eyes shifted back and forth between Adam and him. "I hear a funny noise."

"What kind of noise?" Dan asked. He moved in between Adam and Ned.

"Squeaky."

"Where's the terminal?!" Dan spun around, scanning the galley, and found the computer terminal that linked the galley with the rest of the ship. He leaped to it and began hammering on the keyboard. The monitor flickered to life, with a search program that shifted almost instantly to a bandwidth display.

Ned and Adam crowded behind him.

"There it is!" Dan crowed. "Right there . . . two hundred twelve kilohertz. Plain as day! Higher than any Earth life-form.

Higher than beluga whales. The blasted wasps are communicatin' with each other!"

"Pearl, can you hear that?" Ned asked.

She nodded.

"You mean they're talking to each other?" Leigh asked.

"Not talkin'," Dan said. "Communicatin'. It's not language. It's more like . . ."

"Signals," Ned said.

Dan looked at him. "Well . . . aw' right, yeah. General sorta alarms and like. Calls. Summoning. Kinda like we use signal horns at sea."

"Animals make simple signals," Ned said. "They're not building bridges, so they don't have much to say. So it could be a call, to come . . . or a warning, to run away."

"How can we use it?" Adam asked. "And why can *she* hear it?"

The answer to that was both obvious and unhelpful, Ned noted as they both watched the kilohertz level on the screen go flaring toward the high end.

"Dan," Ned began, "can we artificially replicate—"

But rude interruption clattered at the outside of the galley hatch, sending everyone into a seizure.

"Open the door! Please, open it! Open it, pleeeeeze!"

The shrill scream pealed through the closed hatchway. Over and over the voice of one of the smugglers burned through the metal, actually causing the cabinets in the galley to ring.

The teenagers huddled, shocked, confused, and leaderless. Robin coiled her arms around her foundling and began to weep against his tiny rose-petal face. Her terror had given way to resignation. But abruptly she raised her head again, hearing another wail from outside. "My soul, it's one of the women!"

Ned heard the pounding and the screaming from outside the galley, and his heart tore in half. But something else happened to his brain. Of course it could only be the other woman, the Nordic one. She had some kind of an accent, but Ned couldn't place it. Dutch, maybe.

He shifted his eyes to Adam and the two of them engaged in a moment of resolution. Adam was somehow still himself, still assured and annoyed by life, yet there was something else now.

The cries hit a higher pitch. "*Open! Open the door! Open—God, open it! Help! Please help! Open! Open! Open . . . open . . .*" And the sounds of pitiful sobbing.

The pounding began to weaken.

"Do something . . ." Mary suffered. The noise from outside crushed her.

Dan broke toward the hatch.

Ned snatched out to stop him, swinging him around before he reached the hatch.

"Leave off!" Dan wailed. He shook his arms until Ned was thrown off.

The captain snapped, "Don't open it, you idiot!"

"This is wrong!" Chris countered. "We can't leave her out there!"

"You don't know these people."

"Do I have to?"

"*Pleeeeze! Open! Open! Begging you—open!*"

"Hell, yes," the captain said.

"You're sick!" Dan yanked away from Ned and plunged for the door. "Chris, get ready to pull her in!"

Ned moved toward them as Chris pushed past him and crouched near the hatch and Dan took the hatch lock. "Dan, I don't know . . ."

"Shut your trap! You're not the boss!"

Dylan backed up and ducked under the serving counter. "Captain?"

But Pangborn ignored him. "Don't open it."

Too late, for Dan was already spinning the handle and the oblong clanked free of its housing. He pulled back and swung it open.

And suddenly the captain and Ned were the two smartest people in the universe. At first they only saw the blond woman, her hair half torn from her head, her slashed face turned upward, imploring, as she lay on her stomach, pressed to the deck by a long clawed foot.

Ned dragged Dan back and scrambled to pull Chris. The boys didn't resist, but tumbled against Ned's legs. He rolled them behind him like beach balls.

At first it was just the leg, and behind it a swirling tail, but then the creature hunched its body and looked inside the galley hatch at them. Its head was too big to come in level, so it bent deep, spread its teeth, and drained its gluey resin all over the deck.

A scream rose from Mary. Leigh made a noise just as awful, and Adam put his hands out but couldn't move. Adam's mouth fell open in surprise and his eyes were wide. Apparently even he had not expected this.

Staring upward, Ned shooed the others behind him, but he refused to give ground. The breath of the creature ruffled his hair as it closed its clawed foot on the Nordic woman's spine, one of its claws cracking into her skull. One second alive, the next dead, she went limp with one hand reaching through the hatch.

He sensed the other cadets and the captain shifting back into the depths of the galley toward the freezer, but that would only be another trap. Ned used every shred of experience he'd ever gained in his rural life, operating on instinct almost like an animal himself. He flared his arms out at his sides to appear bigger and didn't flinch or even blink.

"Neddy!" Robin's shriek tore through his head, just as he expected the dragon's claw to tear his flesh.

Without looking at her, without distraction, he simply snapped his fingers to silence her.

The noxious creature parted its silvery jaws and hacked in her direction.

For the second time in half an hour, Ned held his ground.

From his left, he caught a movement in his periphery—a short, round movement, and an arching object. Spiderlegs stepped out from the food prep area, rotated his short arm, and flung the canister of baking soda at the grotesque head just as it came through the hatch. Baking soda fanned out from the can in midair, made a rather elegant beige snowstorm, and went *boof* all over the alien's excuse for a face. The can struck it in the snout and went ringing across the deck. *Tang tang tang rattle-click.*

Startled, the creature snapped its jaws shut and shook its head, scraping its skull case with both prehistoric paws and brushing at its exo-skeleton—the bones were on the outside, weren't they?

Without a pause, the brave little cook spun forward on his short legs and heaved the butchering cleaver with quite a lot more strength than he appeared to have. The heavy cleaver, big and solid and perfectly formed for its task, turned one perfect revolution and *crack*—embedded itself in the creature's skull case.

The animal shrieked and rotated its great head as green acid spurted from the wound, but the cleaver was sunk in mighty well and acted as a plug.

But not quite—the baking soda stuck to the creature began to sizzle and bubble, reacting with the acid! What was happening? The acid was neutralizing!

The animal shook its head again, disoriented. It opened and closed its claws, looking for the utensil embedded in its head, but it couldn't find the wound. Still, it wasn't going down. It staggered a bit, but wasn't wounded enough.

And that might be worse, for now it was wounded and angry.

Standing between the huge pest and everybody else, Ned gave himself up for dead, for the second time today. He would at least not die for nothing. He fixed his eyes on the place where the creature would've had eyes in any other incarnation, and took a step forward.

"*Neddy . . .*"

Somehow over the stridor of the furious creature, he heard his sister's whisper. He wanted to speak to her, but this would have to do. His posture alone would have to communicate his intents to her, his resolution, and his goodbyes.

At least he might be able to back the animal out the door. Somebody would come behind and close the hatch. *Do it, Adam.*

He took another step. The hornet, still shaking off the baking soda, trying to scrape its head clean, stumbled backward off the body of the blond woman. Its claw caught in her neck and dragged her back with it, finally shaking free as if she were a kitchen heap.

Ned put his hand on the hatch, his foot on the coaming—

"Hi! Hi, bird!"

Pearl!

Under his arm she went, quicker than he had ever seen her move.

"Hi!" she rasped again, beaming up at the creature and waving her silly hand. "I heard you singing!"

Ned tried to bring his arm down on her, to coil around her and drag her back, but the alien flared and hissed and snatched out its hand to slap him away. He flew back, right off the deck, and slammed into Adam. The two of them crashed backward into the pantry door.

As they struggled to sit up, pulling at each other for support, the black death pivoted its spined head at Pearl. In a single fluid movement it wrapped its hands around her—and they engulfed her whole torso. She floated up off the deck like a birthday balloon.

"Pearl!" Ned cried out. He pushed his hands and heels into the deck to force himself up.

"No, Ned!" Adam clamped his arms around him and held him down.

The last thing they saw of Pearl were the soles of her orthopedic shoes and her white calves disappearing in a flyblown twist. The last thing he heard was the husk of Pearl's delighted laughter fading down the corridor.

On the deck, all that remained was a puddle of bubbling baking soda as it cooled the rage of nature's poison.

CHAPTER SEVENTEEN

"It took her!" Robin cried. "It took her!"

"What does that mean?!" Leigh also bellowed, agonized.

As Dan slammed the hatch shut and spun the locking handle, Ned twisted around as he lay on the deck and shouted at Adam. "Why did you stop me?! I could've—"

"You could've what?" Adam countermanded.

"Why would they take her instead of killing her?" Leigh asked, dizzy with empathy. "What does that *mean*?"

Captain Pangborn, now with an edge on his words, said, "It means she'll be turned into a human cocoon. They'll beat her and break her bones and condition her until she's barely alive, but still alive. They'll find one of their eggs, if they have them, and the egg will open up. From the egg comes a—"

"Stop!" Ned pushed onto his feet. "Stop frightening them on purpose!"

"If you don't have all the facts, you're not grown-ups. You're just children being soothed until you die."

Favoring his right leg where Leigh had kicked him and on which Ned had landed after the alien batted him away, Adam struggled to get to his feet. Supporting himself on the counter's edge, he moved toward Ned. "Okay . . . how *do* we play by an animal's rules?"

Taken aback, Ned blinked. "I thought you were challenging me."

"No, I was *asking* you."

"Why did the baking soda bother it?" He turned to Spiderlegs. "Mr. Follo, how did you know to do that?"

Spiderlegs shrugged his sloping shoulders and flattened his lips. "Just . . . makes sense, Nedmenzie, every cook knows that . . . pour baking soda on a grease fire and all . . . neutralize it and all . . . pretty simple—"

"Simplicity from a simpleton," Pangborn derided.

Adam spoke up again. "It works because everything reacts with *something*. It's a base. A base is acid to acid." He looked at Ned. "How did you make the dragon back off?"

Ned fought to clear his spinning head. "I . . . I just treated it like the wild thing it is. Everybody who grows up on a farm knows you never back down from a charging animal."

Adam smiled at him. "Looks like we found your talent."

Unsure whether this was a compliment or another snotty remark, Ned said nothing.

But Adam was smiling at him, not something Adam did very often, or at least hadn't done so far.

"Everything backs down from these things," the captain bluntly told them, deliberately diminishing Ned's accomplishment. "Everything in space or anywhere always backs down from these things. Eventually, they kill everything around them. It would've killed you."

"Oh, it was going to kill me," Ned admitted. "But it was already confused by Mr. Follo. I was just hoping it would kill me in the hall after the door was shut and you'd all at least be safer."

Overcome, Robin ran to him, holding her foundling in one cradling arm, and throwing the other arm around Ned. He clasped her tightly in gratitude, though he had little reassurance to give. She smelled of birthing fluids and birthing bloods, like the ewes at the farm after lambing.

"Oh! Oh!" Spiderlegs began. "Know what I got? Not gonna believe this! Just look what I got!" He spun to the other side of the galley and clicked open a narrow spice cabinet. He pushed the button at the side of the cabinet, and the innards of the cabinet rolled through shelf after shelf, bringing him the one shelf he wanted. He reached as deeply inside as his stumpy arms could manage, and drew out a plastic packet about the size of a bed pillow. It flopped in his arms, loaded with containers of different sizes. "Baby food!"

"Baby food?" Robin turned. "But this baby is—too little."

"I got it!" Spiderlegs dumped the plastic bag on the counter and zipped it open, and pulled out several baby bottles and cans of powdered baby formula. "See? It's breast milk! Condensed breast milk!"

"Bless you," Robin whispered. "You blessed man . . . please, let's feed the poor thing!"

"What's baby food doing here?" Mary asked.

"This ship is a contained city," Pangborn said. "We've thought of everything. More than you could ever think of."

As Robin moved away from Ned toward the counter, Ned was left once again with his troubles, and the burden of Adam's lingering question.

"We can't hide . . . we can't camouflage ourselves from them . . . it seems they go after us because we're alive and they know it. What we need is . . . to hide out in the open."

His words floated about for a few moments on their own. Adam, Dan, Chris, Stewart . . . Pangborn and Leigh and Mary

. . . they all watched him, their clever minds toiling to discover some sense in what he had said.

It was the captain finally who spoke.

"How?"

"What's your next move?" Pangborn asked.

"I'm going after Pearl."

"What!"

"I'm going to rescue her."

"Rescue *her*!" Adam echoed.

"Yes."

"Are you nuts? She *belongs* with them! She's a mutant, a deviant, a pink elephant! She should've died in infancy! Maybe this is just nature correcting its error! Did you think of that? Why would you give up your life for that aberration who's doomed anyway?"

"That's wrong to say about her," Ned told him sharply. "She's one of us. She's a person. She's not a throwback and she's not an error, and I'm going to try." He swung away from the distasteful thought of abandoning Pearl to that vile fate, and faced Pangborn again. "It could've killed us all, but it took her and went away. Did it know we were a group? When it's solitary, does it tend to hide?"

Pangborn seemed somewhat amused by the questions, but he was also thinking about answers. "They've been known to hide . . . and when they're in groups, they charge."

"What does that mean?" Leigh asked.

"It means preservation," Ned told her. "It means individuals don't matter to the group, but the group matters to the individual."

"That's our weakness," Adam added. "Individuals matter to us."

Leigh shot him a withering glare. "Which individuals matter to you, except you?"

Ned kept to his own point, and spoke again to the captain. "How can I count them and track them?"

Pangborn shed the initial shock of that idea, and then laughed. "Oh! Okay! Sure, why not? Over on that monitor, call up the ship's mainframe and go to the protocols for emergency search and rescue. Go ahead. I'll give you the codes. Go ahead."

He talked them through it, being surprisingly cooperative, teaching as he went, correcting when necessary. Ned noticed as he learned that if Pangborn had wanted to be a better person, if he liked other people more, he would've made an exemplary instructor. He was patient and careful, and by the time he was done, they had some answers. After a while, they were looking at a top-down schematic of the ship, with little dots of indicator lights, some yellow, some orange, moving about like ghosts on the beautiful picture.

"There are a total of twelve moving bodies out there in the ship," Pangborn finished. "There are a total of sixteen living things, if you add the members of the crew you've put to sleep. You can see that even though they're not moving, the sleeping crew is marked by these heat registries."

"Are these animals warm? Will we know where they are if they stop moving?"

Pangborn shuffled back from the learning station. "I don't actually know that. Never planned on dealing with them. The computer may not be able to register accurately because it's never encountered those animals' body types before. It sees motion and heat. They might have something it doesn't see, or it might register something we don't know they're radiating. I just don't know. Surprise—we don't have all the answers. And we never will."

Trying to be clear, Ned asked, "So there could be more, but they're just not moving."

"Or some of the twelve could be some of the smugglers that aren't dead yet. We only know three of Detroit's crew are dead for sure. There were a lot more on their ship. We only saw seven."

"How many are there on his ship?"

"He doesn't report to me, sport."

"So we could be dealing with twelve monsters, or only eight."

"*Only?*" Mary repeated sarcastically. "*Deal* with them? How can you *deal* with them?"

"We could kill eight of them, and not know there are four more," Chris pointed out.

"Do they breathe?" Leigh asked, her quick mind reeling. "If we hang one by the throat, will it die?"

"What about a vacuum?" Steward asked. "No air?"

Dan snapped his fingers. "Or high pressure!"

"High pressure would kill us too," Adam told him.

Pangborn snickered. "You'll never be able to kill eight of them. You'll never be able to kill *one* of them."

"Are you saying no one's ever won against these animals?" Ned challenged. "Are you flat-out saying that? Because that's the same as giving up and I don't think I'll have that!"

Maybe the captain was thinking about lying, about inventing some story that put him in charge, but he was still leg-ironed and shackled at the wrists, and he measured that in, too.

"No, there've been wins," he admitted, "usually at great cost. One or two survivors in colonies of hundreds of people. One or two survivors on overrun ships. They can be blown apart, we know that, with high-powered weaponry. They don't like fire, so they can be burned. They act different when there are a lot of them than when there's only one. We also know they're abnormally strong for their size. They're fast. They don't care about self-preservation because individuals don't matter. They have a hiving pattern. Everything for the hive. For the queen and the young."

"But there's no queen here."

"You don't know that. Any one of their young could be a queen. Nobody knows till she grows up. They could be forming a whole new hive right here on this ship."

"How would that change their behavior?"

"Nobody knows."

The desolate facts were an abomination, but not much help.

Adam took a grip on Ned's arm and squeezed it, and didn't let go. "How do we fight by animal rules?"

Nature's bounty flowered in the steel halls of the ship *Umiak*. Blending with the supreme technology, humanity's greatest creation, nature put forth its own greatest creation—itself.

From the bosun's observation deck, with its great sprawling slanted windows that allowed viewing of the gigantic port and starboard flank bay holds, Ned Menzie and Captain Thomas Scott Pangborn cooperated for the first time as yet this voyage. For Captain Pangborn it was a minor matter of some small interest. For Ned, it was the hour's victory.

The cadets, the cook, and the captain huddled in the bay after a harrowing sneak through the forward compartments, engulfed in the dread of which had almost peeled their very skins off. They couldn't stay in the galley—there was no way to engage their futures there, and only the hopelessness of waiting for some other twist to dictate their fates. And doing something seemed so much better than hiding.

Now they were here, locked in, betting on luck.

Well, a bit more than luck.

Below in the enormous starboard flank bay, white fog was rising. This was the steamy effect caused by dozens and dozens of cryo-containers suddenly being released from their seals. Inside, as they were programmed and engineered to do, the containers were medically inflicting consciousness upon their residents. Within twenty minutes, there was movement inside the fog.

The cadets and the captain strained to see, looking down from above. The foggy steam filled the hold, except for the top layer. The stacked containers showed like tops of skyscrapers through clouds. The remote bosun's controls could open up selected containers, and indeed that was what they were doing—picking and choosing, mostly containers on the lower levels, and there were hundreds of those.

As the steam began to be drawn out by the automatic filtration system, sucked by the fans into a processing area that would turn it into healthy atmosphere for the ship, the fog began to lower. And there was movement.

Ned pressed his fingers to the cool window. His own breath fogged the unbreakable transparency, seeming to call to its mother, the great fog in the bay.

The fog near the main deck began to stir from inside itself, puffing outward in gouts of action and disturbance. Ned almost stopped breathing.

Then, there was a face—a hint of a triangular shape. Another white puff—a tail—then more triangular faces flashing in and out of the fog.

Suddenly, there was a burst of movement. He recognized it—the herding instinct! Sheep!

He laughed in relief as an entire herd of bulky woolbearers pushed and shoved their way between the containers, desperate to follow the leader, any leader. Sheep were like that!

Hundreds of sheep poured out from the fog as it withdrew.

"Quick!" Ned called. "Open all the entry hatches to the bays so they can move through the ship!"

He had barely said it when there was another movement below.

"Oh—look! Look!" Mary gasped at his side. "Look!"

The cadets pressed to the window.

Even three stories above the deck, they were intimidated by the sight of a giant white curl of bone, as tall as one of the containers—and a second looming near it. Brown bristly fur ruffled the fog and parted it, and what rose through the shroud was enough to shock a rock. A massive blocky head and a long twisting trunk led the way of a gargantuan humped back that sloped downward to powerful hindquarters.

"It's a . . . it's a . . . mmmmm . . . ma . . . mammm . . ." Dylan's mouth kept moving after the first attempt, but no more sound came out.

The animal spotted them. The huge trunk rose, the animal came up on one foreleg, and let blare a trumpet that would've leveled the walls of Jericho. The great Northern Hemisphere woolly mammoth had proclaimed its rise from prehistory.

The sheep bolted and scattered, giving way to the impossibly huge beast coming after them. Behind the mammoth came another surprise—an African elephant placidly tracking behind it, and with the elephant an even more poignant sight—another mammoth, this one but a newborn, with a tiny twist of a trunk and quick little furry legs.

Beside Ned on the other side, Robin was bouncing on her toes with joy as she held her own little baby foundling. "Oh, a baby! A baby one!"

"A baby mammoth," Ned murmured. "Who would ever imagine such a thing? Y'just don't think of it!"

Indeed the parade of towering elegant beasts was like something in a museum or a nature special, and rare was the thought that such enormous historic creatures could ever have just been babies.

"Is the elephant its mother?" Robin squeaked, choked by excitement.

Captain Pangborn twisted his hands in their wrist-irons. "They cloned mammoths by using elephant mothers. Once they figured it out, it was easy. The animals don't care. They've got all sorts of mothers raising their own ancestors. Hell of a project."

The mammoth and its clan, including two more African elephants of teenaged years, trod groggily under the viewing area. How far would they get in the ship? No one could tell, but sooner or later the chamber hatches would be too big for them.

Not so the deer that followed—American whitetails and two bull elk! And—"

"Monkeys!" Mary exclaimed, hammering the glass with her finger at a troupe of what seemed to be spider monkeys or some other long-tailed type, stumbling about comically among the deer. One was even riding an elk, another hanging from its antlers. The elk, nosing around its new surroundings, didn't care or particularly notice.

Ned choked down his amazement and said, "Now open containers of grain and hay. You said there were food sources for all the animals."

"Yeah, all right. Sure," Pangborn said, using his manacled hand to encode the right releases into the bosun's console. "There it is . . . one beastly banquet."

They looked down as more and more animals poured out of the containers, and other containers opened their doors to reveal packaged stacks of grain. The monkeys charged in and immediately began pulling at the containers.

"They can't get the bags open," Robin uttered in empathy.

"They'll get them open eventually," Ned said. "Then the other animals will find the food too."

"Sweet of you to feed them, Mankie." Pangborn cast him a frigid glower. "You're such a soft-hearted shepherd. That'll help a lot."

"If they eat," Ned explained, "they'll be alert. We need them moving about. Dan—"

"Huh? Oh—yeah, mate?"

"That sound they make . . . can you replicate it? Talk to them?"

Dan shrugged one shoulder. "We can make the noise, but there's no way to talk, like make sense or all."

"Might it change their behavior?"

"Shor, I guess, but 'ho's to say their behavior wouldn't get worse? It's a to'al risk."

"Could we . . . call them?"

"Why," Adam interrupted, "would you ever want to *call* them!"

Ned paused. "Seems daft, I guess . . ."

"Daft twice!"

They paused to watch a muscular brace of glossy racehorses trotting past the mammoth, shying sideways as the bigger beast shifted its head to one side to look at them, bringing with it the legendary C-shaped tusks. A half-dozen Canada geese flew past the window in a perfect panic. Gazelles followed by mountain goats flooded the bay decks, dazed, and bolting. From the container opposite came a very skittish pair of mountain lions. American mountain cats, too confused to hunt, slunk out of the hold, spread flat, eyes wide and shoulders up, ignoring a dozen Texas longhorns that came plodding and thumping out toward them.

Chris followed the movements of a skittering flock of fowl, of various breeds and colors, seeking the barnyard. "Look . . . chickens."

"Are those . . . cows?" Dylan asked, craning down at a strange-looking queue of large animals with heavy bristle-wool coats in a bright white-yellow color. They had no horns, but were built almost like buffalo without the hump.

"Arctic cattle," Pangborn explained. "Years of crossbreeding, husbandry—they're bred for lighter gravity, harsher conditions, as a product source for the people living at the poles on

Emerald. Genetic forcing has caused completely new breeds. Even some new species."

Ned glanced at him. Why was he being so . . . was it 'friendly'?

Peering down at a new flock of animals emerging from a container almost under him, Adam asked. "What are those?"

Ned looked down. "Welsh mountain sheep! Robin, we're almost home, girl!"

She gave him a sad smile, for reality was only an inch away.

Adam threw him a grin. "Ned's ark."

A surge of—was it hope?—ran through the mismatched team of cadets.

Perhaps the captain sensed it.

"Not bad," Captain Pangborn said. "I have to admit, this is a not-bad idea at all. Might buy some time. If there are ten killer whales in the water, it's better to be one of ten thousand penguins. Nice going, Mank. Now, unshackle me and let's start working together."

But Adam's tone changed as he warned, "He's lying. He doesn't work *with* others. That's why most of the crew abandoned him at the first chance. The minute they weren't being paid, they left. Crews don't do that when they know their captains care about them. It's not human nature."

"What do you know about being human, you prick?" Pangborn spoke with cold confidence. "You're just a bag of potential that hasn't grown into itself. You think being smart can replace twenty years of adult life? Even Spiderlegs here is better at fighting those things than you. Know why? Because he has experience. He's just been alive longer than you and he paid attention, and that counts for something more than just brain cells. So if *he's* smarter than you, what do you think *I* am?"

Adam's jaw tightened. Something in that speech hit home. At once he was uncharacteristically silent, and the captain's words rang.

"Oh, look! Oh, God! God!"

Mary's shriek split their ears. She was bouncing in fear, pointing down to the far side of the bay, as far as they could see.

Everyone crowded all the way to her side, just as the sound of high-powered weapon fire erupted so loudly that they could clearly hear it even through the sound-dampening glass.

At the far end of the bay, four of the malevolent creatures were dragging humans along the deck, while other humans opened fire on them with flame-throwers and big rifles. At least one alien was blasted into a mash, and another scorched until it dropped the person it was dragging.

Chris pressed to the glass. "Who are those people?!"

"Must be more of Detroit's crew," Pangborn said. "They've got plasma pulse rifles and—who knows what else they've picked up in their 'dealings.'"

Ned shivered at the sight of aliens and humans engaged against each other, each working with withering efficiency. How many people, how many aliens, he could no longer tell, for the end of the bay was still foggy and now also gray with smoke from the flame-throwers. But the scene was atrocious, splayed red with blood and green with acid as the two forces engaged in their personal apocalypse.

But he knew something else. It was time to move, now—now that the aliens were engaged and distracted, and there would be the slimmest chance to get through.

Torn in two directions, he took his own fate in his hands and knew he must ask for more. He turned not to the captain, but to Leigh.

"Leigh," he began. "I'm deeply sorry. I've no right to ask . . . but I don't know the ship well enough."

Fear broke again across her face. But also there was something else. She knew what he was asking. After but a second or two, the fear gave way to determination.

She cleared her throat. "Yeah . . . okay."

And with that she moved to him as if there were two teams being picked.

"I'll go too!" Dylan bravely said. "I've got an idea!"

Ned thought about rejecting the offer, but what could he give the brave fourteen-year-old in its place? Stay here and wait until the dragons come? That was his only offering to his sister and the others, who would have no other or better fate. They might feel safe here, but it was an illusion that would thin with time.

He put his hand on Dylan's shoulder for a moment and with that gesture accepted the help.

Then he looked at Pangborn. "Are there weapons aboard? Have you any guns?"

"No, of course not," the captain said.

"Again, he's lying," Adam insisted. "Nobody does business with those kinds of people without being able to defend himself. They're pirates too, not just smugglers. He'd have to be able to stop them from killing the crew and taking the whole ship."

"You just know everything, don't you?" Pangborn sneered. "Did you also know that if I'm ever caught with heavy weaponry, I could lose my license? It's a line we walk. Yes, I have a few small hand weapons back in my cabin, but that's all the way back through the ship, past the salons, past the guest quarters, past the crew quarters, past the bosun's bay, past the flank bays, past the engine room, past the engines—do you really think you can make it that far? And if you do, you'll find yourselves holding two tiny pistols not powerful enough to give those tough hides a bee sting. So you go ahead and waste your lives trying to break out an arsenal of pop guns. That's about your speed. You think you're dealing with a couple of hyenas here?"

Ned just sighed. "Dan, check the hallway, can you?"

Dan moved to the hatch, while Chris stood by with a heavy pot he'd brought from the galley, as if that would work. Slowly Dan opened the hatch and looked out, then nodded. "Coast is clear, mate."

But now they could clearly hear the ratcheting sound of weapons firing away, the shriek of angry aliens, and the discordant noise of animals.

"Thanks," he said. There was nothing to do but go.

"Wait! Nedmenzie, Nedmenzie! I got it!" Spiderlegs yanked opened the sack he had insisted on bringing and pulled out another cleaver, slightly more gracile but just as heavy as the one he had thrown at the monster. Its curved back and perfectly balanced handle looked serious about its business. Nobody knew what he'd been packing back in the galley, but no one wanted to deprive him of whatever he thought was precious. Now they knew—he was thinking ahead, just like the captain said.

"Take this! And this!" And out he pulled another can of baking soda, waddled down the viewing bay, and pushed the cleaver into Ned's hand and the baking soda at Leigh.

"Thanks, Mr. Follo," Ned told him sincerely. "We'll remember your example."

The stumpy man nodded and smiled and nodded again, swinging his arms to display his humility.

Before a thought could invade his head about how foolish, how dither-headed he was about to be, Ned stepped out the hatch.

He turned to see if Leigh and Dylan were following, but instead found himself toe to toe with not Leigh, but Adam.

"What's this?"

Adam tipped his head. "I'm going with you."

"Why?"

"Why do you think?"

"I'm sure I've no thought."

"You'll figure it out." He started to move forward.

With a firm hand, Ned halted him. "I don't care to be pushed about at this bend in the road. If this is a way to make yourself up in the world, I've no need of you."

He'd had no problem standing up to the alien, but somehow standing up to Adam surprised him about himself. He hadn't expected those words to come out, or this resolve.

The other boy was taller, Ned noticed, but for this particular moment Adam seemed surprisingly young, unsure of himself for the first time. Still he had a bit of swagger about him and Ned came to think maybe he was going along to get away from the challenge of the captain's rocky countenance.

Adam met his eyes, but said nothing. He just shrugged his brows in a kind of surrender. But what kind?

Measuring the ups and downs of rejecting the offer, Ned came to think that more was better.

"Then swallow your heart," he said to him, "for here we go."

CHAPTER EIGHTEEN

"Okay, that's it, they're dead. Now what are the rest of you going to do?"

Thomas Pangborn spoke words right on the closing of the view bay hatch. He watched the postures of the children around him, gauging which ones he would target for manipulation. He was smarter than a kid, he knew that, and sooner or later they would turn to him, because they knew it too.

"They're not dead!" Pushing to her feet with her foster child cuddled against her youthful breast, Robin suddenly had a woman's countenance as she challenged Pangborn's declaration. "Ned knows what he's doing! He's faced down every ram, every stag, every bull, and every stallion on the Isle!"

"Good for him. This is a little different. It's time to let me loose so I can do what should've been done all along." Pangborn lowered his tone to swallow up her rising one. He'd found that such a tactic worked well. When others start yelling, get quieter. "Even if your brother succeeds in rescuing that clothespin, and the chances are microscopic, don't you think we should have another operation in action to save our ship and our lives? It won't hurt to have more, but it could hurt to have less. Don't you know anything about tactics?"

"You're not a military tactician," Stewart charged. "You're the captain of a freight ship."

"Every space captain has military background. Didn't you know that?"

They all fixed on him, rapt with doubts and soaking up what he said like little sponges.

"It's a requirement," he added now that he had them. "I wasn't just a captain. I was a colonel in the Colonial Marines."

"Why aren't you still there, then?" Chris asked.

"I had an injury. In the line of duty."

He watched their faces very carefully. The fact that he didn't elaborate with details actually worked in his favor. Sometimes less really is more.

"Wherever the aliens developed, the competition must be shocking. Like prehistoric raptors—if they were so good, why didn't they decimate everything around them? It was because everything around them was also good at defending and killing. Better than we are. Nothing else matters now. Not the animals in those crates, not the ship or anything. All that matters is survival. I'm going to tell you what survival involves. It works without resting. Without whining. Without hesitating. It works by having a leader and following orders. That's not you and it's not you and it's not you."

"What's your plan?" Chris asked.

"Who bloody cares?" Dan countered. "I'm staying right here! Ned's got a plan and I'm gonna let him have a go at it before I make any moves on my own!"

"Ned's plan is to save the girl," Pangborn said. "My plan is to save the ship. Which one does you more good?"

Mary sniffed. "What *is* the plan?"

"To get to the charthouse or the generator room and put the ship on full squawk."

Mary glanced at Chris, then asked, "What's that?"

"It puts us on a course to the first chance of rescue—the nearest established spacelane or the nearest planetary settlement with the capability to help us. The ship goes to emergency beacons, screams through space at full speed, broadcasting a mayday siren. It suggests a catastrophe has happened and the crew is disabled, but may be still alive. It says, 'Help me, help me, do anything you can to change my situation.' You think people haven't already thought of this? In case a ship is compromised and a crew is disabled? We're all set for this kind of thing. Setting the ship on full squawk also opens the *Umiak*'s control system to accept remote protocol signals. Other captains or the Guard or anybody with the right equipment can stop the ship and control it, then they can board and save us."

"How'll they know what they're up against?!" Dan bellowed.

"Stand down!" Pangborn matched the boy's tone. "Don't speak to me that way on my ship!"

The power of his presence backed the boy off, but didn't cool the heat in Dan's face. There was confusion at work, Pangborn could tell.

"They'll figure it out and board prepared for action," he added, because he liked the sound of it.

Dan digested that, then shook his head. "I'm doing what Neddy told me to do. Anybody else going with me?"

"I will," the Mank's sister said. No surprise.

"Come on."

She held her baby tightly and stood up. "Where are we off to?"

"I have to get to a terminal so I can track the thingies."

"Good luck," Pangborn said, managing not to laugh.

The two kids left and he fully assumed never to see them alive again.

He looked in turn at Chris, Mary, and Stewart. "They've made their choice, and I think you've made yours. Two plans are better than one. I mean to broadcast to the whole sector what's happening and get some professional help for us. Now come over here and unlock these manacles and let's get to work."

Ned's skin prickled as he led the way out into the twisted companionways of the ship. The corridors were darkened now, because the captain had told them to go to emergency status, red alert, and now there was no bright overhead lighting, but only a soft red glow from emergency lighting along the deck. Had it been a trick? Was he working against them? Was Adam right about him?

"It's dark," Dylan murmured. "I don't like this . . ."

"It's for our eyes," Leigh said. "No dilation. Now, shh!"

They were as defenseless as babes in a jungle. Even with their baking soda and their cleaver, and the headset Ned now wore so he could communicate with Dan, they were just naked pink things lurking about in a mine field. His stomach knotted.

They got down two levels through the maze of arteries and corridors and began to work their way aft. Leigh led the way, as bravely as could be, and she was quick too, quick with confidence in the map in her brain. Through the forward chambers, the salon, the crew quarters . . . past the sleeping adults who could tomorrow be slaughtered in their beds.

Ned adjusted the headset on his ear and whispered, "All right, Dan, you there?"

"Ned . . . Ned, come in . . ."

"I'm here!"

"Righto—we're reading you, boy."

"What've you got for us?"

Dan's voice through the mechanism was quiet, just above a whisper, so that Ned almost had trouble hearing. *"Mate, I got the high decibel level goin' down the corridor one level under you . . . moving aft . . . I'm readin' about four moving forms coupled with that noise. No . . . make it three."*

"You're sure they're the dragons?"

"Nothing else can make that noise, Neddy boy."

"Very well. Lead me on, but quietly."

"Will do."

The com unit fell quiet.

They dropped down the metal stairway that led one level down, and as his foot struck the walkway Ned was engulfed with the idea of how bad it was to actually be pursuing these creatures. Every fiber of his existence demanded that he go in the other direction. Standing an animal down was one thing. Following it into its web was another indeed.

"Pangborn's lying about wanting to help us," Adam said, keeping his voice down as they rounded a nerve-wracking corner. "He's in jail if we're rescued. He's smuggling those things. You don't think that's legal, do you? There are probably ten million laws against transporting dangerous things like that. If we're rescued, he knows he'll go to jail for the rest of his life!"

"This isn't helping," Leigh growled.

"We just have to keep him tied up. I'm saying he has a stake in making sure that he's the only one who surviv—"

Leigh let out an involuntary scream, a short high sound, and bumped backward into Ned. He dragged her back and lashed forward to defend her against the menace.

But the corridor blew wild with pink-white flapping and loud honking, not slashing and stabbing. Swans!

And no small Easter-card birds they were, but huge and dominant, their great long necks writhing, giant wingspans

spread, glowing pink in the red-alert lights, for they were as startled as the teens to have been stumbled upon. They honked and
pivoted their wings in a dramatic display, then retreated down
the corridor in the other direction, followed in a dreamlike
punctuation by three beautiful peacocks and two peahens.

Leigh leaned against Ned, one hand on her pounding chest.
"Wow! Did you see that?"

"May all our encounters be so meaningful," Ned said. "Work
the oars and let's move on."

Leigh led the way, with Ned behind her, then Dylan with
his cleaver, then Adam with the two cans of baking soda, not
at all looking as if he knew what to do with them.

Ned braced up against a wall once they rounded a second
corner and came into a small-motor repair area about the size
of a king-sized bed. "Dan! Where now?!"

*"Keep moving aft. I'm getting some sound markers ahead of you,
but can't make out the specific location. Keep your fists up!"*

"When we find her, what do we do?" Leigh asked.

"I've an idea or two," Ned said. "Mostly involving distractions and hoping for divine intervention. You ready, Dylan?"

"Just get me to the container repair zone!"

"Leigh?"

"This way!" The cornrows in her hair were fiercely delineated by the red emergency lights.

They skittered through the small-motor area and into
another corridor which bent sharply left and was crowded with
big thick-wooled sheep.

I can't get through them!" Leigh cried after trying to cross
the corridor. The sheep were up to her thighs and each one
weighed more than she did.

"Here's how to do it." Ned put each hand on a sheep's back,
knotted his hands into the wool, pushed himself up, lifted his
legs clear, then hopped over the next sheep, then did it again.

Leigh shook her hands, then embedded them into the thick wool, grabbed two fistfuls, and imitated his motions. She was not so practiced, but it got her ahead. The other two boys imitated the movements and gradually they managed to move against the stream of shifting animals going down the corridor as if through a farm chute.

Ned moved with great confidence now. He felt protected in the crowd of other mammals and birds, distractions, and with Leigh to make sure they made no wrong turns, for he knew he would be lost by now.

"Here!" Dylan shouted suddenly.

"Quiet, Hobbit!" Adam warned.

"No—here! Look!" Ducking into an indescribable tool chamber that Ned had never visited before, Dylan rushed with renewed vigor to a long rack and pulled from it a gun-like device.

"Is it a rifle?" Adam asked.

"It fires liquid metal!" Dylan shouldered the strange-looking bright orange firing mechanism with a big unwieldy tank hanging from its midsection. It was shaped like a gun, but had many tubes and hoses twisting around it, as if it were being consumed by snakes. "To make the tops of the containers magnetic! Remember?"

"No, actually, I don't—"

"Trust me!" He tucked the not-so-small metallic sprayer under one arm, crossed the narrow work area, and hunted for—and found—a hand-sized control unit of some kind. "Remote for the loaders!"

"What, exactly, do you think you'll be loading?" Adam chided.

"Let's go," Ned said. "We're doing well. Let's not fudge the luck."

He ducked out first and they crowded after him.

"That way," Leigh said, pointing through a rather ominous-looking portal.

That door had a vexed look about it. There was only darkness on the other side, no comforting red lights, but as they approached there was only a weird green glow muddling the shapes of storage units and computer terminals inside. Yes, the ugly glow came from some of the terminals in the shutdown area, which were on a holding pattern.

Ned felt over the coaming with his right toe, then his leg followed. He stepped inside, feeling Leigh's hand on his shoulder. Dylan and Adam followed. Never once in his life had Ned thought of himself as a leader, yet today he had followers. What an odd thing.

They were halfway across the room, heading for the open hatchway outlined in an orange glow at the far end, when they first heard the long low throaty growl of warning.

They weren't alone.

CHAPTER NINETEEN

Like the rumble of a timpani drum, the growl began and did not end. The warning rolled around the cadets, heating their skin with that ancient sensation all creatures recognize. *We are too close.*

Ned would be glad that none of them made a sound as they turned to their left and saw what they saw. No squeaks, no gasps, just stunned silence.

He put out both arms and maneuvered himself so that the others were behind him. He felt Leigh huddle against his spine and Dylan crouch a bit beside him and brandish his metal sprayer. Somehow Dylan managed to hold back and not open fire.

Adam took hold of Ned's arm, but otherwise froze in place, as did they all, out of instinct.

Before them loomed a monstrous form, bigger than any photo ever suggested, with a head as wide as a chair. A grizzly bear . . . one of the most dangerous predators on Earth, with claws longer than Ned's hands. In their hurry to think about the aliens, they had forgotten about something else—other innate killers loose in their midst.

The bear looked at them and shook its head in that quint-essential grizzly manner, rotating its skull quickly in both directions. Its silvery bristled neck ruff, glossy with blood, wagged in the other direction from the head, creating a storm of threat.

"Oh—I'm the world's own fool," Ned gasped. His chest seemed to collapse under the words. Why hadn't he thought of this? Why had he let so many animals go without considering this? He had tripled the danger! They were going to get slashed by a bear before ever reaching the worst of the worst.

But the bear was down on its haunches, sitting over a kill already. It didn't charge, but only snapped its jaws once in warning. *This is mine. You can't have it.*

On the deck below the grizzly was a crushed husk of an alien. The bear was bloodied from many lacerations, sitting among tufts of its own ripped-out fur, which sizzled in alien acid blood, but most of the acid had apparently gone sideways, for there was a huge jagged hole dissolved through the side of the chamber beside the bear. The alien's head case was crushed under one plate-sized paw, its secondary set of jaws lying on the deck like a tongue.

"It killed one!" Adam's whisper almost tore Ned's ear off. He moved his hand to Ned's shoulder and tried to pull him back.

The bear's paws were burning with acid, its hair smoldering.

Without speaking, Ned held out one hand toward Leigh. A can of baking soda appeared in his grip. He thumbed the plastic lid off, swung the canister in an arch, and doused the bear and the deck and the dead alien.

The acid blood of the alien immediately began to fizz and neutralize. The bear shifted back and forth, stomping the powder into the deck, and sufficiently coating its paws. At least it wouldn't have its feet worn away to stumps.

"Take an edge," Ned murmured to the others. "Sideways . . . move sideways."

He inched to his right, moving the whole group with him. They shimmied toward the other hatch and Ned pushed Leigh out of the chamber, then Dylan after. The bear shook its ruff again, then went back to what it was doing—not eating the disgusting flattened alien, but licking its own lacerated foreleg. The bear was wounded in a dozen places, but victorious and passive in its win.

Adam lingered, still watching the bear. "How did it kill one?"

"That's its job. It knows how." Taking a firm grip on Adam's arm, Ned drew him through past the bear and out the other hatch, then pulled the hatch shut in case the bear got any last-minute ideas.

They followed Leigh through two more chambers, and there she paused to point at the next-on hatchway, some twenty feet beyond.

"That's the bay! The starboard bay!"

"Yes, I can smell it," Adam said.

Indeed there was a wafting odor now—manure! And the scent of moist wool and other animal smells. And sounds, plenty of them. Baaing and honking and baying and snorting, like a farm or a petting zoo!

But there was more. Horrid shrieks and the stomping of hooves in panic, confusion—attack!

"*Neddy!*" Dan's voice came over the transceiver. "*You're mighty close to some of them!*"

Leigh got to the hatchway first and peeked in, instantly drawing back to press against a utility cabinet. "They're in there—they're in there!" she gushed, more mouthing than speaking. She was terrified, her eyes ringed with tears. She had seen more than young eyes should have to see.

Ned elbowed her aside and looked into the bay. He was chilled by the sight of a crowding herd of sheep and goats, behind them several horses and three camels, all shuffling and slamming to get away from two of the knob-headed aliens posturing over them, slashing wildly. Bloody parts of animals went flying, as if there were a food processor going in the middle of the herd, chewing up flesh and horn and hoof.

And efficient they were. Slaughtered animals skidded into containers and walkway railings, spattering like loaded sponges. The animals bolted, crowded, changed direction as a single group, as herding animals will do, and displayed the perfect unison panic of a stampede.

But there was nowhere to stampede to, and they couldn't gain much speed. They crowded up, bunching and bolting, then bunching again.

The two slick-skinned aliens had a job on their hands. Though momentarily confused, like true predators they soon bagan to focus on individual animals. They lashed out, as if in planned unison, one seizing a large ewe, the other getting a grip on a young camel. They lifted the kicking animals up off the ground, as if dancing with them.

The camel blared a terrible protest and kicked violently. Its long hind legs cracked into the alien's ribcage. The sound of snapping bones was like paper ripping. The alien hissed, dropped the camel, then drove its tail spear through the poor beast's throat.

The sheep had it worse. With a good grip provided by the ewe's thick wool, the alien held the sheep with one strong arm and pulled the animal's hind leg back with the other. It parted the primary jaws and took a holding bite on the sheep's leg. From where Ned stood, with the alien in profile, he thought he saw the secondary jaws strike forward, then twist.

He heard the sheep's leg bone snap, and the animal blared in pain. But the alien did not kill it next—which was what Ned expected. The alien now had a crippled animal in its grip, and coiled its body around the sheep, then turned and moved away from its partner with what apparently was some kind of trophy.

At Ned's side, Adam said, "They're taking some of them alive!"

Ned almost hit the ceiling, having forgotten that anyone was here with him at all. His mind was so crowded with the sight in the bay that he could almost not think at all.

"Cocooning!" Dylan said from below, peeking out between Ned's knees and the hatch. "They're gonna stick 'em to a wall, like the captain said!"

He spoke out loud, but that didn't matter. Over the blaring, baying, neighing, and roaring, there was just no reason to keep quiet. They couldn't attract any more attention to themselves than the animals were already doing.

"We'd better scat!" Ned said with a gulp. "Leigh! Come on!"

He turned back to her, inside the compartment.

She was pressed back against cabinet, pathetic in her terror, sobbing like a child.

Perhaps she was a child. Perhaps they all were.

"She's all done," Adam evaluated.

With a glance at him, Ned made a decision. He stepped back through the chamber and locked the other hatch, then came back to the girl. He looked down at her in appreciation, for this was no ordinary teenager. Leigh could see the whole celestial sphere of visible intrinsic stars and galaxies in her head, which was a wonder in itself, but this particular girl was more than the sum of her own mind. She knew how to *use* what she knew, and that, from the mundane to the amazing, was remarkable in itself.

"Stay here. Don't come out until someone comes for you. Understand? You must stay right here and not venture at all. You must promise, or I daren't leave you."

Her tear-flooded eyes shifted to him. With a little squeak that might've been "M-hm," she folded herself into the space between the cabinet and a desk, wrapped her arms around her knees, and settled in.

He took her hand and held it between both of his. "A spaceship is the perfect lost city . . . you can't get out of it. Someone will come for you."

Indeed she seemed relieved. She had hit her limit. He didn't blame her a bit and wished he too could hunker here.

"I'll lock you in," he added, and nudged Adam and Dylan through the hatch, then slammed it shut and spun the handle.

The *clang* rang through the hold, briefly startling the herds of animals, almost as if they had heard a signal bell.

And it alerted the alien. Its huge elongated head rolled upward, searching for the noise. But it couldn't tell the humans from the sheep. To it, they were all just warm bodies.

The three boys held suddenly still, grasping each other.

"Dylan . . ." Ned began.

"Closer . . . I . . . have . . . to . . . get . . . closer . . ."

How wild it seemed! Closer to that thing?

The alien scanned the shifting herd. Behind it, the horses found a way out through another entryway and disappeared. Two muscular bull elk, with antlers splayed wide, decided maybe they were horses too and trotted after them.

Overhead, the factory-like appendages of loading mechanisms and disk cranes dangled in repose, creating a contrary industrial sky for the pastoral scene below.

"Follow," Ned quickly said, and moved into the herd of sheep, aiming toward the alien. "Down!" He hunched over, so he was more the size of the sheep, which was all right since they were bulky with wool and fairly large, large enough to provide cover for the humans. He hoped the other two boys imitated his posture, for there was no chance to look back.

In the midst of the bloody slaughtering field, the one alien postured and shrieked a ghastly high-pitched cry.

All at once, they heard barking. Barking! A dog!

Ned craned about, looking for the sound. The huge bay provided a strange echo, and he couldn't—

Suddenly a quick black-and-white form lashed out from between two rows of stacked containers. As if given a divine gift, Ned stood bolt upright. A dog! Not just any average dog— a border collie! The blasted sheep must've come with their own herding dog!

Ned made a single clap of victory with his hands. "Kite!"

No, of course, it wasn't his dog from home, but larger and colored differently, large for the breed, maybe sixty-five pounds, with a long rough coat of coal black and a white tail and chest, white legs freckled with brown, and two brown ears over its black face. The brown streak from the right ear went partway down the dog's handsome pointed face and over a set of wily brown eyes. It hunched down, chin almost to the ground, freckled front paws out, flag-like tail down with the point curled up, in the famous arrowhead attitude of a border collie at work. It would make a poor pet, because it wanted to herd its people more than play with them, but there was never a breed of dog on Earth that knew and loved its job like a Scottish border collie. The smartest dogs in the world.

On any world, apparently.

The dog had its eye on the alien and was actually trying to nip and drive the sheep away from the god-awful danger! Good champ!

He made the bet of his life and shouted, "Kite! Come bye!"

The dog never even looked at him, but instantly broke clockwise around its herd. It moved too fast, though, not understanding the shape of the bay, so Ned shouted, "Kite! Steady!"

Instantly the dog slowed its pace, crossing its paws over each other to keep moving sideways, and continued to drive the sheep, doing better at keeping them away from the dragon. The dog had stopped barking, now that it had a master to give it direction, for it knew they were working together against the destroyer before it.

The unearthly beast snarled at the dog, cradling the body of the camel it had killed.

"Away!" Ned called. "Kite! Away!"

The dog, empowered by Ned's directions, did a little victory jump and circled the sheep now to the right, anti-clockwise, which caused the sheep to bolt directly at the alien. In that short moment of training, the dog had learned that "Kite" had something to do with him. That was brilliant—Ned needed the dog to respond only to certain commands, not jump every time he yelled at somebody, because he had the idea he was going to do a lot of yelling.

Kite continued nipping counter-clockwise, driving the herd, but was unable to change the herd's direction because of the stack of containers keeping them tightly together. The sheep, bunched tight, ran square into the alien and knocked it sideways.

It ran its tail into one of the rams, hoisting it high and casting the sad animal's mutilated body on top of one of the containers. But the rest of the sheep ran on through, and the alien was left standing in an empty spot, ankle deep in entrails.

"Kite, lie down!" Ned called.

The dog hit its emergency brakes and dropped flat to the deck, still as a rug. The alien turned away from the boys, looking now at the dog, which in its ultimate bravery did not flinch even a hair, though its upper lips curled in a snarl and showed its teeth.

"Dylan, now!"

With the alien distracted by the dog, its back to them now, Dylan shimmied forward through the sheep. His short stature and compact form made him the perfect bulldozer to get through the sheep without tripping. He came out of the herd just as the alien got the idea something was up.

"Take this, bitch-kitty!" he shouted, and opened fire with the metallic sprayer.

An arch of lovely shimmering liquefied metal spewed from the nozzle, making a perfect cone. It struck the alien right in the face and body, coating the dragon and the camel's corpse with what seemed like silver paint.

But it wasn't paint—it had a substance about it, a thickness and a gluey texture that drew out in strings as the alien parted its primary jaws and screamed at Dylan. The boy didn't stop spraying, but pressed even harder, until the gun exhausted itself and the alien dripped with glaze.

Dylan dropped the gun, found the utility remote he'd tucked into his belt, and started pushing buttons.

"It's not working!" Adam choked at Ned's side.

The alien shook itself, glowing like a polished jewel in the bay lights. It was enraged now, and didn't seem to care that it was coated head to foot.

"Listen!" Ned held Adam back, hearing a humming sound of electrical activity.

Overhead, one of the crane derricks began to quiver with energy. Hanging from it, the huge magnetic disk used to move containers began also to hum, louder and louder.

The alien arched its bony shoulders and dropped the camel, but the camel didn't go down. It went *up*.

Sucked upward as if into a wind tunnel, the camel's body slammed into the magnetized disk and flattened out, even its tongue pasted upward into the disk. The alien looked up, splayed its hands in fury, and screamed again.

Dylan thumbed the controls. The disk began to hum and whine with power. Two containers nearby, stacked high on other containers, shuddered and actually began to lean toward the disk.

Then the alien's feet left the ground and it was drawn upward like a shot, slamming head-first into the magnetic disk. Its spine and tail hit the disk next, then its hind legs, and it was pinned, shrieking and writhing, clawing at the magnet.

Ned and Adam raced to Dylan's side as the boy thumbed the controls again.

"Stay back!" Dylan warned. "This'll be icky!"

Ned looked at the dog. "Kite! Come bye!"

Delighted, the border collie jumped up from its lie-down position and bolted after the sheep on the clockwise again, which cleared both the sheep and the dog away from under the disk.

With his tongue poking from one side of his mouth, Dylan aimed the remote and cranked.

The humming sound intensified. The containers shuddered. The stuck monster screamed—and the metal on its body pulled all the way through to the magnet, flattening the alien as if it were a bug between two pieces of glass.

The creature's bones and tissue were crushed flat. Acid splattered out in an arch, then struck the deck and began to eat through the sheep corpses and the entrails and the deck itself.

"Brilliant!" Ned slapped Dylan on the back.

"'Bitch-kitty,'" Adam quoted. He looked at Ned. "How did you get the dog to . . . ?"

"Animals know their jobs!" Ned told him quickly. "Border collies are workaholics, by God!"

"Lucky for us—look out!" Adam shoved them both out of the way without warning, knocking them to the deck, just in time to avoid being trampled by a woolly mammoth lumbering out from the canyon between two stacks of containers—with an alien corpse skewered to its tusk!

The mammoth trundled by, shaking its great head, sending ripples down its heavy coat and the underlayer of muscle along its flank. It missed the boys by nothing more than a good arm's reach.

"Say so!" Ned shouted in amazement at the ancient animal that had so efficiently conquered an animal of the future. "Bonny thing, what a champion!"

"Watch out—there's—there are—just get up!" Adam pulled him to his feet and they sidestepped a stream of acid burning its way toward them.

"How many is that?" Dylan asked. "How many of them are dead?"

"At least five we're sure of," Ned said. "The smugglers killed two. The day's with us so far—"

"I thought it was only one."

"No, two, wasn't it? Dylan, didn't you see the smugglers take . . . Dylan?"

But Dylan's expression had changed as he stared over Ned and Adam's shoulders.

"Ah—ah—" he stammered, raising the remote in his hands, and began to push buttons, as if that would help.

A sizzling sound crawled up their backs. Feeling his midsection contract, Ned stopped breathing. Beside him, Adam began to turn to look over his shoulder.

Shock broke in Adam's eyes. He lost that steadyness he had always displayed, and began to shrink sideways.

But it was too late.

A pair of clawed hands drifted down from the top of a container to flank his face on either side.

Dylan fell back, away.

Though he tried to turn, Ned knew they were helpless, without even the spent metal sprayer to throw.

A speared tail twisted down from above and punted him in the chest, knocking him to the deck.

Then the hands closed on Adam's head and lifted him clear off the deck. He hooked his own hands over the alien's arms to keep from having his head torn off and, silent but for a tiny whimper, he was floated away.

CHAPTER TWENTY

"Adam—no!"

Ned's throaty cry had more guff in it than gasp, but he was helpless. Over his head, Adam and the alien disappeared to the top of the container, leaving only the sheer boxy wall looming over Ned and Dylan.

"Oh . . . oh, jeez . . . oh, God, jeez . . ." Dylan began to hyperventilate at Ned's side, choking on the air he was trying to breathe.

"Stop it!" Ned shouted and pushed to his feet. He grasped the other boy and shook him. "Get back to Leigh! Stay with her and don't venture out!"

"But—but—"

"You've done a hero's work! You've killed one single-handed, by God, and scarce that is! Go back, now, and get into cover and don't move! And don't let Leigh move! I need everybody safe!"

"You—you—have a plan?"

"Every animal knows its job and I know mine. Get cracking!"

"Okay!" Dylan slapped him on the shoulder and took off, back the way they had come.

With a silent prayer to any saint that might be listening, Ned steeled himself and began to climb the metal ladder on the side

of the container. What he would do when he got up there, he
had no idea. But a lie of the plan was better than dust, and he'd
spit on the beasts if he had to. Pure anger drove him on. The
idea that these innocent people could be so compromised, and
for no good reason but the captain's greed and the rancor of
cancerous brutes—why, it just wasn't fair in this world or any.
There was wickedness afoot and it had to be faced.

"Dan, still there?" he spoke into the tiny com at his throat.

*"Ned, I can't track 'em so well now! There's interference! I'm
losing touch with some of 'em!"*

"That's because they're being killed. The aliens and the
animals and maybe more smugglers—they're fighting with
each other! Can you replicate that noise they make? Can you
make the same noise in a section of the ship if I tell you?"

"It'll be the devil's own guess what I'll be saying to 'em—"

"Doesn't matter. I'll tell you when I'm ready. Then blare it
through the starboard freight bay, got it?"

"You mean to corner 'em?"

"I mean to drive them."

"Zat so . . ."

"Stand by!"

He reached the top of the container, but it was nothing but
a bare field of that same metal-sprayed stuff Dylan had used
to kill the magnetized one. Seeing that the top was clear, Ned
ran across to another ladder, this one bolted to the actual bay
wall, leading upward to other levels and other scaffolds and
other passageways. It took a leap, but he made it.

Only one level up from the deck . . . he turned to his right and
traveled the only way open to him, along a scaffold walkway over one
of the beautiful aquarium containers. He paused and looked down.

The container was open, probably by the same protocol that
had opened the food containers, but this one wasn't opened
from the end, with a ramp. Instead, the top had retracted,

leaving the turquoise water without a roof. He peered down into the colorful sprawl of a coral reef, with a thousand fish and anemones flitting and winking at him, like an inviting tropical lagoon. Indeed, that's just what it was. A piece of a lagoon cut from the Earth's shallows and venturing out into space to make someplace else beautiful. He wished more than anything to dive in for a swim. He could, right from here, as simple as that. How good that would feel against his clammy, sweat-pasted skin! To forget all this and dive in—to let himself drown passively instead of being ripped to shreds . . .

No. Keep on!

He hoped Leigh and Dylan were all right. He hoped the wonderful collie kept driving the sheep out of the bay. The dog would stay with the herd, he knew, and wait for a command.

Forcing himself to be as dutiful as new Kite, he stepped onward over the beautiful pool, and thought it was the last beauty he would ever see.

"Hurry up. Keep up with me!"

Captain Pangborn led three of the kids through the under-side of the *Umiak*. He chose this route purposefully, and they had climbed down four levels of utility ladders to get here. That Australian kid and the Mank's sister had stayed behind with Spiderlegs, and that was fine with Pangborn. He could control these three. He didn't need an audience.

They reached the lowest level and dropped into a maintenance tunnel that followed the outer skin of the ship and allowed for spot-maintenance of the hull and the inner integrity of the flank bay overhead. The flank bays were almost independent ships, stuck to the sides of *Umiak*. They could actually be taken off and tugged independently, with their own atmosphere and entirely separate systems. He remembered the segment of the educational program when Dana had explained that to the kids, but doubted they had the brain development to really understand the bigger concept. They were following him now, and that was all that mattered. The Mank and that one smartass who thought he was second-mate material were off someplace getting themselves killed, and Pangborn knew things had turned now in his direction.

They followed him because they were children. They hadn't even noticed that he could easily have done this himself. He would let the animals overrun the ship—who cared?—and he would be safe in the charthouse.

Making a sudden right turn, he ducked into a very small closet area, so small that the kids were left outside in the passage, unprotected.

"Can we come in?" the dark-haired kid asked, nervous.

"No room. Stay there."

He used a personal code to open the cabinet inside, and pulled out an extended M-41-A pulse rifle that was almost taller than Mary.

"You said you didn't have any weapons!" the girl exclaimed as he came out with the obvious lie in his hand.

"I was afraid those boys would come get it and try to use it," he told her. "They could just as easily blow their own heads off trying to fire a weapon like this without training. You don't think they'd have let me have it, do you?"

"No . . ."

"Well, I have it now and it's in good hands. Now I can protect you. Go ahead of me and I'll back you up." He pushed the girl and the tall blond kid with the curly hair out in front, then told the squirrely dark-haired kid, "You be the rearguard."

"My name's Stewart," the kid said, with an edge.

"Okay, nidbits, that's fine. My name's 'Captain.' Now shut your impertinent mouth and mind your post." To the other two, he called, "Move decisively, up there, like you mean it. Animals understand confidence."

CHAPTER TWENTY-ONE

Ned wondered what kind of death his would be. Would the shock kill him before there was pain? Or would his mind linger on the agony after his body was rendered? He had stood up to many defiant animals in his life, knowing the things that animals sense, but this hornet was alone, without its pack, and it also knew the danger of backing down. He had called its bluff and it was calling back.

He smelled the gassy stink of its breath and shrank from the soilage pouring from its jaws. In that last moment he thought the creature might feel cornered, isolated, perhaps knowing it was one of the last two dragons, and thus was even more dangerous.

He decided in that final second how he wanted his death to be, how he wanted his soul to remember, if souls remember. With the fatal courage that comes of resignation, he stood up straight and drew his last breath, and held it.

Without letting his mind get ahead of him, he surged forward, following the only track available to him, or to the alien that had taken Adam. There was nowhere else for it to go but straight down the companionway in front of him.

What would he do when he got there? When the dragons laughed at him? St. George he wasn't, and he knew it.

"Dan," he whispered urgently. "Still with me?"

There was a crackle, then a faint voice. "*Still here.*"

"How well can you work the ship's systems?"

"*Got an idea?*"

"I do, but it's dangerous."

"*I'll take it.*"

Ned ducked into a niche at a joint between two companionways and pressed his back to the wall, fighting to think. "Something Adam said. About gravity. We can't cut off the air . . . we can't freeze 'em . . . Can we . . . can we crush them? Can we enhance the pressure and smash one room? One part of the ship? Without crushing the other parts?"

"*Depends which room. Y' know, Captain said something about that—about how the bays are independent vessels, like. They detach 'em and move 'em around to other ships sometimes! Yeah—yeah, we can do that! But it'll crush anything in there—aliens, animals, you—*"

"How?" Ned panted, exhausted. "How would it work?"

"*Lots of failsafes . . . it's not easy . . . there's a reason for that—it's so bleedin' dangerous . . . wish Dana could be here, y' know—I don't know if I'm good enough . . . Ned, I could crush the whole ship. I'm just a little kid in diapers, y' know!*"

"I don't know what you are, but you're no kid. If we can use the acoustics to lure the dragons into one of the bays, can we put the gravity really high? Really high pressure, like? Just in that one area?"

"*Honest—I just dunno . . .*"

"I need you to try."

"*Glory . . . this is bad. I don't know if the hull wall can even stand pressure from inside. I might blow you and the works out into space! Ned—don't ask me, mate. Don't ask me to do that.*"

"I need you to shore up," Ned told him firmly. "This ship is heading for Zone Emerald. All your families are there—thousands of innocent people. If we don't stop the dragons here, they'll infest a whole planet. I'll die every day to stop that. Dying once is nothing. Put the oars down and let's paddle."

There was silence on the other end for several seconds. *"I . . . hear you . . ."*

"Be ready, then."

"Standing by, I guess . . ."

Ned pocketed that conversation and slipped out from his niche. He hoped he would be alive to give the terrible order to a student who had no idea what complex systems the ship would kick up against such a radical protocol. Were they smart enough? Had they learned enough in their short time aboard? Wouldn't the designers of the ship have thought of its possibly being taken over by outside forces and wouldn't they have . . . His brain imploded and crushed his thoughts as he rounded a bend and came to an intersection—and he had company.

At first he thought it was another bear or an elk or mammoth, but no such luck. There, standing in the corridor to his right, a black dragon unfolded its skeletal body before him. It rose to its full height, rolling its banana-shaped head upward to show its craggy teeth. The lips rippled and peeled back. Ned froze in place, almost in a half-stride, bracing for a grisly death and hoping the seconds would go swiftly for him.

The alien unfolded its long hands. One by one the razor claws fanned outward in a display. Behind the alien, the yellow lights from an unknown room cast a glow about the creature, almost a halo, as if it were an angel of vengeful gods.

Instinctively Ned knew he would move no farther forward. He had no magic, no tricks, no way to really stand down an animal that was determined to kill. All he had left was to make peace with himself and his gods.

"I know it's your job," he uttered, his voice ragged. "It's mine to run from you."

Perhaps he could draw it away, fool it somehow.

He began to step back . . . back more . . . retracing in his mind the route back to the bay, where possibly it would lose him in the other animals. Would it work twice for him or had he played that card?

The alien made a long *haaaaaasssssss*. The gassy stink of its breath kissed Ned's face and he shuddered from deep inside his body. Terror ate at him, rattling his knees, his shoulders until he could barely stand.

He took another step backward.

At that moment his ears were assaulted by a guttural jet-engine noise, loud and appalling and close. Hot breath poured down his collar. He twisted around, for the sound came from behind.

Almost filling the corridor was literally the last creature he might've expected to see—a massive assault vehicle in the shape of a cat. A sabertoothed cat right out of the books, right out of the stories and the tales of wilderness predation and the feverish minds of young artists who wanted secretly to ride such animals into the fires of battle fantasy.

But this one was alive—making a terrorizing noise. Ned found his head almost perfectly positioned between the cat's two famous eight-inch canine fangs.

CHAPTER TWENTY-TWO

Tom Pangborn figured things couldn't get much better for him. Circumstances had turned on their edge, but if he played it right, he'd win. The cargo might be lost, the ship in dire straits, but the crew was gone and the rest of the people would be killed, including the brat camp. He just had to make sure he was the one who survived. Terrible how he had been so betrayed, how some of his crew had finagled a deal with smugglers to bring those aliens aboard this ship. How could he have known, after all? Probably the *Virginia* had been in on the deal. By the time he spun the right stories, he'd be a hero. Insurance would move in, he would get a huge settlement, and his pick of commands from now on.

The girl, Marie or whatever, moved in front of him, with the curly-haired boy, and Stewie came behind, not saying a word. Marie was crying, making chicken whimpering noises. The curly-haired kid pulled her behind him and took the lead. *Good boy, you do that. Nobility. Cute.*

"Turn right up here," Pangborn instructed.

They had traveled almost the whole length of the ship, a six-minute walk on a good day, and they had made it in three.

"Up these steps, then left," he instructed.

The curly-haired boy said, "But there's a hatch up there!"

"Go through it."

"What if one of those things is—"

"Stick your head through the hole and look."

"That's not fair!" Marie protested. Mary. Whatever.

"Boys his age are soldiers and cops. He can handle it. Rise to the occasion, kid," he said to the boy. "You'll have something to tell your little classmates back home."

Having his manhood challenged worked on the kid. Pangborn had bet it would. The kids hadn't figured out that he was smarter than a teenager.

By gosh, the punk actually went up the ladder and slowly opened the hatch. It made a metallic crack and a slight sucking sound as it opened. Pangborn watched from the bottom, aimed his weapon, and said, "Go ahead, sport. Push it up. I've got you covered."

He didn't mention that if he opened fire he'd take the boy's head off along with anything else that was up there.

Sweating and trembling, the boy put his foot on another rung and pushed upward. The hatch made a faint creak.

"All clear," he rasped, having trouble finding his voice.

"Go on, then."

"Sweet Jesus, protect us . . ." Mary choked, halfway up the ladder.

"Don't cross yourself," Pangborn said. "You'll fall off the ladder."

She glanced down at him, but kept climbing after the boy.

Only when they were all the way up and there was no sound of slaughter did Pangborn sling his weapon and hurry up the ladder. He came out into the auxiliary staging area for the charthouse, a sort of hallway-slash-meeting room for officers' conferences. Stewie came up after him—Pangborn had almost forgotten he was there.

The two other kids were waiting at the hatch to the charthouse.

"Made it," Pangborn said. "Told you we—"

He froze in place, looking past Mary and Curly to the charthouse, dimmed with red lights for emergency vision. Out of those red lights, in a blood-colored shroud, came the blue-black head of a xenomorph.

Mary felt the acid breath on her shoulder and turned, already screaming. She jumped toward Pangborn, trying to get behind him as he shouldered his weapon, but he stuck a leg out and knocked her back toward the animal with a well-placed knee. Behind him, he heard Stewart yelp with fear. Mary's screams tore through their heads as the xenomorph snatched her by the torso, turned her to face him, and sank its claws into her spine. With one final ragged shriek, she gagged and went limp, falling backward like rag doll in its grip.

Curly made some unintelligible cry of terror and agony, but before the alien could get to him, Pangborn opened fire. On both of them.

His weapon made a deafening machine-gun ratchet noise and sprayed shells all over the forward part of the staging area, cutting the boy in half at the chest and blowing the alien's exoskeleton to shards. Razor-sharp bone splinters blew through Mary's corpse. Acid splattered all over Curly's demolished body parts as they tumbled to the deck, and were instantly eaten through to a mush.

The alien's head, severed clean from its shoulders, did an acrobatic flip backward into the charthouse, and neatly hung itself on an overhead hatch handle over the co-pilot's seat.

"Perfect!" Pangborn shouted. He stopped firing. His weapon smoked from the barrel and cast an aromatic pall through the cabin.

"Aw! Aw!" Stewart gasped over and over. "Aw! Nah! Aw, God, aw!"

"Don't whine," Pangborn said. "A fast death. S'all we can ask for. Stay there. Don't move."

Stewart collapsed into a shivering mass, his head in his hands, staring at the rather shocking bodies of his fellow cadets. Fine. He could stay there.

Pangborn stepped carefully past the sizzling mess, being sure not to get his shoes in the acid.

Hearing the boy whimpering behind him, Pangborn was driven to move that much more decisively, to put on a good show just for the hell of it. Stewart wasn't going to live to be a witness anyway, but it was fun to show off.

"Just stay there. I'm changing the helm protocol to full squawk. This'll take a few minutes, but we'll go to full speed and get to Emerald Sector in record time. They'll hear us long before that and probably send the Stellar Guard. We'll burn up every last vestige of fuel and probably toast half the systems, but we'll get help. Worth it, right?"

The boy wept pathetically and didn't speak.

He turned to reach upward to key in the long-range broadcast system, but paused. Staring down at him with its eyeless case, grinning savagely, was the disembodied alien skull. Torn and smelly, the head hung upside down from the overhead hatch handle.

"Hey, champ," Pangborn greeted. "Whose ship did you think you were on?"

With a grin, he thought about mounting the damned atrocity and hanging it in the main salon. Better than an antique bell any day!

He turned back to the controls, reveling in that image.

That's when he felt it. Something went thwap on the top of his head. He flinched and looked up at the alien head, but it was just an illusion. The thing was dead, not moving. Just his imagination.

He pulled out the command keyboard and hit a key to call up the visuals. Just as the monitor flipped to life and showed him a beautiful view of the exterior of the ship, just as he saw the big painted letters "U M I A K" on the ship's magnificent glossy burgundy hull, he felt the burning begin.

Pangborn grabbed at his head. His fingers came back scorched at the tips. He shook his head, feeling the sensation of a laser burn on the top of his skull.

He bolted back out of the chair, stumbling, knocking the alien head, finally striking the edge of the beverage dispenser with his spine.

Before him, the alien head turned lazily from where it hung on the hatch handle.

As Pangborn's skull sizzled, driving him wild with pain, and sweat broke on his face and neck, he saw the alien head leak again. A single drop of potent green acid formed in its mouth and fell to the seat he had just left. The drop burned through the leather, leaving a trail of green smoke. It burned through the chair and fell next to the deck, and began to burn through the carpet.

His body began to shudder violently as the drop of acid on his head burned through to his brain. He lost motor control almost immediately and slumped forward, seeing his own hands before him, splayed and useless. His mouth began to burn and fell open. The single drop of acid bored through the roof of his mouth and landed on his tongue. The last sensation in this universe for Thomas Scott Pangborn was the taste of alien blood.

CHAPTER TWENTY-THREE

Cats—nature's most perfect predator. From the tailless Manx housecats at Ned's farm to the lions of the Savannah, they were formed by time for the ultimate hunt. Pointy on five ends, this was the quintessence of cats, the best nature had ever done. It was big as that grizzly bear with all the power and ten times the speed, and no fear. In its instinctive memory, this cat had fought with dinosaurs. It was loaded and ready to fire.

Ned looked up, up, up into its huge square jaws, its blocky powerful head, and the neck muscles twitching and cording over his shoulders. But the cat wasn't interested in him. It stared with glowing golden eyes over his head at the dragon. Those eyes—those marvelous machines which could hunt in light or darkness, which sized up an enemy and calculated a thousand details before the strike—

Cramping bodily, Ned crouched. The sabertooth batted him out of the way like a furry toy. Ned tumbled without the slightest control, and slammed into the side wall, landing beside a pile of spark tarps left there by the maintenance crew.

On Ned's right, the dragon hissed, opened its primary jaws wide, and showed its inner jaws, but didn't snap. Not yet. On his left, the giant cat spat and snarled a bestial warning. It lowered its boxy head and the great shoulders rolled. It opened its own jaws—a stunning hundred-degree maw with the lower jaw extended and the eight-inch serrated fangs arching out forward, forty degrees more than a modern lion could open its own mouth. Ah, an historic animal built for historic prey!

Tick-tick-tick-tickit-tick —fanned claws clicked on the deck as the cat moved sideways and maneuvered into the intersection of the two corridors. The alien also pivoted to make room for itself. The cat kept its fangs toward the alien, and they began to circle each other, sizing each other up.

Ned made the near-fatal error of thinking he could move, perhaps slip out while they were so engaged, but the first hint of a step drew the cat's snarl and raised its tail, though it never took its eyes off its primary target—the dragon. Ned shrank into the crack where the wall met the deck, but his movement had triggered the inevitable.

The alien made a savage leap into the air, trying to get on top of the cat. The cat flattened, efficient eyes never leaving its target, never being fooled. But the corridor was cramped and the alien had misjudged. Its long head case slammed into the overhead support bars, which drove it down sooner than it expected.

The cat was there to catch and slash. Suddenly there was a spin of claws and talons, and an ear-splitting rass of snarls.

Now, Ned had heard cats fighting before and terrible enough it was, but this—this noise tore open the hell of all noises. The cat snatched out with both its forepaws fanned, big as car tires, and caught the alien's head and dug in as if clapping a set of concert cymbals. The alien shrieked and rattled, lashing its tail through the pile of spark tarps and taking Ned with them. He felt himself rise and turn in midair, cocooned by the tarps, his arms and legs flying. For an instant he was upside down, sailing over the cat's broad back and the knotted engine of its hindquarters. Its tail whipped up and brushed him on the cheek, almost like a kiss.

But the other tail, the bladed snake-tail of the dragon, was not so kind. The blade tore through the spark tarps, actually slicing them in midair, then grazed Ned's left arm and opened a wound from his shoulder to his elbow. He felt the sting and the burn, and got the taste of blood in his mouth. He came down on his back—on the deck right between the two animals.

Somehow the sabertooth had thrown the dragon off and they were again posturing at each other. The cat was bloodied across its neck and shoulders, but the alien was now missing an arm. Acid spurted from its shoulder joint, sizzling on the wall. Ned shrank away from it to avoid being burned, but there was nowhere to go. The sabertooth's huge left forepaw blocked his way. He was under the cat's chin. The jaws were fully extended in threat and he knew it could stab him with those fangs any time it wanted to. It was an expert at stabbing. For pound-for-pound aggression, the cat matched the dragon as evolution's finest.

The two creatures tore into each other, and there was nothing like the sound of it. Even a housecat could make a horrific noise when riled, and this cat was a mighty air horn of snarls and spits. The alien squealed its own nerve-ripping noise, and they tumbled across the corridor to the other side. Ned clamped his hands over his ears—

Then he saw a narrow slit between the tangle and the wall! He scurried past them, stumbling twice, and slipped into the next chamber, and kept running. Through a hatch, and another he jumped, until finally he came upon a dead end—the ship's lazarette. The repository of tools and miscellaneous storage was crowded to the ceiling with racks of almost anything he could've imagined that a ship might need. He'd only been here once, on a mission to retrieve a spot-welder. He moved forward toward the lazarette hatch, ducked down, and peered inside.

And here he stopped, and there they were. Before him, one of the dragons hovered, hanging from the ceiling as if that were a natural pose for it. This one had glossy bronze skin, almost green, and somehow more hideous than if it were simply black. Beneath it, Pearl sat on a box with her legs swinging happily, singing a song with her raspy weird voice.

"Playmate, come out and play with me . . . and bring your dollies three . . . climb up my apple tree . . . Swim in my rain barrel, slide down my cellar door . . . and we'll be jolly friends . . . forever more . . ."

Though her voice was a scratch and her legs swung in a different cadence, her pitch was perfect with every note—not something Ned would've expected. She even got the high notes.

"Playmate . . . come out and play with me . . ."

The freakish sight almost drove Ned shrinking. The viral savagery of the alien on the ceiling was enough to strike him to the heart and blunt his nerve.

But then, he saw Adam.

And sad it was. The other boy was a mere wisp of the confident young man who would stand up to anything and anyone. He sat on the cold deck, his white shirt now a matted gray, his wavy hair smeared with humectant, his face bruised and his lip bloody. He looked beaten, and was shaking visibly.

Ned could've backed up, but never again could forgive himself for it.

He moved forward, on hands and knees.

"Come out and play with me . . . and bring your dollies three . . . tee hee hee hee hee heeee . . ."

The creature hanging from the ceiling curved its head toward Ned. It saw him. Its segmented tail, moving like a hanging snake, made a figure eight and drifted toward him.

"Swim in my rain barrel . . . slide down my cellar door . . . oh, hi!"

His head throbbing, Ned cautiously looked up at her. She was beaming down at him with her snaggly smile. With the alien behind her, hovering over her like some kind of guardian ghoul, she was a true abomination of nature. Somehow the smile made things even more freakish.

"Hi!" she said again when Ned didn't respond.

He found his voice somehow. "Hi, Pearl . . . hi to your friend there as well . . ."

"We're singing songs. There are twenty-nine million fourteen thousand and four songs to sing."

"That'll take a while."

"This one's my favorite . . . Playmate, come out and play with me . . . and bring your dollies three—"

"Okay if I play with Adam for a minute, eh?"

"He's our audience. He likes our music."

"Sure he does." Ned gathered his guts and crawled forward under the alien's twitching lips and grinding teeth. "Adam, are you—"

The giant wasp made a sharp hiss, hunching its spine, raising those arms from which hung those hands, those talons. The teeth parted, draining liquid resin. The second jaws came out and made a *snap*.

Ned lowered himself to a conciliatory crouch. He could only hope that the creature, like all upper animals, understood the posture.

On his hands and knees now, he moved to Adam, pivoted, and crouched, then took Adam by the forearm in a bridge of simple human contact.

"You all right?" he asked.

"I'm . . . just . . . petrified."

"Makes good sense. What's happening?"

"She's been singing to me. Like . . . courting me."

Pearl smiled her bizarre toothy smile and nodded. "I want him to like me."

"He likes you," Ned told her.

Adam closed his eyes briefly, knowing that Pearl's crush was the only reason he was still alive and not cocooned or slashed to pieces. "Your arm . . . you're bleeding . . ."

Ned glanced at the wound he'd forgotten about. Blood painted his entire left arm. "Not deep. Don't worry."

Pearl played with her fingers and continued performing. "Playmate, I cannot play with you . . . my dollie has the flu . . . boo hoo hoo hoo hoo hoo . . . Ain't got no rain barrel . . . ain't got no cellar door . . . but we'll be jolly friends . . . forever more."

"How's this happening?" Ned asked again. He kept his head down, making certain not to make visual contact with the creature.

Shuddering violently, almost shaking himself to pieces, Adam struggled to answer. As he gripped the other boy's arm, Ned felt the waves and waves of terror run through Adam's body. His voice was almost reduced to nothing. "She turns off their 'kill' mode or something . . . that's how evolution happens . . . out of billions of humans, one mutant turns up different . . ."

Pearl nodded. "I belong with them. I was supposed to be one of them."

"Nature," Adam murmured, "correcting its error . . ."

Ned patted Adam's arm. "Stand by. Eyes down."

Waiting to die, Adam was all too glad to keep his eyes down.

Taking his courage in both hands and rotating to his knees, Ned rose to one knee in front of the girl.

"Pearl . . . listen to me, girl. See this hand? Take my hand."

She looked at his fingers for a moment, extended between them.

Above, the shifting alien peeled back its lips at Ned for reaching out to Pearl.

It took every thread of courage he possessed to keep his hand out, fully expecting to have it bitten off.

"Take my hand," he insisted.

"But they treat me like a queen," she said.

"I know you like them . . . they're pretending to like you. If you stay with them, what kind of life will you have?"

"I'll be a queen."

Ned shifted a little closer, locking onto her intense gaze. She was strange and drifty, but her eyes were focused and she drank in everything she saw and heard. He prayed she heard him now.

"You're not a queen," he said bluntly. "Adam's not a prince. And I, for pity's sake, am no knight. Think, now . . . think!"

She looked up at her befouled friend, or pet, or guard. "But we're different. Alone and different."

"He's not like you, girl. Nature created him to live and kill. He has no choice in the matter and wouldn't take it if he did. You . . . you're something special in this universe of animals and instinct. You're a human being, and a diamond among us. You're born to use your mind and heart. Now . . . *think*!"

She stared down at him now. A true stare—looking deeper and deeper into his eyes, not an empty stare, but one of layered seeking. As if he were a book and she were reading him, sifting the flakes of revelation.

His hand was still out between them. "You belong with us."

The scaffold of alien bones hung over them, tipping its long head and breathing through interlaced fangs. Mucus slathered freely, draining like some bizarre mountain stream over jags of rock, as it had done for eons. Its lips peeled back and it sizzled at him. It knew.

Ned's skin tightened all over his body. He kept his eyes on Pearl's, searching for that human connection.

Pearl looked down at him and raised her brows.

"I'm not stupid, you know," she said.

And she took his hand.

Despite everything, Ned found himself smiling at her.

With new respect, he drew her down from the box she'd been sitting on.

Above, the alien chafed but did not strike. Frustrated, it gnawed and rasped, not sure what to do.

Ned pushed Pearl—gently so the alien would see that he wasn't hurting her—through the hatch, hoping she didn't catch her pigeoned toes. Then he turned back and got a grip on Adam's arm, pulled him to his feet, and moved him forward.

"They'll follow us," Adam uttered.

"Pray they do."

"What?"

As they moved into the corridor, he glanced back to see the alien climbing down from the ceiling.

He herded the two others in front of him, keeping himself between them and the creature behind.

There was no sign now of the sabertoothed cat and the other dragon it had been fighting, but there was plenty of sign of the fight itself. Blood and hair and black torn skin, bits of bone and sizzling streaks of acid all over the deck and bulkheads—it had been a monumental duel for sure. He wondered which one had run and which had chased. He couldn't decide.

"Dan, you copy?" he spoke quietly.

"*I think I've got it, but I'm not sure, not sure enough to bet your life!*"

"That's all right, I'll bet my own, thank you. Turn it all on. Everything, just like we said, but only in the starboard bay. Understand? The starboard bay! Do it now!"

"*What's happening?*"

"You wouldn't believe it. Start the noise, Dan. In the starboard bay—start that noise they make."

"*Will do. Starting now. You think they'll come?*"

"Either they come for the sound or they come for Pearl. I've got all the bait I can think of."

Pearl and Adam shuffled before him toward the starboard bay scaffolds. When they reached the walkway, Pearl shrank back. "I don't like these. I can see down through them . . ."

"Adam, help her! Go in front. Pearl, follow Adam. Go along, now."

Adam stepped out onto the scaffolding, then immediately put his hands to his head. "Aw—what's that? My skull!"

Ned reached out for him, then suddenly felt the pressure too. Pressure! Gravity!

He tore off his headset, wracked with pain, and shouted, "Keep moving, Adam!"

"My legs—"

"Force! Push! Go!"

Pearl looked at Adam. "What's wrong with him? Oh—I feel funny . . . My feet are heavy . . ."

"Keep on!" Ned insisted, pushing her.

They were two levels up, two containers tall, and they had to make it to the ladder that would take them one more level down. But his arms and legs suddenly felt like pure lead and moving them was exhausting.

"They're coming!" Adam gasped and pointed. "Ned, they're coming!"

From behind, the glossy bronze dragon appeared where they had just been, watching them, moving toward them. On the lowest level, among a few remaining sheep and two mule deer, another of the creatures emerged from a hiding place and began to climb one of the containers as if it meant to get to them. The noise! That summoning sound Dan was broadcasting—it was calling them from all over the ship!

How many were left? Ned tried to think, to add up the numbers correctly, but he'd lost track and now his skull felt as if it were in a vise. He choked and tried to keep his eyes from popping out of his head.

Before him, Adam fell to his knees. Pearl wasn't so affected—something about her funny little flat body—but Adam was being crushed by pain and pressure.

Ned came up behind him, threw an arm around him, hauled him to his feet, and pushed Pearl on in front of them. The ladder!

"Down!" Ned ordered, hoping the sound of his voice would drive them.

Below, two more aliens appeared, but no more than that. Was that all of them? It was a good bet.

Pearl tiptoed down the ladder, and Ned pushed Adam down next, then tried to find his hands and feet in the increasing gravitational pull that drew them downward. It wasn't just increased pressure—it was actual directional gravity. They would be crushed!

Ned's feet now moved like rocks. He could no longer feel them, and he slipped on the last rung and fell hard onto the scaffold walkway, one level up from the deck.

"We'll never make it!" Adam tried to lift him, but Ned now weighed twice his normal weight. "We can't get all the way out!"

"Go!" Ruthlessly Ned shoved him along the walkway, by force of will pulling himself to his feet. He managed to drag himself along the rail, keeping his target in sight.

Though Pearl and Adam were trying to reach the next ladder down to the main deck, Ned had other ideas. When they reached the place he wanted them to reach, he drove himself forward until he was between them, took hold of Pearl with one arm and Adam with the other, and shouted, "Deep breath!"

And he made a furious push.

Adam let out a strangled yell, and all three of them hit the water. The lagoon tank sloshed at their increased weight, but the second they were under water Ned felt the weight of his body relieved. *Now hold your breath!*

Salt water burned his injured arm as they sank in the beautiful aquarium, relieved of their intensified weight, drawn downward by the artificially increased gravity. Against the clear wall of the tank, the four remaining alien dragons clawed and scratched to get at Pearl, to get at the boys, for whatever purposes their evolution dictated. They scratched and drooled and reached for the top, but were dragged down as they suddenly weighed a hundred times normal. Even through the water, Ned could hear their screams.

Then the gravity hit the perfect level, a sudden boost, just as Ned's lungs began to hurt. Outside the tank, unprotected, unable to take the Gs, one alien suddenly popped.

Just like a soda can being crushed under a foot!

And a second! Acid made a splat, but before it could eat through the container wall it was dragged down into a puddle on the deck, where it tried to chew through the metal but was not its normal self, and thus was crushed too thin to eat all the way through.

Pop—a third!

All that remained was the bronze guardian ghoul. Pearl, holding her breath, swam with unexpected grace to the aquarium wall, followed by a hundred fish in a cloud of blue and yellow colors. Like a mermaid in a story, she put her hands up to the transparent wall, against the claws of her savage alter ego.

But just as her fingers touched the wall, the alien's skull folded in upon itself and its ribs pushed through to its spine. It dropped to the deck, and was instantly flattened into a mash. Ned reached for Pearl—he had to get to the surface! His eyes began to go dark. He swept his arms frantically, trying to rise, and lost his grip on her.

And lost sight of her. His orientation was gone—a dark tunnel closed in on his vision. His lungs screamed.

All at once the pressure turned off like a switch and he shot to the surface, gagging and choking, splashing as if to continue climbing straight into the air. Somebody had a grip on him.

"Breathe!" Adam called.

Ned choked on the salt water and sputtered, "Where's—where—"

"She's right here!" Adam said. "You all right?"

Ned coughed and tried to nod.

"How did you know that would work?" With a slap on the water's surface, Adam seized Ned in a heartfelt embrace. "That was brilliant! Brilliant!"

Grateful for the support, Ned blinked his salt-stung eyes. "We all have . . . our . . . offerings . . ."

"Here." Adam dragged him to the edge of the tank, where Ned could get a grip and stop struggling. "Are you all right?"

"Half-drowned, thanks . . ."

He was glad for Adam's grip on his good arm, for his left arm was too weak to do much. Still sputtering, he peered down around the bay at the crushed corpses of the last few aliens and the sorry mess of dead sheep and deer that had unfortunately paid the price, too.

But the three of them were alive, and the gravity was quickly returning to normal. Ned felt the pressure ease off his skull and hands.

"Brilliant!" Adam gushed. "Pure genius!" He twisted his hand into Ned's green shirt and shook him joyously.

Beside Adam, Pearl hooked her little hands on the edge of the tank and kicked her feet, enjoying the sensation of the water, in which she was graceful and feminine.

"Like swimming in a rain barrel," she said.

And she smiled at them, and together they all laughed.

CHAPTER TWENTY-FOUR

"Now this, *this*, is the life!"

Dan's declaration was heartily received by the other cadets, and especially by Ned Menzie as he lounged back in his floating chair. Around them, the salt air and warm water lapped at his skin and his crossed legs. Across from where he floated, Adam was reclined on a surfboard, Dan was ensconced in an inner tube, and between them, Robin swam with Pearl as if they were sea nymphs. At the far end of the tank, Stewart made a crazy dive off the scaffold and splashed Leigh as she practiced her backstroke, and Dylan as he retaliated with a sweep that drenched Stewart as soon as he surfaced.

The starboard bay was brightly lit with simulated sunlight, and there was lots of bustling activity, but the cadets were officially off duty, as a reward for their brave actions in saving the ship. Ned was relieved just to be here, to hand responsibility back to the adults. There was an advantage in being a kid and he wanted to take it for all it was worth.

He looked up as Dana came walking down the scaffold walkway toward them, with Spiderlegs spinning behind, carrying a tray of icy drinks with little umbrellas stuck in them.

"Virgin coladas, anyone?" Dana invited.

The kids cheered and crowded toward that side of the tank.

"What?" Dan protested. "No rum?"

"Just use your imaginations," Dana merrily told them. She crouched at the edge of the aquarium and said, "Robin, guess what, honey? Your baby's being adopted by a really nice couple on Zone Emerald. They have a vineyard, and they say you're welcome to come visit him any time. They named him Robin, after you!"

Robin's face dissolved into pure joy as the cadets broke into applause for her.

"Oh, I'm that grateful!" she chirped. "Poor wee thing!"

"Well, the poor wee thing's going to grow up rich, romping among the grapes, and have all the benefits of two parents who are just gigglin' thrilled to have him. I sent him off this morning on a high-speed shuttle. They'll be meeting him at the spacedock. Lots better than growing up in a pirate ship, huh?"

"So much!"

"What about those pirates?" Adam asked as Spiderlegs handed out the drinks.

"We rounded up three of them, including Detroit himself," Dana said. "The rest were killed. They're in custody. They're facing the death penalty for trafficking in dangerous contraband. We've flushed the ship completely, so it's all safe now, stem to stern. It's going to stink for a while, because suddenly we're running a cattle train, but that's okay, right?"

"Just like home in the twigs!" Ned told her.

They all laughed together, and Stewart splashed him.

"I'm still impressed," Adam said to Ned, "that you knew we could take all those Gs under water. How do you get that kind of knowledge living in the middle of a farm all your life?"

"The farm's on an island, mind," Ned told him. "We know a bit about water."

"Oh, look!" Leigh called, and pointed down onto the main deck. "They found the bear!"

Below, a makeshift series of corrals had been set up to separate the sheep from the deer, the geese and fowl from the horses, and the various breeds of cattle milling together, and other manners of animal into their own enclosures. Even the mammoths and the elephants were boxed in by four carefully situated containers, the only fencing big enough to hold them. The dangerous animals had been hunted down with tranquilizer darts and were being held subdued in special box-cages. The cadets watched as a robotic pallet rolled across the deck with the tattered grizzly bear placidly lounging inside. He shook his big drowsy head only for a moment, when they moved him past the cage with the sabertoothed cat soundly drugged and sleeping inside, rolled onto its back with its legs bandaged up and happily sprawled. It stretched its front leg and yawned, like big kitten, with mighty big fangs.

Ned looked down at that cat with deep gratitude. It would go on to its own life on a new planet, never really knowing what it had done, to live as the wild thing it was meant to be, in a new unspoiled wilderness. He was glad for it.

And there were people below, too, dozens of professional crewmen and veterinarians and wildlife specialists brought from other ships, and Mr. Nielsen down there enjoying the sights and recording the captures. They knew now who was alive and who was dead, and they had come to accept the facts.

"We'll all be attending memorial services for Mary and Chris on Zone Emerald," Dana went on, pulling them back to a sadder reality. "Mary's parents and Chris's aunt and uncle are donating a children's medical research wing to the university in their honor. It's hard, but this is space. Tragedies do happen."

"They do," Ned murmured, thinking back.

Everyone looked at him, aware of the burden he had carried. He wished they would stop looking.

"Dana," Adam spoke up.

She looked at him. "Yes."

He sat up on his surfboard, letting his legs hand in the water. "I want to apologize for what I did to you. It was immature. I put everybody in danger because I didn't trust you and your authority. In fact, I owe all you guys an apology. I thought I was somebody. I didn't respect anybody else. I'm really sorry for it."

The moment grew quiet. Adam held his ground.

Just when things were becoming too intense, Ned cupped the water and splashed him in the face. "And don't forget it."

With that he released them to laugh and move on.

"That's so nice," Spiderlegs uttered, and sniffed back a tear. "Kids are so nice . . . good kids. I love kids."

"We love you, Mr. Follo!" Robin cheered.

Dana gave him a little smile, then turned back to Adam. "Guess there's hope for you, Mr. Bay."

Adam nodded, but he didn't smile. It wasn't an act. Not this time. Ned looked at him, and they shared a private moment of mutual appreciation.

"Hey!" Dana turned as one of the veterinarians appeared on the scaffold walkway. "Ned, look who we found!"

She was echoed by a happy ruff! and the tick-tick of toenails down the metal walkway.

"Kite!" Ned splashed to the edge of the tank to meet the delighted border collie who had worked so flawlessly when the hard moment came. "Kite, that'll do! That'll do, boy! What a dog! What a good dog, good dog!"

The others had no idea, but he knew and the dog knew that this was border collie command, saying that a good day's work was done, and come thee now to me. The dog ruffed again and almost pulled the veterinarian off his feet to get to Ned, who greeted the collie with open arms.

"Kite . . ." Adam gave him a quizzical look as the dog joyously licked the salt water from Ned's face, and Ned returned the joy with his own.

"Cosmic!" Dylan exclaimed. "You've got a dog!"

"He also has a sabertooth," Leigh said. "And I think that bear likes him now."

"I want the mammoth!" Stewart claimed.

Dan laughed. "I really want to see your skinny bum riding a mammoth!"

The dog, the Kite of space, overcome by delight, could no longer contain itself and leaped into the water beside Ned, then came up and shook its head as it paddled, and indeed seemed to actually be smiling. Ned helped Kite stay afloat with a sincere hug, and smiled at Adam over the dog's head. Could a day so dire have turned out so bright? Could this be real?

Pearl looked up at Dana with special admiration. "Are you the captain now?"

"Yes, I am. That's how things work on a ship. And as soon as you're all done swimming, there's a lot of mess to clean up."

They let out a collective groan of protest.

"What?!" Dana declared. "Did you think you'd get out of sailors' work? What do you think you came here for? A vacation? What do you think this is? A resort? Now, float around till you're good and pruny, because that's when we start spittin' and polishin'! Snap to! Brace those yards over! Let fly those sails! Sheet her home and smartly now! Hup to, you salty monkeys! There's a ship to run and a galaxy to tame! Bedad and argh and all them clichés!"

ABOUT THE AUTHOR

DIANE CAREY is a best-selling science fiction writer with more than forty-five novels to her credit, including nine *New York Times* bestsellers for her Star Trek work and several number one chain bestsellers. She holds the distinction of having written many of the episode-to-novel adaptations of seminal Star Trek episodes, including the novelizations of the finale for *Star Trek: Deep Space Nine* and the premiere of *Star Trek Enterprise* and has gained a reputation for her care and attention in expanding and extending the rich backstories of the characters she works on. An avid sailor of historic tall ships, Carey lives in Michigan with her husband, writer and computer programmer Greg Brodeur and children Lydia, Gordon, and Ben.